# Suburb, Slum, Urban Village

*Carolyn Whitzman*

# Suburb, Slum, Urban Village

Transformations in Toronto's
Parkdale Neighbourhood,
1875-2002

**UBC** Press · Vancouver · Toronto

17   16   15   14   13   12   11   10   09              5   4   3   2   1

Printed in Canada with vegetable-based inks on FSC-certified ancient-forest-free paper (100% post-consumer recycled) that is processed chlorine- and acid-free.

**Library and Archives Canada Cataloguing in Publication**

Whitzman, Carolyn
   Suburb, slum, urban village : transformations in Toronto's Parkdale neighbourhood, 1875-2002 / Carolyn Whitzman.

   Includes bibliographical references and index.
   ISBN 978-0-7748-1535-2

   1. Parkdale (Toronto, Ont.) – History. 2. Parkdale (Toronto, Ont.) – Social conditions. I. Title.

FC3097.52.W44 200    971.3'541    C2009-900748-7

Canadä

UBC Press gratefully acknowledges the financial support for our publishing program of the Government of Canada through the Book Publishing Industry Development Program (BPIDP), and of the Canada Council for the Arts and the British Columbia Arts Council.

This book has been published with the help of a grant from the Canadian Federation for the Humanities and Social Sciences, through the Aid to Scholarly Publications Programme, using funds provided by the Social Sciences and Humanities Research Council of Canada.

UBC Press
The University of British Columbia
2029 West Mall
Vancouver, BC V6T 1Z2
604-822-5959 / Fax: 604-822-6083
**www.ubcpress.ca**

# Contents

# Maps and Illustrations

# Preface

The streetcar emerged from the underpass, and we entered a new world.

On this sunny afternoon in July 1986, we were newcomers to Toronto. I had come to undertake a master's degree at University of Toronto; my husband was looking for work as a journalist. "Don't bother looking for an apartment in Parkdale – it's a real slum," said our host, a friend of my brother's, who lived on a street that seemed none too savoury. But Parkdale was the only central neighbourhood that had a range of apartments cheap enough for us to rent.

I had no clear idea of what a slum was supposed to look like. To the extent that I had thought about the term, I would have associated it with a public housing project like Benny Farm, near where I had grown up in Montreal. Benny Farm was a visually barren set of low-rise apartments that looked like army barracks – indeed, it had been built for veterans of World War Two. There seemed to be no reason to enter the pedestrianized vicinity unless you lived there or were about to do something illicit, since there were no licit businesses there.

Instead, beyond the Dufferin Street underpass we saw a lively and bustling section of Queen Street West, one of Toronto's main commercial arteries. A multicultural crush of people of all ages were strolling, shopping at grocery stores, hanging out on the few benches provided in front of the library. As we walked down Jameson Avenue, an imposing corridor of eight-to-twelve-storey apartment buildings, "farm fresh" bananas and mangoes were being sold off the backs of trucks. It looked like a good place to live.

We rented an apartment on the southernmost street of Parkdale, Springhurst Avenue. It was a one-bedroom unit on the second floor of a once-grand three-storey detached villa. The rent was $650, double what we had paid for our last apartment, a considerably larger and more pleasant flat in Montreal. But we had looked around enough to realize that the

Toronto rental market was superheated, with a low vacancy rate and dozens of applicants for each apartment. And the living room and tiny kitchen had a grand view of Lake Ontario, if you ignored the expressway in the foreground. Besides, our landlord, "call me Andy," seemed friendly enough.

My husband started work, but I had the month of August with nothing to do and no money with which I could pass the time. I spent my days exploring every block of my new neighbourhood. Unlike much of Toronto, locked in a tight street grid, Parkdale was a place of hidden alleyways and cul-de-sacs, tree-lined avenues that never quite joined up, glimpses of history. It also featured daily in the newspapers, in stories of street prostitution, drug dealing, ex-psychiatric patients burning down their buildings, and casual violence. All accounts agreed that Parkdale had been developed as a middle-class neighbourhood in the late nineteenth and early twentieth centuries, and had somehow gone terribly wrong in recent years. But my eyes registered a different story. Yes, Queen Street in the evenings had street prostitutes and people engaged in loud conversations with invisible partners (this was before mobile phones made this occurrence commonplace). But there were also many other people walking the streets after dark and I did not feel particularly unsafe. On my travels, I would see tiny wood-framed cottages behind grand villas, factories next to houses, a few middle-class cafés next to the dollar stores. Historical Parkdale did not seem to have been all middle-class, nor was modern-day Parkdale entirely poverty-stricken. Perhaps I would do some historical research on Parkdale for my master's thesis.

But by the end of 1986 I wanted to forget Parkdale. The trouble had begun almost immediately. We noticed the day we moved in that the quite solid-looking lock on our apartment door had been replaced by a flimsy bathroom doorknob some time after we had viewed the unit. Our landlord explained that he changed the locks every time tenants moved. He had temporarily run out of "real" doorknobs, and would replace it within the week. The bathroom doorknob stayed, and we were never given a key to the front door of the building, which was never locked anyhow. We are not nervous people, but there did seem to be a lot of coming and going in the hallway beyond our apartment at all hours. With flimsy drywall between us and our neighbours, we could hear everything. The good news was that we did not hear the door-knocking and financial negotiations we might associate with drug deals. Instead, the middle of the night noises consisted of drilling and hammering. We would almost have preferred a quiet drug deal or two. A few days later, there would be battered suitcases and cartons in the hallway as someone moved in. Then the drilling and hammering would start again. There were six apartments in the building when we arrived in August. By October, three more units had been created.

We tracked down the previous tenants of our apartment, to give them some mail. We discovered that they had paid $400 for the apartment in 1985, but when Andy had bought the apartment in January 1986, he told them that the new rent was $450, payable immediately. They had refused, and threatened to take him to the Rent Review Board. "Have you met Cousin Frank?" they asked, referring to the man with the physique and expression of a sumo wrestler with a wedgie, who lived downstairs from us and helped Andy with the renovations. "He's a really scary guy. Watch out for him."

Despite the warning about Cousin Frank, we called on Parkdale Community Legal Services. As we suspected, Andy did not have the right to a 62 percent rent increase, and he was also obligated to provide us with a secure apartment door. Two weeks later, we returned home one evening with a paralegal friend and an armload of flyers from the Parkdale Tenants Association. We began knocking on doors. Andy must have received correspondence from the Rent Review Board, because he and Frank appeared at the bottom of the staircase and yelled at us that we were evicted, effective immediately. When we did not scurry to our apartment to pack, Cousin Frank decided to include us in his renovation plans, picking up my husband by the shirt and pounding him into the wall. I screamed, ran into our apartment, and called the police, while our paralegal friend, who probably weighed a third of Cousin Frank dripping wet, tried to pull him off my husband. The police officers, when they eventually arrived, did not lay charges, and to our eternal regret, we took their advice to let the matter rest. "You should move out of this neighbourhood," one officer advised. "It really isn't safe." The paralegal would have stayed to argue, but he had to run off and visit another client, whose altercation with his landlord the same night had led to his admission into hospital.

The next month was hell. I still did not think that we lived in a slum, but we had certainly met a slumlord. Andy followed up his terrorizing opening gambit with a series of slightly more subtle moves. We received an eviction notice under our door the morning after the assault. Apparently, Andy's mother, not currently resident in Canada, wanted to move in. Then our hot water was turned off. One evening, I returned home to find that someone had been in the apartment. Although nothing was taken, the bathroom window had been broken and there was glass all over. We now had the building inspection office on speed dial. When we moved out, there were seventeen outstanding work orders on our unit alone.

But finding a new place in a 0.01 percent rental market was no easy task. We applied to move into non-profit housing in Parkdale, but there was a three-year waiting list. A friend told us about a new non-profit housing co-operative just east of downtown that was having trouble attracting tenants who could pay market rent, since it was located across the street from Regent Park, Canada's largest public housing project. We viewed an apartment. "The previous tenant had some cleanliness issues," said the maintenance worker, as she unscrewed an overhead vent in the kitchen, and hundreds of dead cockroaches tumbled out. "We'll take it," we said.

We were very lucky, then and afterwards. Our parents loaned us first and last month's rent. My brother helped us move. When our case finally came before the Rent Review Board, six months after we moved out, Andy presented some receipts from Cousin Frank's "construction service" indicating that the improvements justifying the rent increase consisted of drywalling a hundred-year-old stained-glass window. Nothing could have outraged our judge's yuppie sensibilities more, and she awarded us the full amount of the rent increase, along with our last month's rent and moving costs. Remarkably, after we pursued Andy in small claims court, we finally got a cheque. We learned later that Andy had sold the building to an overseas investor who wanted all outstanding claims settled before taking over.

Seven years later, in 1993, we returned to Parkdale. Our material circumstances were now quite different. Now I worked as a senior policy planner at City Hall, and my husband was a lobbyist for the Canadian book publishing industry. We had a one-year-old son and were ready to move into a neighbourhood with mature trees, less traffic, and real front yards. We also did not want to pay more on a mortgage than we were paying for rent, which was becoming a tricky proposition in central Toronto. Some of my work colleagues raved about Parkdale. It was a different world north of Queen Street, they insisted. The schools were good and there were a growing number of young families, but it was still "colourful." We found a tiny old three-bedroom semi-detached house, behind a tangled garden and a big porch. The wiring and the roof needed work, but with a 10 percent down payment, the mortgage would carry like rent.

I am not arrogant enough to fancy myself Everywoman, but it was easy to see that we were part of a demographic trend. Within a month, the house next door had a couple with a young child, and by the end of the year, six more houses on our block had sold to families with young children. In the majority of cases, an older, first-generation Canadian household, originally from Eastern Europe, had been replaced by a younger, second- or third-generation household. We got to know our neighbours, the old-timers as well as the newcomers. We felt safe in the knowledge that the older woman across the street, whose family had owned that house since it was first built in 1912, kept an eye on our house during the day. In late summer, the Hindu temple on the corner had a harvest festival procession down the street, and the neighbours gathered to watch the "parade." I found grocery stores, a pharmacy, banks, parks, and a library on Roncesvalles, one block away. High Park, the largest green space in the central city, was a short stroll from our house. My son went to the childcare centre at our local public school, and then to the school itself. When my second child was born, I stayed at home with her for a year and took full advantage of the parent-child drop-in at the school, the newly renovated playground and wading pool around the corner, informal parents' get-togethers at neighbourhood coffee shops, swimming lessons at the new community centre, story time at the library. One afternoon, a couple of months after she was born, I took the streetcar downtown with my daughter to meet my work colleagues at lunch. I was appalled at the noise, the traffic, the tall buildings that seemed to block out light, the grit sailing through the air. I could not wait to return to my clean, green, safe, quiet enclave. I had become a suburbanite, living in the central city.

This personal story is only one of the millions of stories of home in a big city like Toronto. It is about a place that simultaneously contained elements of "suburb," "slum," and "village," which we had experienced as both a place of fear and (temporary) poverty, and a place of safety and affluence. The story of Parkdale similarly seemed more complex than simplistic narratives of a stable, middle-class neighbourhood gone terribly wrong in the post-World War Two era, or of an inexorably gentrifying neighbourhood returning to its former status as a stable, middle-class "good place to live."

In the rest of this book, I explore the relationships between discourses, social conditions, and planning policy over time in Parkdale, as a way of illuminating these relationships in other English-speaking large cities since the late nineteenth century. But in this preface, I would like to remain personal and thank some of the people who helped me in the writing of a doctoral thesis on this topic, and then supported me in writing this book.

First and foremost, I would like to acknowledge the excellent supervision and advice of Professor Richard Harris of McMaster University's School of Geography and Geology, whose timely, lively, and supportive assistance made the process of research and writing the thesis on which this book is based such a pleasant learning experience. I would also like to acknowledge the thoughtful contributions of Professors Beth Milroy, John Weaver, Gunter Gad, and Vera Chouinard, my ideal supervisory committee. At the University of Melbourne, Professors Ruth Fincher and Kevin O'Connor have been extremely helpful in the process of revising my thesis into a book. Discussions with U.K. gentrification researcher Tom Slater and Melbourne historian Seamus O'Hanlon also gave me insight into my topic.

The staff at many archival collections went above and beyond the call of duty to lend a hand in research. I would especially like to thank the gang at the City of Toronto Archives, where I spent many a happy day calling up hundreds of boxes of City Council reports and correspondence from their huge collection. Thanks are also due to the staff at the Parkdale, High Park, Toronto Reference, and Urban Affairs branches of the Toronto Public Library system; Mills Memorial Library at McMaster University; Robarts Library at the University of Toronto; Archives of Ontario; Ontario Land Registry Office; City of Toronto Assessment Office; and the Toronto office of Statistics Canada, for their cheerful and expert assistance.

The Social Sciences and Humanities Research Council of Canada financially supported the research and writing of the thesis that is the basis of this book, through a three-year doctoral fellowship. I also received financial support from McMaster University's School of Geography and Geology, and considerable assistance from graduate secretary Nancy Brand in cutting red tape. Ric Hamilton provided patient assistance with the maps and illustrations.

The journey from thesis into book has been long and sometimes frustrating, complicated by my move to Australia immediately upon completion of the thesis in 2003. I would like to thank Melissa Pitts of UBC Press for her constant encouragement, Sarah Wight for excellent copy-editing, Anna Eberhard Friedlander for ably overseeing the production of the book, and two anonymous reviewers, whose contributions were constructive and helpful. Research assistants Jana Perkovic and Tranh Nha Nguyen assisted with copyrights and getting my bibliography in order.

As the daughter of a real estate agent, I must thank my mother, Sheila Whitzman, for teaching me all about "location, location, location" as a child. Without her, I would not have developed my fascination with cities as a good place to live. I would also like to thank my father, Earl Whitzman, for his constant encouragement and support, particularly when he muttered curses at my examiners during my thesis defence.

Last and certainly not least, I would like to acknowledge the emotional support of my immediate family and friends. David Hunt, my husband, is always a source of inspiration, a thoughtful editor, and a friend whose faith in my abilities has carried me through many a rough period. My children, Simon Hunt and Molly Hunt, who grow more remarkable every day, were also sources of encouragement, support, and enjoyable breaks from three years spent in the basement. Jennifer Ramsay, Deborah Hierlihy, Elisabeth Szanto, Deborah Hasler, and many other friends kept me from being a dull dog. My love and thanks to all of you.

# Suburb, Slum, Urban Village

# Introduction

> Cities, like dreams, are made of desires and fears, even if the
> discourse is secret, their rules are absurd, their perspectives
> deceitful, and everything conceals something else.
>
>          – Italo Calvino, *Invisible Cities*

Today, the central Toronto neighbourhood of Parkdale, like many older
neighbourhoods in North American, Australian, and British cities, simultaneously evokes images of a revitalizing urban village and a declining
slum (Beauregard 2003, vii). As early as 1970, Parkdale, with its charming hundred-year-old houses, streets lined with mature trees, and history
as a well-to-do suburb, was being promoted by urban redevelopers eager
to attract middle-class homebuyers (*Toronto Star*, 8 August 1970). At the
same time, newspapers began to report some residents' concerns about the
growing number of "boisterous welfare recipients, drunks and drug
addicts" inhabiting cheap apartments and rooming houses in the community (*Globe and Mail*, 7 April 1972). A two-page 1980 feature in Canada's
national newspaper, the *Globe and Mail*, described Parkdale as "shaped by
city trends, but outpacing them" in a growing division between "costly
enclave" and "dumping ground" for the poor (13 September 1980). In
1997, the *Toronto Star* triumphantly proclaimed the "bowery to bohemia
conversion" of the neighbourhood (16 January 1997). Three years later,
however, the *Globe and Mail* ran another two-page feature on growing disparities within Toronto neighbourhoods, and used Parkdale, with its
repeated juxtaposition of "an elegant reno next to a rundown rooming
house" as an example of a place that was simultaneously bowery and
bohemia, ghetto and gentrified urban village (5 August 2000).

I use the term *image* here to mean a description or representation. This
book focuses mostly on representation in written sources, such as newspapers, government reports, real estate advertisements, and literature (both
fiction and non-fiction), but I also include visual materials, predominantly
photographs. Often images evoke something else, as when Van Gogh
paints a field with crows or a poet uses metaphor. In this book, I use *dream*
to mean a series of images that are intended to evoke certain desires or

fears, as in the words of Italo Calvino above. The three main dreams I will be discussing are the suburban dream of the late nineteenth and early twentieth centuries, the slum nightmare, particularly as it pertained to so-called declining neighbourhoods in the early twentieth century, and the urban village dream, closely linked to gentrification, of the late twentieth century. In each case, the image of Parkdale may have had more to do with changing ideas of "a good place to live" than the more concrete socio-demographic qualities of its residents and houses.

The importance of dreams in defining certain types of places – cities, suburbs, neighbourhoods, housing projects – and in shaping public consciousness and influencing policy has been a common theme in much recent writing on cities, including US planning historian Christine Boyer's *Dreaming the Rational City: The Myth of American Planning* (1983), Australian geographer Louise Johnson's edited collection *Suburban Dreaming: An Interdisciplinary Approach to Australian Cities* (1994), and Canadian historical geographer James Lemon's *Liberal Dreams and Nature's Limits: Great Cities of North America since 1600* (1996). These works deal in the broad strokes of urban history. Few studies, however, focus on the succession of images in a local place such as a neighbourhood, the extent to which these successive images reflect or conceal social conditions, the relationships between past and present, and the impacts particular dreams of place might have on policy.

What are the relationships between images of place, social conditions, and planning policy in Anglo-American cities? When, how, and why are some neighbourhoods labelled as suburbs, slums, and gentrifying areas? When, how, and why, in the continual process of conflict over neighbourhood change, does the perception of a neighbourhood alter decisively? Which voices are most influential in creating and disseminating these labels? Do changing labels simply reflect the reality of local economic and social conditions, as objectively reported by newspapers and government documents? Are changing evaluations of neighbourhoods based on evolving social norms and understandings of "a good place to live"? Or are they responses to structural economic forces, such as the availability or withdrawal of development capital? What impact do changing discourses of the "good neighbourhood" have on government policies, particularly planning policy? And what impact do planning policies, in turn, have on social conditions in these neighbourhoods? In short, how are dreams attached to urban places, and do these dreams matter?

This book is not about a unique place, except in the sense that all neighbourhoods, like all people, are unique. Parkdale is not a fabled neighbourhood of literature or film. It is not Hollywood or Whitechapel, the

Upper West Side of Manhattan or Back of the Yards in Chicago, West-mount in Montreal or the Downtown Eastside in Vancouver. What inter-ests me is how Parkdale is a typical place, like many other places I have visited and read about in the United States, Canada, Australia, and the United Kingdom, places that were supposedly developed as middle-class suburbs, then seemed to decline to the point where they were called slums. Now they are reportedly being revitalized as gentrifying neighbourhoods, or urban villages. But coexistent with this new wealth there is often poverty that appears to be worsening. These places include Jamaica Plain in Boston, Clifton in Cincinnati, St. Kilda in Melbourne, and, of course, the mostly commonly cited examples, Greenwich Village in New York City and London's Islington (see, respectively, Von Hoffman 1994; Miller 2001; Howe 1994; McFarland 2001; P. Williams 1978).

However, as the studies of these places suggest, the neighbourhood trajectories were not so clear-cut as is generally assumed. Alexander Von Hoffman, for instance, takes a part of Boston whose development as a middle-class residential suburb was documented in Sam Bass Warner's clas-sic 1962 urban history *Streetcar Suburbs* (1978) and contends that "although it contained suburban elements, Jamaica Plain never conformed to the usual notions of a suburban community" (Von Hoffman 1994, 24). Sim-ilarly, Renate Howe (1994, 149) maintains that inner suburbs in Melbourne labelled slums in the early twentieth century did not have particularly dangerous or unhealthy housing or social conditions. Instead, the slum "label was freely applied to those areas which did not meet the criteria of the suburban ethos as it was defined in the later part of the nineteenth century." In the latter part of the twentieth century, as the supposed "'dys-functions' of city life [were] reconstructed as advantages ... what was once termed slum housing now became 'heritage' property" (155-57). In other words, the evolving image of a neighbourhood is as related to changing societal norms as it is to actual housing or social conditions.

## The Chicago School and Development of the Suburb/Slum Dichotomy

This proposition is intriguing given the continuing impact of the Chicago school of sociology and, particularly, Ernest Burgess' 1925 mapping of "concentric zones" in that city (Burgess 1974). According to the Chicago school's paradigm of city structure and growth, cities sorted themselves into a moral and social order of concentric rings, which expanded out-wards as the city grew. The laws of human ecology dictated the natural inclination of families to move to the outer edges of the expanding city, where there was space for children to grow up healthy. There too, women and children would be far from urban hazards such as polluting industries, crime and greed associated with capitalism, and the underclass engendered by the dense and close-grained mix of land uses and social classes in the central city. Surrounding the central business and industrial district lay a "zone of transition," where once-grand houses were being converted into multiple units for new immigrants and down-and-outers as part of those buildings' inexorable decline into obsolescence and inevitable absorption into the central district. Peripheral rings contained progressively lower densities, newer houses, and richer and more nativized families. Burgess was explicit about the norms that informed this model, taking American suburban family life as the apogee of social evolution. But the Chicago school and its successors did not doubt that they were describing real, measurable, and inexorable changes in social and economic conditions within these zones, despite a reliance on ethnographic qualitative research over statistical comparisons (Park 1974; Zorbaugh 1976).

The Chicago school drew upon an Anglo-American tradition of distrust and dislike of urban life that led many middle- and upper-class families in Britain, the United States, Australia, and Canada to establish suburban residences at the outskirts of rapidly expanding industrial cities in the nineteenth century (Jackson 1985; Fishman 1987; Rybczynski 1995). As Peter Goheen (1970), David Harvey (1973), and others have pointed out, Burgess was merely elaborating on a structure first described in Manchester by Frederick Engels (1969), and expanded upon in Charles Booth's accounts of London's slums (1971) and Jacob Riis' similar accounts from New York City (1957). Burgess and his contemporaries codified a consensus on suburbs and slums that had emerged by the early twentieth century.

The Burgess concentric ring model bore no relation at all to the largest non-English-speaking cities of the time, such as Paris, Vienna, Berlin, Buenos Aires, and Tokyo, where the poor and immigrants were generally found in the outskirts (Jackson 1985, 7-10; Hall 1998). The model also did very little to explain the structure and growth of what were then the world's two largest cities, New York City and London, where large sections of the central city were dominated by the housing of the affluent and middle class. Burgess' assumptions and findings were attacked in detail as early as 1948, when Walter Firey pointed out that slums had been transformed into middle-class areas in Boston, and that the land use pattern had little to do with concentric rings. But despite being a simplistic model that became even more simplified over the years, the Chicago school's explanation of why suburbs were middle-class and white, while central cities were poor and ethnic minority, underlay endeavours as disparate as American and Canadian "red-lining" mortgage patterns (Jackson 1985,

197-207; Harris and Ragonetti 1998) and the study of urban history (Harris and Lewis 1998, 2001). The Chicago school was the dominant mode of urban sociological thought until the mid-1980s (Gottdiener 1985, 12). And the dichotomy between the poor and diverse central city and the socio-economically homogenous middle-class suburb continues to inform urban theory, planning discourse, and popular opinion in the United States, the United Kingdom, Canada, and Australia (on the United States, see Dreier, Mollenkopf, and Swanstrom 2001; Duany, Plater-Zyberk, and Speck 2000; on Canada, see Leo and Shaw 2002).

Since the 1980s, the dominant discourse has shifted to an equally simplistic dichotomy. Now the contrast is made between densely populated, multicultural, and vibrant central cities, and sprawling, boring, car-dependent suburbs. Whether advocating for environmental sustainability or promoting "creative capital" as economic development, the notion of concentric zones has been turned on its head. Living in the central city connotes progress, moral and physical health, and social responsibility. As households move further out into the suburbs, they are considered to lose access to once-despised and now sought-after attributes: land-use and social mix, and proximity to the new non-polluting industries of information technology and finance. Living, working, and playing in the central city is now lauded the way that strict separation of land uses in the suburbs used to be (Newman and Kenworthy 1999; Florida 2002).

Of course, most cities do not have simplistic gradients between distance from the central city and car dependence, cultural mix, or economic innovation. Many new migrants gravitate to cheaper housing in outer suburbs, many central city residents drive their cars as much as those in lower-density or more peripheral areas, and economic innovation happens in a variety of settings. There have always been, and continue to be, countervoices to the dominant discourse. Suburbs and suburbanites were mocked by many in the late nineteenth and early twentieth century, just as downtown "latte liberals" and "chardonnay socialists" are mocked today in the central city/suburb culture wars that have erupted in the United States, Canada, Australia, and the United Kingdom.[1] The changing dichotomous relationship between suburbs and slums over the past 150 years forms a backdrop to this study.

## Suburb, Slum, and Urban Village in Parkdale

The changing image of Parkdale in newspapers and magazines, planning reports, and books about Toronto has been inextricably linked to the notion of concentric rings. From the first promotion of Parkdale as a place for "those whose avocations require them to spend much of their time

amid the bustle of Toronto [yet desire] a quiet home in an agreeable locality" (Scott 1881), the westernmost edge of the city (as it was then) continued to be portrayed as a stable, wealthy, residential outer-zone suburb
during the twenty years of its initial development. The "fact" of Parkdale's
well-to-do beginnings is taken for granted today. The current standard
two-volume scholarly history of Toronto describes Parkdale as a "well to
do residential retreat" in the 1880s (Careless 1984, 124), while an article
in *City Planning* magazine, the Toronto Planning Department house organ,
contains this thumbnail sketch: "Developed at the turn of the century,
South Parkdale was originally an upper middle class residential suburb"
(summer 1987).

By the mid-twentieth century, when the growth of Toronto had left
Parkdale closer to the centre than the periphery (Map 1; Harris and Luymes
1990), the neighbourhood was attracting very different descriptions. The
1934 report of the Lieutenant-Governor's Committee on Housing Conditions in Toronto, known as the Bruce Report, was considered Canada's
"bible for social housing" and urban redevelopment (Bacher 1993, 10). It
said Parkdale was "becoming a serious slum," due to the influx of immigrants and industry into a "formerly prosperous district" (Bruce 1934, 23).
In 1959, the proposed metropolitan region master plan used a concentric
ring model to determine that Parkdale, simply because it was in Toronto's
"inner ring," needed significant urban renewal (Metropolitan Toronto
Planning Board 1959, 23). The second volume of Toronto's standard history agrees that by the 1930s, "in a very real sense, Cabbagetown [a part
of Toronto traditionally considered a slum] was moving up to South
Rosedale, to the Annex, and out to South Parkdale," and that by the 1980s,
Parkdale was a "notable poor area" (Lemon 1985, 65, 177). Michael Dear
and Jennifer Wolch, in their 1987 book on "institutional service ghettoes," credit Parkdale's remarkable concentration of rooming houses (48
percent of Toronto's total beds in the early 1980s) to its location in the
"zone of transition," close to the city centre and near psychiatric services.

Parkdale's initial attraction as a well-to-do suburb, and its deterioration
from suburb to slum, has thus been seen as an inevitable outcome of its
location within the larger city, reflecting an uncritical reading of concentric ring theory. The explanations of its rise and fall parallel famous North
American studies of urban development and change, from Homer Hoyt's
1933 *One Hundred Years of Land Values in Chicago* (1970) and Sam Bass
Warner's 1962 *Streetcar Suburbs* (1978), to Larry Bourne's *Internal Structure
of the City* (1971) and John Stilgoe's *Borderland* (1988). Although Marxists
criticized the human ecology explanations and liberal positivist perspectives of the Chicago school and its followers, Marxist explanations of

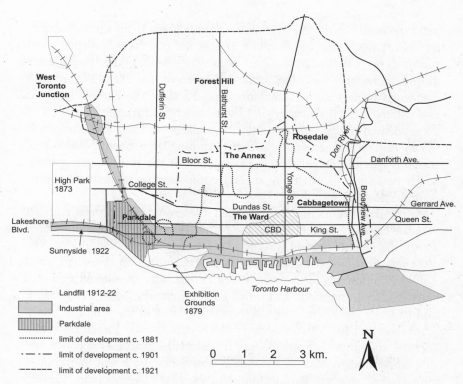

*Map 1.*    Parkdale within the context of central Toronto, 1881-1922
*Sources:* Harris and Luymes 1990, Lemon 1985, map 2. Map courtesy of Ric Hamilton, McMaster University.

urban structure also applied the concentric ring model, at least until the 1980s (Harvey 1973; Castells 1977; Dear and Wolch 1987). But to return to the Toronto example for the moment, the Annex and South Rosedale, two neighbourhoods roughly the same distance from downtown as Parkdale, had successfully resisted decline by the 1980s. Similar examples of central neighbourhoods that resisted decline could be found in the cities described by the classic writers: Chicago, Boston, and New York City.[2]

Why did Parkdale get an expressway and high-rise apartment corridors while similar projects were successfully opposed in other parts of Toronto's "zone of transition"? Jon Caulfield, in his book on gentrification in Toronto (1994, 33), contends that Parkdale was a "less fortunate middle class area," somehow unluckier than other districts that were able to turn back the tide of urban renewal. But are there explanations for neighbourhood decline that fit somewhere between the inexorable structuralism of concentric rings and the pure agency of luck and the acts of key individuals?

Parkdale, like so many older districts, is now in a new phase of transition. It is no longer simply called a suburb or a slum, but is something else, a place where decline seemingly coincides with revitalization. The binary view (declining/revitalizing) of neighbourhood transition no longer suffices, which raises the question: did a binary view of neighbourhood transition ever suffice? Can a comparison of Parkdale's images and social conditions over time lead to reconsideration, not only of one neighbourhood's history, but of the way we generally look at neighbourhood transition over time?

## The Study of Neighbourhood Transitions

There have been many excellent case studies of neighbourhood transitions, both in the tradition of the Chicago school and critical of it. Since the early-1960s work of H.J. Dyos (1961) in the United Kingdom and Sam Bass Warner (1978) in the United States, neighbourhood case studies have been commonly used to elaborate on an increasing understanding of how cities grew and became more complex in form and structure. Dyos and Warner described the development of two very different kinds of late-nineteenth-century suburbs. Whereas Dyos focused on the mixed-use, mixed-income neighbourhood of Camberwell, South London, Warner provided a case study of the "weave of small decisions" that created a middle-class residential streetcar suburb in Boston. During the subsequent twenty years, Warner's work was more influential, at least in North America. Scholars tended to emphasize the origins of what they saw as the greatest issue facing cities: the divide between the poor, visible-minority inner city and the white, middle-class suburb (Wright 1980; Edel, Sclar, and Luria 1984; Hayden 1984; Jackson 1985; Teaford 1986; Fishman 1987; Weiss 1987). In the last decade, as the pricing out of poor and even middle-class households from many central city housing markets and the decline of many post-World War Two suburbs became apparent, a more nuanced portrait has emerged. This approach includes revisiting the past to challenge the simplistic opposition of rich suburb and poor central city, by paying attention to the development of working-class, ethnic-minority, and heterogeneous suburbs (Von Hoffman 1994; Harris 1996).

The years between 1960 and 1990 saw many historical case studies of middle-class suburbs declining into slums: Richard Sennett (1974) described the decline of Union Park, Chicago, in the late nineteenth century, and Jerry White (1986) wrote about *The Worst Street in North London* in the mid-twentieth century. In the past decade, some urban historians' research has turned to a critical analysis of how the slum label got attached to what were often viable and vital communities (Mayne 1993; Metzger

2000; Beauregard 2003). Other urban historians have turned to the hitherto neglected stories of working-class and ethnic-minority suburbs, including Suzanne Morton's study (1995) of domestic life in working-class Richmond Hill, Halifax, in the 1920s, Richard Harris' work (1996) on the self-built housing and the development of Earlscourt, Toronto, Becky Nicolaides' examination (2002) of Los Angeles' blue-collar suburbs 1920-1965, Robert Lewis' edited volume (2004) on industrial suburbs from the mid-nineteenth century to World War Two, Mark Peel's history (1995a) of Elizabeth, Adelaide, from its development in the 1950s to the current day, and Andrew Wiese's history (2003) of African American suburbanization since the early twentieth century.

After the 1960s, two warring streams of research on contemporary redevelopment of the central city became common: one celebratory (Rapkin and Grigsby 1960; Ahlbrandt and Brophy 1975; James T. Little and Associates 1975; Teaford 1990) and the other highly critical (Smith and Williams 1986; Zukin 1989; Smith 1996). As was the case with suburban histories, recent years have seen case studies that explore both positive and negative outcomes of central city gentrification, along with those that seek to complicate the trajectories of gentrification and to extend analysis of gentrification beyond the central city (D. Rose 1984, 1989; Beauregard 1986, 1990; Bondi 1991; Caulfield 1994; Ley 1996; Lees 2000; Robson and Butler 2001). In general, these re-examinations of gentrification have come from Canadian, British, and Australian writers, as opposed to those writing on American cities, perhaps because the gentrification of central cities is close to complete in Toronto, Vancouver, London, Sydney, and Melbourne (Ley 1996, 81). There, the battle between gentrification and inner city decay seems to be over, at least for now, with "islands of decay" retaining a precarious hold within "seas of renewal" (Wyly and Hammel 1999, commenting on Berry 1985).

Despite this plethora of historical and contemporary case studies, few recent case studies of neighbourhood transition cover the life of a community from development to the present. This seems odd to me, since a study of the development, decline, and redevelopment of Beacon Hill was the centrepiece of Firey's 1948 attack on the Chicago school. Yet few followed in his footsteps, at least not for the next forty years. Howe, in her article "Inner Suburbs: From Slums to Gentrification" (1994) provides an overview of changing images of Melbourne's central city. Richard Rodger, in "Suburbs and Slums" (2000), gives a broad-brush history of British urban development in the nineteenth century that focuses on the evolving meanings of these two terms; in doing so, he elaborates on an influential study by H.J. Dyos and D.A. Reeder, similarly entitled "Slums and

Suburbs" (1973). Michael Doucet and John Weaver (1991) offer many case studies of suburban development and changing cultural attitudes towards the city within their history of North American housing from 1880 to 1980, but without much material on gentrification or long-term change within neighbourhoods. Rosalyn Baxandall and Elizabeth Ewen (2000) provide a history of neighbourhood succession in Long Island, New York, that takes the reader from the development of a wealthy outer suburb in the late nineteenth century to a far more mixed community, in terms of income, race/ethnicity, and land use, in the late twentieth century. Christopher Mele (2000b) describes a century of characterizations of New York's Lower East Side as it moved from slum to gentrification. Of all the recent works that I draw upon, only two take a neighbourhood from development through decline and into gentrification while paying equal attention to changing images and social conditions: veteran urban historian Zane Miller's book (2001) on Cincinnati's Clifton, and an article by Marian Morton on Cleveland Heights (2002).

In short, there appears to be that situation so beloved by academics, a research gap. Moreover, this research gap matters. Sharon Zukin (1989), Neil Smith (1996), and Gerald McFarland (2001) all show how the past of a neighbourhood can be reimagined to justify present and future urban policy. The revisionist histories of Alan Mayne (1993), Richard Harris (1996), Alexander von Hoffman (1994), and Andrew Wiese (2003) give us new models of viable communities that, in their opinion, were unjustly condemned, forgotten, or misrepresented by others. The simplicities of an earlier era of research on industrial cities are being revised to reflect a more complex understanding of cities in the developed world as they face the post-industrial twenty-first century. Of course, urban studies may be in a period of transition towards new and equally simplistic paradigms (Dear 2002). As E.H. Carr (1961) has pointed out, it is arrogant enough to presume to know the reality of the past, let alone to predict the future based on one's understanding of the past. The most anyone can expect from history is greater understanding of the past in light of the present, and perhaps, greater understanding of the present in light of the past.

## Parkdale as a Case Study of Neighbourhood Transition over 125 Years

Although now considered part of downtown Toronto, from 1879 to 1889 Parkdale was a politically independent suburb five kilometres (three miles) due west of City Hall. Parkdale continues to have a strong sense of neighbourhood identity, partly because of its clear boundaries (Map 2). The historical boundaries of Parkdale are identical to the present North Parkdale and South Parkdale planning districts. The lake to the south provides one clear limit, as does the industrial district east of Dufferin, whose existence predates Parkdale's development. North of the intersection of Dufferin and Queen Streets, the neighbourhood's boundary curves westward along the tracks of what were once four mighty railroads. Parkdale's western boundary is only a little less clear: starting at a complicated intersection where King, Queen, Roncesvalles, and the Queensway intersect, it follows Roncesvalles Avenue northward. Roncesvalles has long been a fifty-cent street on its Parkdale east side and a dollar street on its High Park west side, with cheap commercial properties facing upscale residential ones. Parkdale's northern boundary along Wabash and Fermanagh Avenues, a jumble of small industries and semi-detached homes, is perhaps the most difficult for the casual observer to discern. Queen Street, Parkdale's major commercial artery, divides the neighbourhood into two roughly equal halves, South and North, each with its own distinct character.

According to the 2001 census, the 35,663 residents within Parkdale's boundaries are, on average, among the poorest in Toronto: the median annual household income of the neighbourhood was approximately $34,000, 58 percent of the median income for households within Toronto's census metropolitan area (CMA).[3] There are large and growing disparities within the neighbourhood: one census tract in the relatively gentrified area north of Queen Street had a median household income of $55,814, close to the Toronto CMA average, while another census tract south of Queen Street had a median household income of $23,070, with 45 percent of households defined as low income in the census.

In South Parkdale in 2001, 93 percent of the housing stock was rented. The majority of rental units are one-bedroom and bachelor apartments in approximately forty post-World War Two apartment buildings, ranging from eight to eighteen storeys, which line the wide north-south avenues of Jameson, Dowling, Spencer, Dunn, and Triller. There are an equal number of small three-to-five-storey apartment buildings, dating from the early twentieth century, along the east-west arteries of Queen and King and on some of the smaller side streets. Approximately 150 of the larger houses in South Parkdale have been converted into small apartments. The casual observer of South Parkdale can thus see a cluster of high-density housing, much of it visibly poorly maintained, and a preponderance of dollar stores, social service agencies, doughnut shops, and cheque-cashing establishments along King and Queen Streets east of Jameson. But, depending on the street you visit, you can also view more than five hundred detached, semi-detached, and row houses with single-family owners, including the grandest Victorian architecture in Toronto. Some of these houses command

**PARKDALE TODAY**

N

Fermanagh Av
Wabash Av
Lukow Ter
Wright Av
Rideau Av
Fern Av
Garden Av
Lansdowne Av
Galley Av
Sorauren Av
West Lodge
Pearson Av
Cunningham Av
Marion St
Roncesvalles Av
Seaforth Av
Brock Av
Harvard Av
Virtue St
Margaret Lane
Earnbridge
Callender St
Saunders Av
Fuller Av
MacDonell Av
West Lodge Av
O'Hara Pl
Maple Grove
Strickland Av
Grafton
Noble St
Abbs
O'Hara
Queen St. West
Triller Av
Laxton Av
Milky Way
Melbourne Pl
Wilson Park Rd
Beaty Av
Dowling Av
Leopold
Grove
Elm Av
Gwynne Av
Melbourne Av
Maynard Av
King St West
Lake Shore Blvd West
Glenavon Rd
Springhurst
Jameson Av
Close Av
Dunn Av
Cowan Av
Spencer Av
Tyndall Av
Dufferin St
Temple Av
Gardiner Expwy
Trenton Ter
Thorburn Av
Spencer Av
Tyndall Av
Fort Rouille St

*Lake Ontario*

0    500    1000m

*Map 2.* The streets of Parkdale, 2002
*Source:* MapArt Publishing, Map 119 (West Toronto), 2002. Map created by
Ric Hamilton, McMaster University.

prices well beyond $800,000, while the greater Toronto median house price hovers around $400,000.

North Parkdale, in contrast, has a 60/40 mix of rental and owned housing units. With the exception of the eighteen-storey, 720-unit behemoth that is West Lodge Apartments and a handful of other high-rise apartment buildings, the housing stock north of Queen consists of detached, semi-detached, and row houses, along with duplexes and low-rise apartment buildings. Quite often, all these house forms are found on a single street. Along the rail lines, there are also several dozen small industrial buildings that have recently been converted into loft-style condominiums. The visitor alert to the signs of gentrification might see them by walking west of Jameson along Queen Street and then north: the well-designed cafes and art galleries in the "Antique Alley" stretch of Queen Street east of Roncesvalles, elaborate gardens and expensive cars in front of some of the houses, a gourmet shop or two, the Film Buff video store on Roncesvalles, as opposed to the Blockbuster on Queen Street. According to a regular report distributed by a local real estate agent, house prices just east of Roncesvalles doubled between 1996 and 2002 (Chaddah 2002).

The resultant situation bears some resemblance to the "dual city" model proposed by John Mollenkopf and Manuel Castells (1991), with rich and poor living in close proximity but in different perceptual worlds. More precisely, it resembles two of the four sectors of the "quartered city" in Peter Marcuse's modification (1989) of the dual city metaphor: the "gentrified" alongside the "tenement" city.

Using the case study of Parkdale within a context of other theories and studies of neighbourhood change, with a particular focus on the Anglo-American societies of Canada, the United States, the United Kingdom, and Australia, this book has two purposes. First, at an empirical level, I wish to compare the changing images of a single neighbourhood with social and housing conditions over time, in order to ascertain (for instance) whether Parkdale was a residential upper-middle-class suburb at the time it was being so described, and whether Parkdale predominantly contained poor people who were poorly housed when it was being described as a slum. Second, at a theoretical level, I wish to explore the relationships among perceptions of a place's past, present, and future, its evolving social and physical conditions, and planning policy, and thus contribute to the literature on neighbourhood transition and urban social policy.

Case studies are a common form of urban historical research. At best, a neighbourhood case study allows a "deep understanding of one place which is transferable, with modifications, to others" (Harris 1996, 4). At worst, case studies can become local history, interesting in its details, but resistant to generalization. Longitudinal case studies can run into difficulties in finding comparative data over time.

The temporal scope of this book begins with Parkdale's initial marketing and development as a suburb in 1875, and extends to the present day. The starting date of 1875 is when the name Parkdale was first used by the Toronto House Building Association to distinguish its fifty-acre subdivision from the adjacent Irish working-class suburb of Brockton. Parkdale was developed during a period, 1875 to 1912, when Canadian urbanization and industrialization began to resemble trends in Great Britain, the United States, and Australia. Parallels will be made between these four societies, although Britain had a stronger tradition of government intervention in the housing market (Fishman 1987), and Canadian suburbs seem to have had a higher level of homeownership than in the United States, with more reliance on affordability strategies such as self-building and taking in lodgers (Harris 1996). Parkdale was also an early product of a change in house production and marketing in North America, the transition from small-scale individual developers to corporate involvement (Doucet and Weaver 1991, chap. 2).

I divide Parkdale's history into three distinct eras. These eras are based on changing perceptions of the neighbourhood, as shown in newspapers and magazines, government reports, academic studies, and marketing materials. Parkdale was initially marketed and generally described as a middle-class residential suburb, although its land use and income mix was diverse. A turning point for Parkdale can be detected from the second decade of the twentieth century, when the rhetoric of decline began to be applied to the neighbourhood. In 1912, a Toronto City Council debate over a bylaw to ban apartment buildings, which were described by local politicians as "breeders of slums," drew the newspaper spotlight to Parkdale, which contained a third of Toronto's larger (twenty or more unit) apartment buildings by 1915 (Dennis 1989, 1998). By the end of World War One, housing demand had begun to shift to smaller units, lower densities, and, for the upper middle class, more exclusive districts than Parkdale. This was true not only in Toronto, but across Canada (Sendbuehler and Gilliland 1998), the United States (Fishman 1987), and Britain (Rodger 2001). The largest residential developer in Toronto, Home Smith, planned to eradicate houses in lakeside Parkdale for a highway leading to his new suburban developments, according to the Toronto Harbour Commission's master plan for the waterfront, released in 1913 (Reeves 1993). As planning interventions in North American societies increased after World War Two (Doucet and Weaver 1991), Parkdale became a target for the urban renewal experiments characteristic of the time (Bacher 1993; Metzger 2000;

Beauregard 2003). Parkdale's status as a declining area was by then taken for granted in planning documents and in newspaper coverage.

The third era for Parkdale's image, that of becoming an urban village, began in the late 1960s. This period has seen the neighbourhood described, in local government reports and in news coverage, as simultaneously gentrifying and becoming a social service ghetto. There has been considerable reinvestment, both by private developers and by local and senior government. Unlike the urban renewal of the 1950s and 1960s, the emphasis of both private and public investors has been on renovating existing housing stock, rather than tearing down and replacing buildings. Therefore, I use a starting date of 1967, when community opposition led City Council to reject a neighbourhood plan recommending further destruction of the housing stock. The 1967-2002 period has been marked by increasing disparities within the neighbourhood. The number of poor people has rapidly increased in relation to the Toronto average, while local house prices have increased to exceed the Toronto average and the proportion of business and professional workers has risen to just below the Toronto average.[4]

## Data Sources

One of the chief methods I use in comparing social conditions with images in Parkdale over 125 years is the construction of a set of indicators to measure population, residential tenure (renters as opposed to owners), income, occupation, and number of housing units per building. In gathering indicators, I have been guided by popular stereotypes of suburbs and slums as they have evolved over the years. Suburbs were generally represented as places with relatively high homeownership and low population turnover, predominantly residential, and far from industries and other workplaces. They were considered to offer lower densities and more privacy than the city. Suburbs were seen as relatively well-to-do, homogenous in terms of class, race, and ethnicity ("the middle class suburb of privilege," as Fishman calls the stereotype), healthy, with lots of green space, and lived in by nuclear families with young children and unwaged mothers. Suburbs were described as modern in design but old-fashioned in values and virtues (Dyos and Reeder 1973, 369; Jackson 1985, 5-10; Fishman 1987, 5-6). Slums, in contrast, were considered crowded, with high-density rental housing. They were characterized by a transient, non-English-speaking and immigrant racial/ethnic-minority, and generally outcast society, with little privacy and much street activity, and consequent crime, violence, and morality concerns. Furthermore, slum inhabitants were of a low social and economic class, unhealthy and possibly genetically inferior, backward in social norms. They suffered from abnormal family life, such as adult men not in the paid labour force and mothers or children working for wages (Dyos and Reeder 1973, 364; J. White 1986, 2; Mayne 1993, 2-12). Above all, I have been guided by Dyos and Reeder's dictum (1973, 363) that suburbs and slums were defined in relation and in contrast to one another (see also Howe 1994 and Rodger 2001). I therefore compare Parkdale with similar neighbourhoods in Toronto and other North American cities, and with Toronto as a whole.

In 1939, Hoyt set out nine sources for studying urban growth and change, which resemble the sources I use to describe Parkdale's changing social and housing conditions in relation to the rest of Toronto. These sources are survey maps, city atlases, development maps showing locations of structures, early photographs, city histories and newspaper accounts, testimony of older inhabitants, building permits, property surveys such as assessment rolls, and appearance and style of remaining buildings. Fortunately, all of these primary sources of information are readily available. Fire insurance atlases indicating building footprints, materials, and number of storeys exist for the entire period of the study. Late-nineteenth-century street directories give householders' workplaces, providing valuable information about their journeys to work. And the city archives have an excellent collection of early photographs of houses and streets. Council minutes, reports, and correspondence for York Township (Parkdale was an unincorporated part of York Township until its incorporation as a village in 1879), the independent municipality of Parkdale, and the City of Toronto have been used to illuminate local government policy responses to perceived problems.

Toronto daily newspapers (eight in the late nineteenth century) extensively covered the suburb of Parkdale, especially during the years of its development and battles over amalgamation with the City of Toronto. In the early years of Parkdale, several newspapers had resident reporters in Parkdale who provided daily updates on the development of the new suburb. A relative lull in coverage from the early 1910s to the late 1960s was succeeded by another flurry of almost daily articles since the early 1970s. The three newspapers that continue to the present day, the *Toronto Star,* the *Telegram/Sun,* and the *Globe and Mail,* have searchable computer databases.

Oral histories were preserved in several 1970s projects, with audiotapes available of interviews with several early inhabitants of Parkdale, and a considerable number of reminiscences published in community newspapers and memoirs. While I have made particular efforts to search out and use the narratives of as wide a variety of residents as possible, in terms of gender, class, and ethnicity, the quotations from memoirs, oral histories, and newspaper articles are of necessity selective and unrepresentative. Because of the relative wealth of existing oral history sources, I did not carry out my own interviews with older inhabitants.

In the case of assessment records, I have been particularly fortunate. Richard Harris (1992) has developed a Toronto database comprising a one-in-twenty sample for the 1901 and 1913 assessment records, and a one-in-thirty sample for the 1921, 1931, 1941, and 1951 assessment records, broken down by subdivision. This database provides information and comparison of Parkdale's population density, occupational class of household head, tenure, subdivision of single-family housing, and multiple occupancy of buildings. I have supplemented this database with the entire assessment roll for Parkdale in 1881 and a one-in-ten sample for 1891, and can compare my data to similar information for Toronto during the late nineteenth century (Goheen 1970; Harris 1996).

Assessment rolls, and samples based on them, are not unproblematic. Assessments tend to underestimate the number of mobile and low-income transients, especially lodgers and other tenants (Harris 1996, appendix 2). The "class" of household heads is based on simplistic categories. The occupations of other members of the household are not taken into account, and no occupation is listed for female household heads, who were simply labelled by their marital status (single, married, or widowed) until 1951, regardless of whether they had paid employment. There are also some flaws in terms of the completeness of my assessment data. From 1891 to 1951, the majority of the study area was covered by the southern portion of Ward 6, and assessment area 6.1 is used as the equivalent of Parkdale for social and housing statistics from 1901 to 1951. Unfortunately, this assessment area deletes eight blocks in North Parkdale, west of Sorauren Avenue and north of Galley Avenue, approximately one-eighth of the study area (Map 3). This results in population figures being slightly underestimated from 1901 to 1951. The omission also may skew the occupational classification somewhat, underestimating the number of lower-middle-class salespeople, clerks, and skilled industrial workers in the suburb.

From the 1951 census onwards, when data are available by census tract, assessment roll information can be replaced with more accurate census tract information, which covers a wider range of factors: not only population density, tenure, subdivision of single-family housing, and multiple occupancy of buildings, but occupational class of all household members in the workforce, unemployment, residential stability (proportion of households that have lived in their dwelling for over five years), ethnic background, education, median household income and number of households living in relative poverty/wealth, average house prices and rents, and substandard houses.

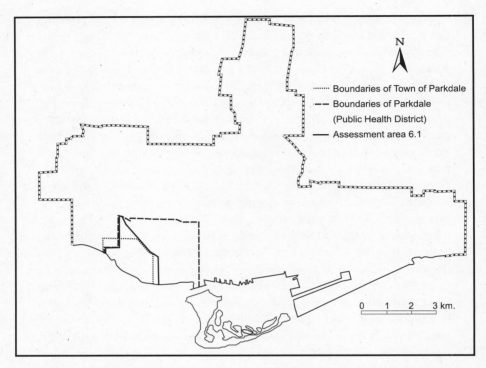

*Map 3.*   Boundaries of data sources: Village of Parkdale 1879-1889, assessment area 6.1, and Parkdale public health district
*Sources:* Laycock and Myrvold 1991; City of Toronto Assessment Rolls 1891-
1961; City of Toronto Public Health Department 1921-1975. Map created by
Ric Hamilton, McMaster University.

A particularly rich source of data is land registry records, which provide
sale prices and mortgage amounts, sources, and repayments. Because local
area information on changing house prices and mortgage availability is so
difficult to access before the 1951 census, I have gathered land transaction histories for all the buildings on six block faces in Parkdale. (A block
face is one side of a street between two intersecting streets.) There were
both practical and empirical reasons for sampling block faces, as opposed
to random properties. Land registry records in Toronto were, until they
were computerized in 2003 (after my research was finished), archaic and
difficult to use. Sales, mortgages, leases, and liens were hand-recorded in
huge and heavy books using the number of the original plan of subdivision, undifferentiated by street name or address until the 1980s. Conse-
quently, information on dozens of properties on a number of streets was

recorded together, sorted simply by the date on which a transaction was formally registered, which could be years after the actual sale or mortgage. I was given permission to use the land registry records free of charge for a six-week period, but this meant I had to focus on a small number of subdivision plans, ignore the actual deeds for the most part, and gather all information about owners beforehand using assessment records, so I could track which property was being referenced. A positive effect of sampling block faces was that it allowed me to understand how the occupancy of streets changed dramatically at certain points in time: for instance, the influx of Eastern European immigrant families on Galley Avenue between 1949 and 1959.

I chose the six block faces to represent the diversity of housing and land-use types, development eras, and locations in Parkdale, and cross-checked tenure and household head's occupation for 1901, 1921, and 1941 to ensure that the information was broadly representative of the neighbourhood. Three sample block faces shifted from working-class dwellings to a more mixed set of inhabitants over time, one sample block face was built up in upper-middle-class villas that slowly became subdivided into ever more substandard accommodations, one sample block face remained mixed in both land-use and social composition, and the final block face was expropriated for an expressway in the 1910s, with the houses torn down by the 1950s.

The first sample block face, in order of development, is the east side of Gwynne Avenue between Melbourne Avenue and Queen Street West (see Map 2). Part of the first Parkdale subdivision registered in 1875, it was developed in the early 1880s, mostly with small two-storey row houses. Clusters of low-priced row housing were typical of many streets close to the railroad tracks and industries east of Dufferin Street. Gwynne's original population was mostly working-class tenants, and homeownership increased slowly throughout the twentieth century. There was some gentrification, and considerable house price inflation, from 1970 onwards.

The second sample block face is the north side of Noble Street between Strickland and Brock Avenues. It was subdivided during the 1880s land boom by one of the many female developers who populate Parkdale's early history, Pamela Noble, daughter of a local landowning family, and built up immediately in a combination of small industries and row housing. Both industrial and residential properties changed hands infrequently until the 1970s. In the late 1990s, the industrial buildings were converted into live-work lofts and condominium apartments.

The third sample block face is the north side of Queen Street West between O'Hara Avenue and West Lodge Avenue. Subdivided in the 1870s, built up in the 1880s and 1890s, and relatively unchanged in physical form to this day, this is a handsome set of properties at the centre of Parkdale's main commercial street. The shops, and the tenants of the apartments above them, reflect Parkdale's changing fortunes over the years.

The fourth sample block face is the east side of Dowling Avenue between Lake Ontario and King Street West. Subdivided in the 1880s and built up intermittently between the 1880s and the 1910s, this block face is typical of the grand avenues lined with the villas of the wealthy that were once taken to represent Parkdale as a whole. Conversion of these villas into flats was common from the 1910s onwards. In the 1920s, two low-rise apartment buildings were constructed on what had been empty lots. From the 1950s to the 1970s, a large developer bought up many properties in this block face, resulting in the construction of two privately owned high-rise apartment buildings, and a controversial parcel of land was eventually developed as public housing. Today, the block face consists of three original villas, all converted into single-room-occupancy apartments, plus two low-rise and three high-rise apartment buildings.

The fifth sample block face is the south side of Empress Crescent between Dunn and Jameson Avenues. It is one of eight streets, with a total of 170 houses, destroyed for the construction of the Gardiner Expressway in the late 1950s. Like most of these streets, its housing was built relatively late, between 1900 and 1913, and many of the villas and semi-detached houses were soon converted to multiple occupancy. After 1913, the houses were slowly expropriated and torn down by the City of Toronto for road allowance or parkland.

Finally, I sample the north side of Galley Avenue between Macdonell and Sorauren Avenues. This avenue was subdivided in the 1880s but not built up until the tail end of the 1906-1913 Toronto housing boom. The substantial two- and three-storey semi-detached and row houses were initially sold to British immigrant working-class and lower-middle-class families. There were very few re-sales until 1949, when many houses began to be sold to Eastern European working-class families. Another changeover began in the 1980s, as middle-class homeowners began to predominate.

Unfortunately, it is difficult to find comparative information on Toronto house prices, mortgage financing, and ethnic/class change before 1951. Some limited data exist on mortgage financing in particular neighbourhoods or parts of the city in the mid-twentieth century (Murdie 1986, 1991; Paterson 1991), and some comparative data are available on central neighbourhoods between 1981 and 1996 (Ley 1996). I also compare Parkdale trends with the limited data on land prices, including house price inflation, in other North American cities and internationally (Hoyt 1970 in Chicago; Edel, Sclar, and Luria 1984 in Boston; Ball and Wood 1999 internationally).

Further data can be gathered from secondary sources. Housing quality can be gauged not only from fire insurance atlases but from City Council reports in 1934 and 1942 mapping "substandard houses" and further reports in 1946 and 1956 judging housing quality on a neighbourhood level. Public health annual reports give information on death from infectious disease and child mortality, common health indicators, broken down by district, although the Parkdale public health district is much larger than the boundaries I use, comprising all of west-central Toronto from Bathurst Street to High Park.

Information on ethnic origins of inhabitants is harder to find. Toronto was a more homogenous city than many of its US counterparts in the pre-World War Two period. The 1951 census shows that 73 percent of Toronto's population was of British (Anglo-Celtic) origin, and Parkdale's average was the same. However, it is sometimes possible to identify the presence of ethnic minority individuals and, in a few cases, communities in Parkdale, by the last name in assessment records, some oral or local history sources, and insurance atlases (which mark places of worship). Information on crime rates was not available broken down by police district for most of the period of this study, and therefore was not included in my set of indicators.

For the changing images of Parkdale, I rely on both the writings of outsiders – journalists, marketers, politicians, civil servants, social reformers, academic researchers – and on neighbourhood oral histories and memoirs (Harney 1985, 8-9). Representations of the community in newspaper photographs, maps, advertisements for new and renovated property, and historical markers have also been used as evidence of changing perceptions (Sies 2001). As will be discussed in the next chapter, an influential theory of "urban growth machines" was developed in the 1970s to explain how local politicians, land developers and marketers, and some social reformers and members of the media worked together to shape public opinion and influence policy (Jonas and Wilson 1999). In all three eras of Parkdale's history, journalists, local politicians, social reformers, property developers, and real estate agents played powerful roles in creating images to describe the neighbourhood and in developing policy in response to these images. There was never an easy consensus over these images, and full play will be given to the relative power of conflicting images of place over time. Aside from the primary sources of newspaper articles and oral histories, secondary sources include an excellent local history of

Parkdale before its annexation by the City of Toronto in 1889 (Laycock and Myrvold 1991), numerous planning reports, especially from the late 1960s onwards, and mentions of Parkdale in many academic and popular non-fiction books, plays, memoirs, novels, and articles written about planning, history, and neighbourhoods in Toronto (Goheen 1970; Moore 1979; Ganton 1982; Kaplan 1982; Careless 1984; Lemon 1985, 1986; Murdie 1986; Reeves 1992a, 1993).

# 1
# A Good Place to Live? Perceptions and Realities of Suburbs, Slums, and Urban Villages

> Now he was warming to his theme: to chart the life of each word, he continued, to offer its *biography,* as it were, it is important to know just when the word was born, to have a record of the register of its birth ... And after that, and for each word also, there should be sentences that show the twists and turns of meaning – the way almost every word slips in its silvery, fish-like way, weaving this way and that, adding subtleties of nuance to itself, and then perhaps shedding them as the public mood dictates.
>
> – Simon Winchester, *The Professor and the Madman*

Parkdale has been described over time by a succession of key words and phrases: *suburb, slum,* and *urban village.* The definitions of the terms *suburb* and *slum* have changed over the years, and have been supplemented by other terms used as urban locality describers, such as *bowery, bohemia, ghetto,* and *urban village.* These labels are, of course, not unique to Parkdale, but are products of the broader Anglo-American discourse related to the suburban ideal in the nineteenth century, fears of central city decline in the early twentieth century, and the new rhetoric of central city versus suburb in the late twentieth century. The relationship between such perceptions of a place and social conditions is described in this chapter.

## Perceptions of Place and Urban Differentiation in Three Intellectual Traditions

As Edward Relph (1976, 3) posits, "Places have meaning: they are characterized by the beliefs of man [sic]." Throughout the nineteenth and twentieth centuries, as developed English-speaking nations became more urbanized, cities and the components of cities attracted considerable description and analysis. Both statistical and perceptual descriptions sought to discover meaning in these urban places.

For some theorists, a description was an uncomplicated dissection of an underlying objective reality that could be universally discerned and applied. This view is evident, for example, in the writings of sociologists associated with the University of Chicago in the 1920s. The members of the Chicago school were influenced by the great German and French sociologists of the nineteenth century: Emile Durkheim, Georg Simmel, Ferdinand Tonnies, and Karl Marx (Chorney 1990, 100-102). They were also influenced by evolutionary theory, especially as these biological theories had been adapted to human society by writers such as Herbert Spencer (Sibley 1995). The Chicago school sought to apply the sociological traditions of Europe to American cities, while removing any hint of class struggle that might attach the label *communist* to them in the highly politicized university environment of the 1920s (Chorney 1990, 102).

According to Robert Park's seminal 1925 article, "The City," urban growth and differentiation are results of "sympathy, rivalry and economic necessity." These forces are neutral, structural, and essentially unchangeable. Rich and "fashionable residential quarters" simply "spring up," "from which the poorer classes are excluded because of the increasing value of the land." Slums arise because some people are weaker than others: "There grow up slums which are inhabited by great numbers of the poorer classes who are unable to defend themselves from association with the derelict and vicious." Communities within the city change through a natural and inevitable progression: "The past imposes itself upon the present, and the life of every locality moves on with a certain momentum of its own" (Park 1974, 5-6).

Ernest Burgess, another key member of the Chicago school, argued that the purpose of urban research is to facilitate the process of business and state planning, although the agency of planners is inherently limited to small interventions such as the creation of settlement houses and playgrounds in some "evil neighbourhoods" (Burgess 1974, 48; Park 1974, 8-9). The prognosis for particular neighbourhoods was bad: as cities were "invaded" by waves of immigration, neighbourhoods would inevitably become "junked" as they aged and were overtaken in popularity by newer communities on the periphery. However, the prognosis for urban society as a whole was good: these urban forces of "disorganization and organization may be thought of ... as co-operating in a moving equilibrium of social order toward an end vaguely or definitely regarded as progressive" (Burgess 1974, 54-58). As the city grew outwards, more and more families would attain homeownership, and more immigrants would become Americanized. Vice, crime, and poverty would remain a "natural, if not normal part of city life," but only among those who were "peculiarly fit for the environment in which they are condemned to exist" (Park 1974, 45).

As David Sibley (1995, 127) points out, "a model like Ernest Burgess' representation of the organization of social space in the western city attained the status of a universal statement, with the effect that other read-ings of the city, representing other world-views, were not seen." For the next fifty years, the Chicago school's moral map of the city dominated discourse on urban differentiation and growth, not only in the United States but in Canada (Harris and Lewis 2001) and Australia (Howe 1994) as well. Although the Chicago school accepted that the "city is ... a state of mind, a body of customs and traditions" (Park 1974, 1), its adherents maintained that this urban mind and body were universal, able to be mapped, understood, and analyzed across cultures.

Intellectual descendants of the Chicago school perfected tools to dissect the urban form. In the 1930s, Homer Hoyt modified the concentric ring model of the city to accommodate the notion of growth along radial sectors such as highways and rail lines. He elaborated on the uses of the rules and maps he provided for city planning and zoning, slum clearance, and mort-gage providers (Hoyt 1939). For Hoyt, as for many others who followed in the footsteps of the Chicago school, the role of the urban analyst, whether based in academe, government, or business, was to provide rational and scientific advice, based on perception and understanding of an underlying reality. Throughout, this reality was informed by a binary moral order. The central city was bad for people, and the people who were left there, after natural selection had removed those most fit to live in the suburbs, were bad.

David Harvey's *Social Justice and the City* disrupted the relationship between perception and reality posited by the Chicago school, and became an influential text for a new generation of urban analysts. Published in 1973 by an author previously known as a torchbearer for scientific mod-ernism, the book reinserted class conflict into the discussion of urban growth and structure. According to Harvey, the ruling class provides the dominant ideas, including the ideas about where rich and poor should live (147). Harvey sees postwar suburbanization (the movement of the majority of city dwellers into politically separate suburbs) as a logical out-growth of middle-class movement after jobs that have decentralized, along with a desire to avoid negative externalities associated with poor people, such as degraded public services and depressed property values. The pro-vision of new residential and industrial space in suburbs allows excess capital to be used to create new products, "new wants and needs, sensi-bilities and aspirations" (311). Discriminatory practices, including zoning out low-income housing, stop the poor from also moving outwards to fol-low the jobs (57-66). Spatial structure is thus derived from the economic basis of society (293), and perceptions and values arise from the prevail-ing social and political norms.

Harvey Molotch also drew his inspiration from a Marxist view of the city to analyze urban politics. He was specifically critical of pluralism, the dominant discourse of American political science into the 1970s. This school of thought, closely allied to the Chicago school, held that decisions taken were the result of equally competing interest groups. In contrast, Molotch argued that urban politics could be seen as a machine for urban growth, which was supported by an ad hoc coalition of real estate interests (property developers, mortgage lenders such as banks, and realtors), local media, and politicians (both local and federal). The urban growth machine theory, further reinforced by the insights of sociologist John Logan, remains influential today (Jonas and Wilson 1999).

The first feminist critiques of urban form and power were influenced by the Marxist perspective. Beginning with a 1973 article, "Social Change, the Status of Women, and Models of City Form and Development," published by Pat Burnett in *Antipode*, "the radical journal of geography," and continuing with the founding of *Women and Environments Magazine* in 1976 and the publication of *New Space for Women* ( Wekerle, Peterson, and Morley 1980) and *Women in the American City* (Stimpson et al. 1981), an underlying socio-economic structure of patriarchy as well as capitalism was held responsible for the dominant ideology. This ideology promoted the city as an appropriate space for men, and the suburban home as an appropriate space for women. Feminists explicitly critiqued the moral values behind the view of suburbs as safe havens, positing central cities as places of economic opportunity and relative social freedom.

For Harvey and many of the critical urban theorists who followed in his footsteps,[1] perception is mediated by the largely invisible and taken-for-granted power system of capitalism and, in the case of feminists, patriarchy. The role of the critical analyst is to strip away the veil of seemingly natural behaviours in order to reveal the exploitative system that lies underneath. Despite the omnipresence of this underlying structure, urban agents have opportunities to subvert power and make positive changes. The most eloquent explanation of this urban agency is found in the work of Harvey's contemporary Manuel Castells (1983). However, Marxist and feminist urban analysis of the late 1970s and early 1980s continued, rather than disrupted, several assumptions behind modern quantitative research. For a radical urbanist of that era, there remained a reality to be uncovered, and furthermore, a reality which is universal, largely structural, and rational.

A third wave of theories on urban growth and structure began to be popularized in the 1980s and 1990s under the umbrella title of postmodernism. Postmodernists consciously reject the notion that there is a simple or universal reality that can be perceived through research and analysis. Indeed, the role of the researcher, according to David Sibley, the author of *Geographies of Exclusion* (1995), might be to show "how exotic [the previous] constitution of reality has been," to "emphasize those domains most taken for granted as universal ... [and] make them seem as historically peculiar as possible." Like Marxists, postmodernists tend to assume that divisions within space are a reflection of unequal power relations. Unlike Marxists, postmodernists generally see that superstructure as encompassing inter-related forms of oppression on the basis of gender, ethnicity, sexuality, and abilities, as well as class. Thus, Sibley begins his book by contending that "power is expressed in the monopolization of space and the relegation of weaker groups in society to less desirable environments" (ix). In one way, this echoes Burgess and Harvey in their formulations of urban succession: the strong overcoming the weak in an eternal struggle over living space. Like Harvey, Sibley attributes socio-spatial differentiation to unequal division of power, not to some natural force, as was the case with the Chicago school. Power is socially constructed and thus mutable.

Unlike Harvey, Sibley posits a complex face to power. Attempts to create a totalizing or universalizing critique of the city based on an underlying binary worldview, however progressive or even radical in nature, are wrong. Christine Boyer (1983, 60) adapts Michel Foucault's aphorism, "Against the plague, which is one of mixture, discipline brings into play its power, which is one of analysis," to urban studies. "So too," says Boyer of the birth of modern planning, "against the chaos of the city with its simultaneity of land uses, jumble of vehicles, multitudes of people, corrupt politicians, and labour unrest, there stood an ideal: the city as a perfectly disciplined social order." In the postmodern worldview, the first order of the researcher is to uncover past "myths" and "constructs of the imagination," as Alan Mayne (1993, 1) defines the historical slum, not to create a new layer of urban mythology. Complexity is not only inevitable but good: simple solutions do not work.

I have a considerable amount of sympathy with this perspective. If we say, for instance, that a century of urban planning was dead wrong, what claims allow us to say that an alternative path is right? Can we still say, as Jane Jacobs did forty years ago in *The Death and Life of Great American Cities* (1992, 4), that it is possible to create maxims for successful cities based on "how cities work in real life," if there is no shared understanding of real life?

Postmodern writers on the city have been critiqued, perhaps most effectively by Harvey, as theorists who privilege arcane analyses of discourse over concrete issues of social disparities and what to do about them. After all, asks Harvey (1989, 291), if it is "impossible to say anything of solidity and permanence in the midst of this ephemeral and fragmented world, then why not join in the game?" Ironically, emphasis on unpacking perceptions was pioneered by several cultural analysts who wrote from a Marxist perspective, such as John Berger and Raymond Williams. As the latter wrote in *Keywords*, changes in the meanings of words both reflect and can shape changes in a society (R. Williams 1976, 9-10). The question for Harvey, and for myself as a researcher, is how unpacking changes in the meanings of words can lead to some form of positive social change.

In order to talk about positive social change, I believe it is necessary to accept that there is some level of social reality, however imperfectly discernable. As Mayne (1993, 1-2) says in his dissection of slum discourse in English-speaking societies between 1880 and 1914, "deplorable life choices available to inner-city residents were real in material and absolute senses," although "the term slum, encoded with the meanings of a dominant bourgeois culture, in fact obscured and distorted the varied spatial forms and social conditions to which it was applied." Mayne argues that the prevalent discourse shapes the choice of which statistics are used and which voices are heard, a point also made by Robert Beauregard in his analysis of a century of popular writing on the American city (2003, 239). Discourse analysis also allows hitherto obscured voices to have a say. For example, Sibley (1995) resurrects the relatively neglected writings of Jane Addams and W.E.B. Du Bois, two contemporaries of the Chicago school; Beauregard (2003) uncovers surprising ambivalence within a predominantly anti-city twentieth-century American discourse; and Elizabeth Wilson (1991) shows how cities have offered women pleasure as well as danger.

A discussion of positive social change also requires a generally accepted goal against which progress can be measured. Current feminist and postmodernist writers such as the late Iris Marion Young are developing a politics of difference that posits tolerance of the "other" as a basis for a just urban society (Fincher and Jacobs 1998). Tolerance evokes, for these writers, not only an end to exclusionary practices that seek to discipline and punish those who do not fit societal norms. Tolerance also connotes a commitment to inclusion, choice, diversity, and rights to a basic set of urban goods, including housing, health, and rewarding work (Young 1990).

## The Binary Rhetoric of Suburbs and Slums

As discussed in the Introduction, cities and their component parts are often described in binary terms. For much of the nineteenth and early twentieth centuries, the most popular rhetorical opposition in talking about cities was to compare them to the countryside (R. Williams 1973). This was hardly surprising, since most migrants to the city were from rural areas and small towns, and thus had to accommodate themselves to a way of life significantly different from the one known by themselves and their parents. Sociologists like Georg Simmel and Emile Durkheim compared urban and rural mindsets, while visionaries like Ebenezer Howard proposed a new form of community, garden cities, that would combine the best of both city and countryside (Hall 1996). As suburbanization increased in the later twentieth century, the suburb/city dichotomy received a great deal of attention from scholars, who compared political representation, taxation levels, access to jobs and services, urban architectural form, and again, ways of life (e.g., Jackson 1985; Teaford 1986; Sewell 1993; Duany, Plater-Zyberk, and Speck 2000).

In this section, I propose to analyze a third dichotomy in "the rhetoric of urban space" (Wilson 1995): the relationship between the terms *suburb* and *slum*. For about a hundred years, from the mid-nineteenth century to the mid-twentieth century, these two terms were used as binary opposites, thesis and antithesis, in attempts to describe a good place to live. Slums were seen as urban problems, suburbs as solutions. Slums represented the societal nightmare: a shifting and shiftless population of renters and slumlords who destroyed the urban fabric; a mixture of noxious industries and a diseased and immoral underclass; a place to be avoided and feared; a cancer that might spread if not contained. Suburbs represented a dream for both individuals and the city as a whole: families owning homes and thus having a financial stake in improving their communities; separation of workplace and residence (for many men, at least); and the shared expertise of architects, planners, and enlightened developers promoting the best housing and community designs. Slums were, in short, unstable, unhealthy, and bad; suburbs stable, healthy, and good.

Forty years ago, US urban historian Sam Bass Warner (1978, vii-viii) summarized the "central event of the 1870-1900 era" as the "creation of a two part city, an old inner city and a new outer city, a city of slums and a city of suburbs, a city of hope and failure and a city of achievement and comfort." Harold Dyos and David Reeder (1973, 370), writing ten years later in the United Kingdom, took a far more critical approach to the reality of late-nineteenth-century suburbs and slums, but echoed the rhetoric: "the convulsions of the city became symbolic of evil tendencies ... while the serenity of the suburbs became a token of natural harmony."

Despite a vast literature on suburbs, and an equally impressive literature on slums, few writers have tried to come to grips with the historical trajectory of this rhetoric. Dyos, in his pioneering case study of an English nineteenth-century suburb, and more recently Kenneth Jackson (1985), Robert Fishman (1987), John Stilgoe (1988), and Witold Rybczynski

(1995), in their US-focused overviews of the origins of suburban life, all provide examples of the rise and fall of the suburban ideal, from pre-1800 descriptions of suburbs as bad places where bad people lived (i.e., slums), to late-nineteenth- and early-twentieth-century descriptions of suburbs as opposites of, and solutions to, slums. The change coincided with the large-scale industrialization and urbanization of cities in Europe, the United States, Australia, and Canada. These writers also grapple with the future of suburbs, coming to dissimilar conclusions about their popularity and viability.

Similarly, writers on slums, such as Gareth Stedman-Jones (1984), Thomas Philpott (1978), Terry Copp (1974), and Alan Mayne (1993) have all provided short histories of the origin of the word *slum* in the early nineteenth century, and its adoption as a problem with local, national, and international dimensions during the last quarter of the nineteenth century and the prewar years of the twentieth century. Philpott, Copp, and Mayne identify a similar time frame (between 1870-1880 and 1914-1930) as the heyday of government reports, surveys, and sensationalist literature on slums. Robert Beauregard (2003) describes the second flourishing of slum literature in the United States: the series of slum reports during the Great Depression of the 1930s and the integration of slum stereotypes into post-World War Two urban renewal schemes, even as the term *slum* was superseded by *inner city* (see also the debate between Metzger 2000 and critics Downs 2000, Galster 2000, and Temkin 2000).

The rhetoric of suburbs and slums lingers today as gentrification has brought on the "class remake of the central urban landscape" (Smith 1996, 39). According to Beauregard (1986, 36), "The image of a city and its neighbourhoods are manipulated in order to reduce the perceived risk and to encourage investment." Peter Williams (1986, 56) describes how the "original features" and "period charm" of nineteenth-century suburban housing are highlighted for Melbourne and Sydney gentrifiers, while Caroline Mills (1993) gives a similar example in a case study from Fairview Slopes, Vancouver. Certain artifacts associated with slums, such as abandoned industrial buildings (Zukin 1989, 73) or a "heroic" immigrant past (Mele 2000b, 643), can also inspire nostalgia in middle-class homebuyers. These safe versions of the older city (the industries no longer spew out smoke, the period charm of older houses has been altered to provide indoor toilets and central heating, the descendants of heroic immigrants are now second- and third-generation citizens) are contrasted with the supposed "anonymity and homogeneity" of current suburbs (Howe 1994, 157; see also Caulfield 1994). Gentrification can be seen as a way to restore a past order to the current urban wilderness, wherein a new generation of urban pioneers harvests what is best from the central city's past, leaving the now old-fashioned outer suburbs to those with less courage and fore-sight (Smith 1996). Gentrification can also be described as a cyclic reversal of the centre-periphery dichotomy: the urban village is now the repository of community spirit and civic virtue, while the bad city of bad people is embodied in Los Angeles-type suburban sprawl (Peel 1995b).

The rhetoric of suburbs and slums also features in the urban theories described in the first part of this chapter. The Chicago school and its suc-cessors see suburbs and slums as a natural, evolutionary, structural re-sponse to competition between individuals for space (Park 1926; Burgess 1974; Zorbaugh 1976). Positivists like Hoyt (1939, 1970) and Hoover and Vernon (1959), and Marxists like Harvey (1973) and Smith (1978), in their early works, share the belief that the divide between suburbs and slums is an economically rational outgrowth of conflict within industrial capital-ist economies. Feminists like Gwendolyn Wright (1980), Dolores Hayden (1984), Margaret Marsh (1990), and Elizabeth Wilson (1991) see suburbs and slums as a socially constructed and not particularly rational product of struggles over gender roles. Postmodernists of various stripes claim that the division between suburbs and slums is a discontinuous, fluid, and highly contingent reflection of oppression, which encompasses class, gen-der, ethnicity, and other grounds of difference (Boyer 1983; Harvey 1989; Mayne 1993; Sibley 1995; Smith 1996).

## The Development of the Suburban Dream

The word *suburb,* derived from a Latin term meaning "beyond or below the city," has a long history. The suburban dream itself is even older. Jack-son (1985, 12) cites a letter from a nobleman to the king of Persia in 539 BC: "Our property seems to me the most beautiful in the world. It is so close to Babylon that we enjoy all the advantages of the city, and yet when we come home we are away from all the dust and noise." Like the anonymous Persian, a few wealthy people throughout European and Asian history could afford to spend weekends in a villa, near the commerce and culture of walled cities, but far from their noise and pollution. The com-bination of proximate access and psychological distance remained a com-mon theme in the suburban ideal for the next 2,500 years.

More commonly, suburbs housed those on the fringes of urban society. They included, in medieval Europe, the craftsmen not associated with guilds, obnoxious trades such as leather working, immigrants not yet accepted into their adopted societies, and places of amusement beyond taxes and moral laws. In both suburbs and cities at the beginning of the eighteenth century, "the poor were living cheek by jowl with the rich to an extraordinary degree" (Dyos 1961, 34). Even in the first stages of the industrial revolution in Britain, migrants to cities tended to settle in outer districts. Only when industries concentrated within cities, in the early and mid-nineteenth century, did the demand for casual labour bring a wave of impoverished newcomers into the heart of the city, while the proliferation of wharves, warehouses, stations, and offices began to cut into housing and increase land rents, expelling those residents who had any choice about where to live (Stedman-Jones 1984).

A great deal of the imagery later associated with central city slums was developed to describe pre-industrial suburbs. Six hundred years ago, in *The Canterbury Tales*, an alchemist's servant could describe his "sly" and "crafty" master living in "the suburbes of a toun," "lurkinge in hernes [hedges] and lanes blinde / Whereas thise robbours and thise thieves by kinde / Holden hir pryvee fereful residence" (Chaucer 1974, 90). Suburbs were the home of the outlaw, a hidden and sinister landscape of dark dead ends. The Mephistophelean alchemist has the capacity to "infect al a toun" if allowed within its safe and regulated boundaries (103). Suburbs were also described in feminized and sexualized terms. In 1548, Nash, who wrote an early travelogue of Britain's capital city, asked: "London, what are they Suburbes but licensed Stewes [brothels]?" *Suburb sinner* was a common synonym for *prostitute* in the sixteenth and seventeenth centuries (Fishman 1987, 7). In Shakespeare's *Henry VIII* we find: "There's a trim rabble let in / Are these your faithfull friends o' th' Suburbs?" Mobs of potentially dangerous poor people, as Hall (1998), Wilson (1991), and others have pointed out, were a common concern in cities of the industrial era, and mobs, like pre-industrial suburbs, were often described as debased females (see the *Oxford English Dictionary* definition of *suburb*).

During the latter half of the eighteenth century, the term *suburb* went through a radical, although gradual, change. Stilgoe contends that eighteenth- and nineteenth-century English literature drew upon a classical thread that contrasted the morality of country life with the sinful city. American intellectual leaders like Thomas Jefferson propounded the belief that democracy would flourish only in smaller communities. And as basic knowledge of the origins and spread of infectious disease grew, densely packed urban centres were seen as less healthful (Stilgoe 1988, 38-45). By 1752, the novelist Samuel Richardson could receive a get-well note stating, "I hope that ... the air of your agreeable suburbane North-end, will restore you." The *Oxford English Dictionary* uses this example and others to support its statement that, by the 1820s, suburbs were associated with "professional men and artists." But negative imagery still lingered: in 1820, another writer of travelogues, the aptly named Crabbe, observed "Suburbian prospects, where the traveller stops / To see the sloping tenement on props." Fishman (1987, 62-63) says that *suburb* lost its negative connotation only in the 1840s.

The British were the "first predominantly urban-dwelling people in the long history of human settlement" (R. Williams 1973, 2), so it is hardly surprising that England, Scotland, and Ireland were experimenting with new urban forms in the early nineteenth century. St. John's Wood in London saw the first semi-detached houses, a compromise between villa and row house, in 1800, and Regent's Park in 1820 introduced the concept of a suburb planned around a green space (Fishman 1987, 64-65). However, it was Manchester, the "shock city" of the early nineteenth century, in historian Asa Briggs' phrase (1993), that drew most attention from contemporary writers. Manchester's growth was phenomenal: from a town of 17,000 in 1750, it grew to 70,000 by 1801 and 303,000 by 1851. And Manchester suburbanized as it grew. By the 1830s, a pattern was discernable: a central business core surrounded by an industrial zone with working-class dwellings interspersed, in turn surrounded by the houses of the new middle class (Fishman 1987, 74-75). The development of middle-class suburbs in Manchester was supported by a combination of low land prices in the periphery and hyper-inflated central city land prices. In other words, a middle-class household could sell a house in the central city for a good price and use that money to buy a much more spacious house and lot in the suburbs, commuting by the new technologies of rail or horse tram. There were also push factors that drove the middle class from the central city: fear of industrial riots, for example, which translated into a fear that lower classes would follow the middle class to the periphery and depress the value of their new homes (81-87).

Frederick Engels, who lived and worked in Manchester, wrote in 1845 that: "The town itself is peculiarly built, so that a person may live in it for years, and go in and out daily without coming into contact with a working-people's quarter or even with workers ... The facades of main thoroughfares mask the horrors that lie behind from the eyes of factory owners and the middle-class managers who commute into the city from outlying suburbs" (1969, 78-79). A little more than a century later, but in the same vein, Dyos and Reeder (1973, 369) described "the middle class suburb" as "an ecological marvel. It gave access to the cheapest land in the city to those having most security of employment and leisure to afford the time and money spent traveling up and down; it offered an arena for the manipulation of social distinction to those most adept at turning them into shapes on the ground; it kept the threat of rapid social change beyond the horizon of those least able to accept its negative as well as its positive advantages." The growth of suburbs can thus be seen as an example of successful middle-class control over space, a symbolic wall protecting the middle class from "the foul-smelling environment of the poor, the smell of the poor – and the poor themselves," in the words of Sibley (1995, 24).

There are, of course, many ways to divide the city by class, and Sibley is actually referring to the radical replanning of Paris by Baron Haussmann in the mid-nineteenth century. Haussmann's wide boulevards, lined with luxury apartments and exclusive stores and theatres thanks to generous government loans to developers, made the central city safe for the middle class by clearing out slums and effectively banishing the poor to the periphery (Harvey 1985). The contrasting experience of Paris indicates that another factor needs to be taken into account to understand the flourishing of the middle-class suburb in Anglo-American cities during this period: the growing cult of the nuclear family. The rise of a new set of meanings for *suburb* in Anglo-American culture coincided with the rise of new meanings for *family* (Marsh 1990, xii). According to Raymond Williams, the term *family* evolved between the Middle Ages and the nineteenth century from meaning everyone living in a household, including servants, to meaning a small kin-group sharing a house. Thus in 1631, a description of a family could read, "himself and his wife and daughters, two mayds [sic] and a man," while in the early nineteenth century, the economist James Mill defined a family as "the group which consists of a Father, Mother, and Children" (cited in R. Williams 1976, 108). Sibley talks of "sites of nationalist sentiment, including the family, the suburb, and the countryside, all of which implicitly exclude" others, while Wright devotes an entire book to the intertwined relationship between the idea of a "'model' or typical house and the notion of the model family" (Sibley 1995, 108; Wright 1980, 1).

Influential designers of pattern-book homes and early planned suburbs doubled as moralists for suburban family life. A.J. Downing, the Beecher sisters, and Frederick Law Olmsted, all prominent in the development of mid-nineteenth-century US suburbs, held that they were the only way to protect women and children from the evil influences of the city. Suburbs also provided opportunities for women to exert positive influences on society through their moral leadership in the home (Wright 1980). Fishman (1987, 110) contends that the main difference between Anglo-American and continental European culture was a religious concern in Anglo-American culture with the sin found in the city, primarily in evangelical religions such as Methodism and Presbyterianism. Wilson (1990, 6) elaborates on this Anglo-American notion: "Nineteenth century planning reports, government papers and journalism created an interpretation of the urban experience as a new version of Hell, and it would even be possible to describe the emergent town-planning movement – a movement that has changed our cities almost beyond recognition – as an organized campaign to exclude women and children, along with other disruptive elements – the working class, the poor, and minorities – from this infernal urban space altogether."

Thus a tension existed within the new notion of the suburb, between those developers and property holders who valued exclusivity and increasing land values for the middle and upper classes, and those evangelical visionaries who wanted everyone living in the suburbs for the sake of their souls (not to mention their acquiescence and productivity as workers and begetters of the next generation of workers). Brooklyn is an example of the latter type of "big tent" community. The *Brooklyn Star* proclaimed in 1815 that the suburb "must necessarily become a favorite residence for gentlemen of taste and fortune, for merchants and shopkeepers of every description, for artists, artisans, mechanics, laborers, and persons of every trade in society," and Walt Whitman, writing of "Brooklyn the Beautiful," observed fifteen years later: "men of moderate means may find homes at a moderate rent, whereas in New York City there is no median between a palatial mansion and a dilapidated hovel." Brooklyn developed its own commerce, industry, and culture (cited in Jackson 1985, 27-32). In 1870, Brookline, outside Boston, called itself the "richest town in the world," although only 25 percent of its household heads were executives, professionals, or manufacturers, and 40 percent were blue-collar, first-generation Irish immigrants, most working in nearby industries (100). Another Boston suburb, Jamaica Plain, had streets where affluent businessmen and their families lived adjacent to parks, but also streets that housed every other occupational group, including industrial workers and labourers working small market gardens (Von Hoffman 1994, 7, 33).

While the big tent suburb may have been the norm, other pre-existing settlements at the periphery of large US cities tried to maintain or increase their exclusivity through early attempts at zoning and residential restrictions. The town council of Cambridge, Massachusetts, for example, promoted residential over commercial or industrial expansion in the mid-nineteenth century. Meanwhile, newer developments like Beacon Hill in Boston, Gramercy Park and Washington Square in New York, Germantown in Philadelphia, and Nob Hill in San Francisco marketed themselves to an exclusive group of homebuyers (Jackson 1985, 21-25). In the later nineteenth century, restrictive covenants became increasingly common. These could ban non-residential uses and subdivision of land, prescribe a minimum value for a house along with nature and colour of materials and architecture style, or exclude particular racial or ethnic groups (most commonly blacks and Jews) from buying property (Fishman 1987, 151; Doucet and Weaver 1991, 100-101). Suburban communities also incorporated new residential designs to add value. Highbury New Park in Islington, London, used curving streets and a large central park to attract buyers in the 1850s (Hinchcliffe 1981), and in the 1860s Riverside outside Chicago was designed in the same fashion by Frederick Law Olmsted, the famed landscape architect of New York's Central Park (Fishman 1987). Perhaps most importantly, this period saw the beginning of a corporatization of the urban land process, although master-planned suburbs, developed and sold by one company, were not the norm until after 1950. Whereas subdividers, home builders, estate agents, and mortgage financiers had once worked separately, these functions began to be brought together within one firm. A more efficient housing production process allowed much more efficient social segregation by the developers themselves ( Weiss 1987; Doucet and Weaver 1991).

Mixed suburbs of the nineteenth century were often the result of a land marketing process that resembled today's discount fashion stores, where the worth of a product decreases rapidly with time. A developer would lay out multi-acre lots. If a few choice lots were taken but the majority remained unsold, the developer (who usually had borrowed short-term money on high interest to purchase, subdivide, and resell a piece of property) would further subdivide lots in order to sell them for less. Builders, in turn, would buy lots on speculation; if there was a glut in the middle-class housing market, they would erect two or three row houses rather than one villa on a lot. This process was seen in Manchester in the 1830s (Fishman 1987, 89), Islington in the 1860s (Hinchcliffe 1981, 33; J. White 1986, 12), and most North American suburbs until the turn of the twentieth century (Doucet and Weaver 1991, 33). Clifton, a hilly suburb three miles (five kilometres) north of Cincinnati's municipal boundary, comprised multi-acre country estates in the 1840s. By the 1890s, there was a much more varied mix of housing and apartments, lived in by blue-collar and white-collar workers and small businessmen, as well as merchants. Still, the image of "park like grounds, splendid residences, magnificent prospects" and inhabitants of "American stock" remained long after Clifton had become a mixed community (Miller 2001, 1-20).

Although a preponderance of small-scale developers made sense in highly unstable housing markets, some developers realized that profits could be realized by buying land while it was cheap and then marketing it over a longer period (Doucet and Weaver 1991, 81, 44). Potter Palmer used his influence as a member of Chicago's elite to make the Gold Coast the wealthiest section of Chicago in the 1870s. This involved draining and filling marshy land, and then changing the whole high-value commercial orientation of the city from an east-west to a north-south axis (Keating 1988; 66). William Harmon of Cincinnati and Samuel Gross of Chicago are usually credited with being the first home builder/developers to provide instalment-plan mortgages for more modest homebuyers, in the 1880s (Doucet and Weaver 1991, 84; Ward 1998, 83).

Gross was also a pioneer in place marketing, providing picnics at new home sites and running lushly illustrated newspaper and magazine advertisements extolling the virtues of suburban homeownership. According to Gross' advertisements, owning a home in the suburbs would ensure that children grew up with clean air and water, and that women were protected from immoral influences. Images of "good women" were common in illustrations marketing suburbs, just as illustrations of "bad women" were common in slum literature: an 1891 Gross advertisement shows a young lady, dressed in white, pointing at "virgin soil" (Ward 1998, 120). Freed from the depredations of "house renting sharks," families would enjoy personal and financial security by owning a house in the urban frontier. New suburban houses were advertised as having the latest in modern, labour-saving devices, and as being connected to central cities by efficient public transportation (railways and streetcars). Subdivisions were advertised as being on higher land, closer to nature, and upwind from smoke (which meant, generally, to the west of the city in the northern hemisphere, and east of the city in the southern hemisphere). The names of subdivisions used signifiers such as *park, heights, hill,* and *west* to convey these attributes. Gross possessed a particularly American melting-pot sensibility: he targeted advertisements to immigrant families in German, Swedish, Italian, and even Yiddish newspapers, while excluding black Americans from his working-class suburbs (90-91, 120-31).

By the beginning of the twentieth century, Anglo-American culture had fully embraced the notion of the suburban future, while developers provided a range of suburbs, from industrial working-class to exclusive to minority-culture (Harris and Lewis 2001). The developing suburban dream was based on the material realities of cheap land and quick profit, as well as ideological constructs of strictly separated gender roles, the moral purity of family life, and fear of the mob. The problem with the future, however, is that it keeps becoming the present, and the highly valued periphery had a tendency to merge into the central city with dizzying speed. Although in the 1890s a British observer noted that "the process of urbanisation has been modified by one of suburbanisation," Eric Lampard (1973, 29) adds that the "late Victorian belief in suburban 'purity' was belied by the fact that the suburbs of one generation were often indistinguishable from the town of the next; sometimes yesterday's suburb became today's slum." In 1925, Harlan Douglass' *The Suburban Trend* (1970, vi) pointed out what was becoming increasingly obvious, that suburbs were "intermediate in form. They are parts of evolving cities." The corollary to this statement was that "nearly all suburbs are either being made or being unmade" (164). Development was followed by decline as surely as birth led to death.

## Central City Decline and the Slum Nightmare

As suburbs developed their reputation as good places to live, living in the central city was increasingly derided by researchers and reformers. Compared to *suburb*, *slum* is a young word, which emerged along with the industrial city in the early nineteenth century. Slums in their original meaning were associated with rooming houses. The first written mention of a slum is in a British "flash," or slang, dictionary of the 1810s, where it derived from *slumber* and meant a short-term rental room. The term *back slum* gradually widened in the 1820s to encompass "a street, alley, court in a crowded district of a town or city, inhabited by the poor," then, by the 1840s, "a number of these streets or courts forming a thickly populated neighbourhood or district where the houses or conditions of life are of a squalid or wretched character" (*Oxford English Dictionary*).

Late-nineteenth-century suburbs were associated with good women, virtuous daughters and wives who were separated from the paid workforce; hard-working immigrants and migrants of European origin who were anxious to assimilate; and healthy children. From the first, slums were associated with their binary opposites: bad, immoral, working women; despised ethnic groups such as Gypsies, Irish, people of African origin, and Chinese; and physically and mentally stunted children and adults. In an 1824 history of gaming cited by the *Oxford English Dictionary*, we find this early use: "Regaling ... in the back parlour (*vulgo* slum) of an extremely low-bred Irish widow." By mid-century, the term *slum* also described "gypsy jargon" (the origin of Cockney), begging letters, and as a verb, "to do substandard work." Mayne provides a lexicon of dehumanizing descriptions of slum dwellers in the late nineteenth and early twentieth centuries: "savage nations," a "degenerate race"; in Birmingham, "trollops ... idle around"; in San Francisco, Chinese immigrants "live like prairie dogs" and are "human scum" (1993, 167, 181, 188). An 1894 US report, *Slums of Great Cities* (New York, Philadelphia, Baltimore, and Chicago), defined them as "an area of dirty back streets, especially when inhabited by a squalid and criminal population" (cited in Philpott 1978, 22). These attitudes lingered among those who focused on the physical and social problems of slums. A 1963 textbook, *New Towns for Old: The Techniques of Urban*

*Renewal,* instructed: "The Dwellers in a slum area are almost a separate race of people, with different values, aspirations, and ways of living ... Most people who live in slums have no views on their environment at all ... When we are dealing with people who have no initiative or civic pride, the task, surely, is to break up such groupings, even though the people seem to be satisfied with their miserable environments and seem to enjoy an extrovert social life in their own locality" (cited in Wilson 1991, 100).

Even such a progressive and scientific observer as the British social reformer Charles Booth contended that "the lowest class of occasional labourers, loafers, and semi-criminals," which he estimated at 1.25 percent of London's population, "are perhaps incapable of improvement" (1971, 54-56). But although some slum dwellers would not change, in the nineteenth century it became considered increasingly necessary for governments to destroy their homes, under the rationale of social and economic progress. A mid-century British observer of slums hyperventilated: "We fear them for what they are – beds of pestilence, where the fever is generated which shall be propagated to distant parts of town ... not only the lurking places, but the *nurseries* of felons. A future generation of thieves is there hatched from the viper's egg" (cited in J. White 1980, 9). The medical officer of health from Glasgow told the parliamentary Dwellings Committee in 1873, "The destructive part of the duty of the authorities is of more importance, if possible, than the constructive; the first and most essential step is to get rid of the existing haunts of moral and physical degradation, and the next is to watch carefully over constructing and construction, leaving, however, the initiative of these usually to the law of supply and demand" (cited in Stedman-Jones 1984, 198). From the 1830s onward, slums in London were "ventilated" by the construction of wide new roads. These were supposed to help slum dwellers by bringing in air, light, and police supervision, but the underlying impetus was to assist commercial growth (J. White 1980, 9-10). Between 1830 and 1880, approximately 100,000 people were displaced from central London by a combination of road, railway, and dock construction, with virtually no new housing constructed to accommodate those made homeless (Stedman-Jones 1984, 167). Similar case studies of the destruction of working-class slums in the late nineteenth and early twentieth centuries are provided by Mayne (1993) for Birmingham, Sydney, and San Francisco, and Philpott (1978) for Chicago. In every case, regulation and demolition of substandard housing was favoured over construction of low-cost housing in the central city. In the few cases in which low-cost housing was constructed by the state or private philanthropists, the rents were too high for the impoverished residents displaced by slum removal.

Unsurprisingly, there was enormous pent-up demand from working-class people for housing close to central workplaces in large cities. Booth pointed out in the 1870s that the middle-class "demand is for new houses, not old," which meant that they constantly migrated to peripheral areas where "streets are wider and houses have gardens of some sort." This "centrifugal action" left "inner ring" neighbourhoods to become increasingly filled up with "workshops and extensions," and eventually to become "overcrowded" (Booth 1971, 51-52, 421-22). Jacob Riis, writing at the turn of the century about New York City, distinguished between purpose-built "rear house" slums and "tenant houses" that had once been "decorous homes." As middle-class "residents moved out, once-fashionable streets along the East River fell into the hands of real estate agents and boarding house keepers." Although "in the beginning, the tenant house became a real blessing to that class of industrious poor" who needed to live near work, further subdivision resulted in a "class of tenantry living from hand to mouth, loose in morals, improvident in habits, degraded, and squalid as beggary itself" (Riis 1957, 5-6).

Jerry White describes the origins of the "worst street in North London," "Campbell Bunk" in Islington. Campbell Road's six-room houses were built for clerks and artisans in the 1860s, but speculative overbuilding for the lower middle class, combined with demand from workers at nearby industries, resulted in one or two houses being converted to lodgings. By the 1871 census, only twenty-six of the sixty-three occupied houses on the street were home to a single household, while five houses contained eighteen people each (for an average of three people per room). A few years later, a lodging-house keeper named John King obtained a licence to lodge ninety men in his six-room house (J. White 1986, 8-10).

An even more spectacular decline is recorded in Richard Sennett's case study of Union Park, Chicago. At the edge of Chicago in the early 1870s, Union Park housed "only the best families." By the 1890s, "only the worst families" would live there (Sennett 1974, 9). Sennett presents Union Park's rise and fall as a complex story. In the 1830s, when Chicago was still a tiny settlement, the area west of the Chicago River had stockyards and a tavern, plus the mansion and extensive grounds of Philo Carpenter. In 1837 Carpenter was forced to sell his land at a loss to a bank where he held loans, and the bank commenced developing the area as an exclusive neighbourhood for the upper middle class. A park and broad commercial avenues were laid out, and volunteer improvement societies, made up predominantly of women, began to organize family entertainments such as Saturday afternoon concerts and good works with female inebriates and foundlings. By 1860, the suburb had between six hundred and eight hundred mostly upper-middle-class residents.

But in the late 1860s, Potter Palmer began to promote the Gold Coast just north of the city as an elite commercial and residential hub. Some properties on Lake Street, Union Park's main commercial thoroughfare, became warehouses and bars. A more precipitous change occurred after the Great Fire of 1871, when tens of thousands of temporary refugees moved west of the river while the central city was rebuilt. Inevitably, most of the central city housing was lost, and developers wedged in smaller houses between mansions and in the back streets and alleys of Union Park. By 1880, twelve thousand people were living in the same forty-block area that, two decades before, had accommodated a hundred socially homogenous households. While there was "no sudden break from affluence to poverty," the suburban character of the area was forever lost. By the turn of the century, Dreiser's Sister Carrie lived near the new elevated railway in Union Park, trapped with her respectable poor family in the house that had eaten up most of their savings and was now declining in value (Sennett 1974, 12-50).

The decline of Union Park can be seen as the result of aggressive marketing of a competing elite area, along with an intensification process exacerbated by a natural disaster. Put simply, the decline was caused by investors investing elsewhere. But accounts of the rise and fall of residential areas by members of the Chicago school mention neither development industry boosterism nor the impacts of the Great Fire. Instead, Park (1974, 4) talks of "the inevitable processes of human nature [that] proceed to give these regions and these buildings a character." Slum residents are drawn to particular neighbourhoods, not by cheap rents or because there is nowhere else to go, but because "they are particularly fit for the environment in which they are condemned to exist" (45). The process of housing filtering to ever-lower classes is described by Burgess (1974, 57-58) in biotic terms: immigrant "invasion of the city has the effect of a tidal wave inundating first the immigrant colonies, the ports of first entry, dislodging thousands of inhabitants who overflow into the next zone, and so on and on until the momentum of the wave has spent its last force on the last urban zone." Despite a "relative degree of the resistance of communities to invasion," such resistance is futile (51-52). All that urban planners or social reformers can do is provide settlement houses to Americanize slum inhabitants and speed them on their generational progress towards the outer suburban zones. Change is inevitable, yet change is bad. Neighbourhoods in the process of "disorganization" are associated with "juvenile delinquency, boys' gangs, crime, poverty, wife desertion, divorce, abandoned infants, vice" (59).

A decade later, in the depths of the 1930s depression, Hoyt (1939) sought to give the insights of the Chicago school a more quantitative basis. He was more specific than his predecessors in two ways. First, he suggested "a series of techniques by which the 'terra incognita' of a city may be mapped and charted and the growth of its various parts measured" in fifty American cities (see Introduction). Based on this historical research, his findings suggested one major amendment to concentric zone theory, namely, the importance of sectoral paths in the outward movements of high-rental, industrial, and some low-income neighbourhoods. But the equation of the periphery with high status and centrality with low status remained largely unchanged: "From the high rental areas that are frequently located on the periphery of one or more sectors of American cities, there is a downward gradation of rents towards areas near the business centre. The low rent areas are usually large and may extend from this center to the periphery on one side of the urban community" (112).

Second, Hoyt was more specific about the causes of decline, while maintaining the basic thrust of the Chicago school argument. The proportion of buildings requiring repairs reduces the value of adjacent residential property, as do older buildings and centrality in general, a low proportion of owner-occupiers, and overcrowding, for which Hoyt (1939, 31-44) used the common measure of more than one person per room. Perhaps most important, "the presence of even one non-white person in a block otherwise populated by whites may initiate a period of transition," and, as already established by the Chicago school, transition equals decline (54). Third, Hoyt was specific about the uses of his theories: "city planning or zoning, slum clearance, and market surveys all require a knowledge of the patterns formed by types of neighbourhoods within the urban community" (81).

Indeed, urban planners, real estate developers, and mortgage guarantors were hungry for this kind of scientific information. The US government set up the Home Owners' Loan Corporation in 1933 to refinance long-term residential mortgages. This initiative was intended partly as an economic boost for the home construction industry, and partly to stimulate growth of new suburbs, which by this time were seen as the panacea for all urban evils. The Home Owners' Loan Corporation used maps based on the works of Burgess and Hoyt, which divided cities into four classes of neighbourhood. First-grade neighbourhoods consisted of new and homogenous homes, occupied by "American business and professional men." Neighbourhoods, no matter how well-to-do, that had experienced an "infiltration of Jews" were never "best" or "American." Second-grade neighbourhoods had "reached their peak" but were stable. The third class of neighbourhoods was "definitely declining," with an "appearance of congestion" due to factors like a lack of front yards. Houses in the fourth-class neighbourhoods, those given a "D" rating, were refused mortgage guarantees. New and good-quality homes in St. Louis, for example, were given a "D" rating (or "redlined," because of the colour code used in the maps) because they had "little or no value today, having suffered a tremendous decline in values due to the coloured element now controlling the district." Later programs such as the mortgage insurance offered by the Federal Housing Administration and the mortgages provided under the GI Bill also used these maps (Jackson 1985, 197-204).

By 1944 in New York City, it was assumed that the "almost complete removal of upper-middle income groups from the city and their replacement by unskilled coloured people" had occurred (Swan 1944, 1). Edgar M. Hoover and Herbert Vernon, in their 1959 analysis of that city, identified five stages of "residential evolution": from new single-family houses, to apartment buildings and other sources of increasing density, through a "slum invasion" by immigrants and non-whites, to a "thinning out" due to abandonment of "obsolete housing," and finally, urban renewal (192-202). In the 1970s, guides to urban revitalization reiterated these inevitable stages of housing decline (Ahlbrandt and Brophy 1975, 6-9).

This assumption of inevitable house value decline, buttressed by scientific maps and formulas, was devastating to individual homeowners. As Matthew Edel, Elliot Sclar, and Dan Luria (1984, 30, 7) point out, "filtering penalizes each group of investors," trapping most of their savings in a highly depreciable asset whose value is determined as much by neighbourhood perception as household maintenance. White homeowners in Chicago frightened of losing their equity threw themselves into ratepayer associations, advocated for zoning, restrictive covenants, and other conservative measures, and, when all else failed, smashed windows and set off bombs in black homes (Philpott 1978). Both active terrorism and passive redlining created black ghettoes in American cities, ghetto inhabitants being differentiated from slum dwellers by their total, involuntary, and perpetual segregation from better housing and neighbourhood conditions (xv).

The terms *slum* and *ghetto* had been used interchangeably by the Chicago school, despite different connotations. Slums have been considered to be creatures of poverty, places where poor housing and health conditions combine with a different and possibly dangerous population (such as foreigners) to evoke a mixture of sympathy and fear in authorities, which in turn generally leads to reform. Ghettoes, whether for Jews in Europe or for African Americans in the United States, have been places of total, involuntary, and perpetual segregation of a group considered inferior by the dominant society (Philpott 1978; Marcuse 1997). They are not necessarily places of deep poverty, although poor living conditions are almost inevitable, given an expanding population and limited land and capital resources. But they are places of entrapment. Individuals or families can, with luck and effort, move out of a slum. In ghettoes, mobility is severely limited by external discrimination: edicts in European Jewish slums, restrictive covenants in early-twentieth-century US black ghettoes, lack of cheap small units for single people with long-term mental or intellectual disabilities in many cities today (Philpott 1978, xv). Ghettoes may be torn down, as they were in many US cities in the mid-twentieth century, but they immediately reappear, for instance, as public housing projects. Barriers to escape may no longer be as blatant as restrictive covenants, but a combination of single-family zoning in better neighbourhoods, poor educational and employment opportunities within ghettoes, non-existent public transit to good jobs, and other less obvious methods of discrimination operate effectively to keep people in the ghetto. It can be argued that the ghetto, not the slum, is the obverse to the ideal of the middle-class residential suburb. Suburbs were supposed to keep unwanted land uses and people out, while the underlying purpose of a ghetto is to keep a particular group confined in order to avoid contaminating the rest of the city. The ghetto is a landscape of power, created by powerfully inequitable social relations. The ghetto is also a landscape of despair for those who live within it and cannot escape (Dear and Wolch 1987, 9).

In the latter years of World War Two, governments in all Anglo-American societies began to plan for massive postwar central city reconstruction and suburban expansion. The identification of slums and ghettoes in the central city that could be replaced by modern roads and housing was an important aspect of that planning. Both John Bacher (1993, viii) and Jane Jacobs (in Sewell 1993, x-xi) argue that Canada's traditional suspicion of government intervention, along with a variant history of immigration and racism, spared Canadian central cities the worst depredations of the US "federal bulldozer." It is true that the government-funded expansion of the US urban expressway system in the 1950s and 1960s, a vital aspect of urban renewal, was fuelled by Cold War plans to move troops and evacuate cities (Fishman 2000, 199). But the Canadian understanding of neighbourhood transition, and resultant plans and government policy, were clearly influenced by American reports maintaining that slums drained civic coffers through costing more in fire prevention, police, and public health services than they brought in through property tax (Bacher 1993, 72). The notion that central city blight would inevitably spread unless checked was prevalent in both nations, as well as in Australia and the United Kingdom (Sewell 1993, 150).

Few central city neighbourhoods were untouched by the assumption of decline. A 1937 slum report divided Melbourne's central city into three zones, all with negative connotations: congested areas, where houses were built on narrow lots; blighted areas, where factories mixed with housing; and decadent areas, where once-fashionable houses had been converted to apartments and boarding houses (Howe 1994, 149). Similarly, because Clifton was by then considered part of central Cincinnati, planning reports of the 1940s called it a "once exclusive residential section, a suburb of mansions and huge estates," now "middle aged" and facing inevitable decline (Miller 2001, 50-54). Society Hill in Philadelphia, a wealthy neighbourhood in the mid-nineteenth century, was threatened with destruction in a 1959 urban renewal plan, shortly before the housing became upgraded (Smith 1996, 53). And Boston's West End was demolished in the 1950s, just as a similar neighbourhood, the North End, was beginning to be rehabilitated by its residents (Gans 1962; Jacobs 1992, 8-11).

By the 1960s, urban renewal was under sustained attack in influential books written by Jane Jacobs and Herbert Gans, and in less populist policy reports as well. In a US policy report published in 1964, Martin Anderson argued that urban renewal was an inefficient use of government resources, since land was usually sold to private developers for about 30 percent of what it cost the city to acquire, clear, and improve it in preparation for sale (Anderson 1964, 2-3). Urban renewal was racist in impact if not in intent, since "approximately two-thirds of the people forced out of their homes are Negroes, Puerto Ricans, or some other minority group" (7). It was also a disaster for low-income city dwellers, since over 90 percent of newly created housing commanded rents that could not be afforded by displaced residents (93). A 1968 Canadian federal task force on urban renewal echoed these concerns: "In order to eradicate the 20 to 30 per cent of buildings that were rotting beyond repair, whole blocks were demolished. Thousands of sound houses capable of being rehabilitated at reasonable cost, together with thousands of others in perfectly good conditions were destroyed. The economic waste was enormous. But far more important, the sense of community, that certain intangible something that gives a district life and meaning, was eradicated" (cited in Bacher 1993, 227).

Sense of community, economic rationalism, and avoiding racism were thus being put forward as grounds for a complete turnaround in policy. In order to understand these attacks on urban renewal, it is necessary to back up once again and look at the changing image of the Anglo-American central city during the latter half of the twentieth century.

## The Urban Village, A New Urbanist Dream

As discussed above, a consensus had built by the mid-twentieth century that central city neighbourhood change was inevitably downward. The only solution offered by researchers and policy makers was to entirely replace so-called obsolete housing stock with more modern buildings. Where there was a perceived need for commercial uses, offices, or express-ways, the process was straightforward: expropriate, demolish, and rebuild. After World War Two, piecemeal philanthropic efforts to provide central city housing for low-income people displaced by slum removal were re-placed with large-scale public housing efforts. These were led by the United Kingdom, which by the interwar years was creating large public housing estates in the suburbs, and the United States, followed in a less ambitious fashion by Australia and Canada (Fishman 1987; Howe 1994; Bacher 1993; Hall 1998). Unfortunately, these efforts almost always produced neigh-bourhoods with even worse housing, employment, and health conditions, and greater marginalization of the poor and racialized, than the places they had replaced (Teaford 1990; Jacobs 1992).

A few dissident voices questioned the inevitability of central city decline. One of the most insightful was Walter Firey (1948). For Firey, space is a "neutral arena" rather than a "determinate and invariant influence," and he disputes Burgess's and Hoyt's assumption that high-income households all eventually migrate to the periphery (3). His case study of the growth of Boston emphasizes the "importance of cultural values in determining space," and he stresses the agency, or "positive human volition" as he called it, of both individuals and local governments in attributing values and symbolic meanings to neighbourhoods and places (45, 53, 170).

Firey uses the example of Boston's Beacon Hill, which was subdivided by a development syndicate in the late eighteenth century. By the mid-nineteenth century, Beacon Hill was adjacent to the central business dis-trict. Despite its central and congested location, the eastern (uphill) part of the neighbourhood attracted and maintained an elite set of residents, while the western (downhill) part of the neighbourhood "gradually lost its families and the dwellings [were] taken over by landladies who rented out rooms to single men," followed by redevelopment into tenements (Firey 1948, 45-49). By the mid-twentieth century, the eastern portion of Beacon Hill had successfully resisted the encroachment of apartment buildings. It was still considered an elite district, largely because of the "weight of past his-tory," and despite the proximity of a lower-class district and non-residential uses (94, 63). Of course, Beacon Hill was only one of the elite central city neighbourhoods that successfully resisted decline during the era of mass suburbanization: Baltimore's Roland Park, Philadelphia's Chestnut Hill,

Pittsburgh's Squirrel Hill, Cincinnati's Hyde Park and Mount Lookout, and Minneapolis' Lake District are a few other US examples (Teaford 1990, 309). Mayfair and Kensington in London, Westmount in Montreal, Rosedale in Toronto, and Toorak in Melbourne are among a long list of other elite central city neighbourhoods that retained or heightened their status during the twentieth century.

Moreover, Firey points out that becoming a slum is not the terminal phase in a neighbourhood's life, even if the housing is not demolished to make way for a higher use. He uses the example of the North End, often considered the "worst part of Boston" in terms of density and house repair (Firey 1948, 172). Here, at the time he wrote, the residents were attached to the place, and many were renovating their buildings. Firey believes that local government should encourage this private-sector rejuvenation, instead of threatening the neighbourhood with demolition.

Firey is perhaps most radical when he speaks of the need for housing to accommodate a low-income, transient population. This is a significant break with the Chicago school and Hoyt, who had continued the quasi-medical metaphors of earlier slum literature, such as "growths" and "cancers," in describing areas with cheap apartments and rooming houses. While Firey supports the enforcement of housing standards and the amelioration of vice, he does not suggest tearing down viable multi-unit housing. Rather, he suggests small improvements that retain this function while making the lives of their inhabitants better (i.e., more moral). For instance, he is in favour of requiring parlours in all rooming and boarding houses, so residents do not have to entertain their friends in their bedrooms or in a tavern (Firey 1948, 336-37). Such prescriptions might seem both limited and condescending today, but his ideas represent a quantum leap forward in working with the realities of poor people's housing.

Whereas Firey's work was largely ignored, Jacobs' *The Death and Life of Great American Cities*, published in 1961, was enormously influential in its "attack on current city planning and rebuilding" (1992, 3). According to Jacobs, "cities are an immense laboratory of trial and error," but instead of looking at cities as they are, practitioners and teachers of urban issues ignore "success and failure in real life," while elaborating simplistic theories in a false science of separating people and land uses (5). Like Firey, Jacobs recognizes that density and centrality could be construed as advantages by some housing consumers, and that some neighbourhoods, regardless of income or adjacent land uses, retain people because they like living there. She returns to the example of Boston's North End, where housing was rehabilitated using local money because the area was redlined and effectively off-limits for institutional mortgages. In the 1950s, the neighbourhood had a low rent-to-income ratio, safe streets, and good public health indicators despite its high density and older housing (8-11). San Francisco's North Beach and Chicago's Back of the Yards are two other examples of what she calls "unslumming," working-class neighbourhoods generating their own investment capital for housing and commercial rehabilitation (271, 297-300). In successful districts, she says, "old buildings filter up," in part through residents getting wealthier while remaining in the same place (193). Jacobs goes much further than Firey in her attack on the principles of urban planning as they had developed by the mid-twentieth century. For her, a mixture of land uses and incomes in a neighbourhood, which she calls "intricate and close-grained diversity," is to be treasured, not separated, because it is part of what makes a city diverse, healthy, and safe (14). Small, narrow streets do not cause traffic congestion, but cure it, by deterring car traffic and thus making the sidewalks more pedestrian-friendly (222).

Jacobs does not deal much with housing per se, partly because she sees housing in the larger context of a city's economic life, and partly because she believes that wholly residential areas are boring. She also does not particularly engage with the issue of class, or at least, she discusses it in a way that seems problematic in hindsight. At one point, she contends that "unslumming" is not a question of "bringing back the middle class as much as it is retaining people who become middle class," and that "gradual money" helps a neighbourhood more than a sudden influx (1992, 281). Yet she takes issue "with a common belief about cities – the belief that uses of low status drive out uses of high status. That is not how cities behave ... People or uses with more money at their command, or greater respectability (in a credit society the two often go together), can fairly easily supplant those less prosperous or of less status, and commonly do so in city neighbourhoods that achieve popularity. The reverse seldom happens" (97).

In other words, Jacobs returns to the Chicago school's notion of an ecological process whereby groups with more power (i.e., money) force out those with less power, a notion later accepted by Marxists and one that appears to be borne out by the trajectories of gentrification in most cities. Given the potential problem of the rich supplanting the poor in the successful districts, she does not offer much in the way of prescriptions for maintaining income mix over time. She suggests that governments should subsidize dwelling units rather than buildings (1992, 321). This measure was successful in non-profit co-operative housing in Canada in the 1970s and 1980s, and perhaps has some applicability in a city with strong rent controls (New York City had rent controls on apartments built before 1947 at the time Jacobs was writing; Mele 2000b, 117). But it is hard to see, forty years later, how subsidizing dwelling units would not contribute to rent inflation, and how this measure alone could maintain a large stock of dwellings affordable to lower-income people once central city neighbourhoods became popular and housing prices started to rise rapidly. This was already beginning to happen in some places, as Jacobs (1992, 70-71) concedes, by the late 1950s: the "rich and near rich" were moving in and "crowding out" middle-income and poor people in "Yorkville and Greenwich Village in New York ... Telegraph Hill in San Francisco ... [and] Georgetown in Washington."

The incipient gentrification of Greenwich Village, where Jacobs lived and worked at the time, offers an interesting example of how central city housing stock could increase its cachet over time. Gerald McFarland (2001, 1-3) describes how Greenwich Village was developed as a suburb in the early nineteenth century, when there was a buffer of fields between the original agricultural settlement and the northern outskirts of New York City. While there were fine houses around Washington Square, the majority of the suburb's inhabitants were middle or working class. By the 1850s, Greenwich Village was surrounded by development, and during the second half of the nineteenth century it was "left to decay into a picturesque ... slum," with its row houses and tenements settled by successive waves of Irish, German, Jewish, and Italian immigrants.

On the eve of World War One, US magazines like *Collier's* were describing Greenwich Village as "American Bohemia," after the Parisian immigrant suburbs of Montparnasse and Montmartre, where artists and free thinkers were drawn to the combination of cheap accommodations and a sort of working-class authenticity they felt was lacking in the wealthy quarters (Hall 1998). Greenwich Village had become a hotbed for similar political and cultural activism, and free love, feminism, and new writing and art were being promulgated in a heady mix (McFarland 2001, chap. 6). Traditionally, there had been tensions between the patricians who were still associated with the Washington Square Association and the settlement-house-led Village Improvement Society, which articulated a commitment to represent every ethnic community except African Americans (105). However, the two groups worked together in 1913 to promote a zoning plan that would keep the neighbourhood's core area a residential and small business zone, with height limitations and restrictions on large manufacturing uses (215). Real estate developers based in new migrant communities, like the Italian immigrant Vincent Pepe, began remodelling older houses into studio apartments. Their marketing efforts included a 1914 pamphlet advertising the cheap and accessible units to single and married office workers, entitled, "How would you like to open a door to this – Ten minutes after you 'punch the clock'?" (cited 212). The fact that these developers also emphasized the existence of good schools in the area suggests that they were also trying to attract families to this central city neighbourhood. Thus by the second decade of the twentieth century, at least one place in the United States was using heterogeneity and centrality as selling points to attract what would later be termed the "new middle class."

The example of Greenwich Village shows how a new lexicon was developing to combat the conflation of central city with slum. The notion of bohemia gradually lost its countercultural connotations as it was approvingly taken up by both developers and the popular press. The Chicago school had had an equivocal and somewhat patronizing attitude towards bohemias and bohemians. Burgess (1974, 54-56) referred to Chicago's zone of transition as containing the "mainstem of 'hobohemia,' the teeming Rialto of the homeless migratory men of the Middle West" along with the "Latin Quarter, where creative and rebellious spirits resort," while Harvey Zorbaugh (1976, 87, 91) sneeringly referred to Towertown, a Chicago neighbourhood, as a Bohemia of students, artists, and writers "whose radicalism runs to long hair, eccentric dress, lilies, obscenity, or a Freudian interpretation of dreams" as well as "free love." But it was also during the 1920s that the term *bohemia* was becoming a valuable marketing tool for an area in transition. Towertown's rising land values and rents were making it too expensive for young artists and students by the end of the 1920s, and Greenwich Village became unaffordable to a new generation of artists by the 1950s (103; Mele 2000b, 143).

In the meantime, the term *village* was being unhitched from its rural connotations. Transported to the central city, it became a signifier of community spirit in a heterogeneous yet socially integrated neighbourhood (Peel 1995b), a Sesame Street for grown-ups, a place, in the words of the theme song for the TV show *Cheers*, "where everybody knows your name." Developers in the Lower East Side, like their confreres in adjacent Greenwich Village, used centrality and heterogeneity to market new apartment buildings to clerks, professionals, and corporate workers in the 1920s. Images of the heroic immigrants of past decades were contrasted with the current "queer, unadjusted, radical, bohemian and criminal ... neighbourhood of lost souls" to justify tearing down tenements. But the quaint Eastern European and Jewish stores remained to serve those who had moved outwards as well as the "logical future residents of the East Side," the new middle class (Mele 2000b). By the 1950s, the name East Village was replacing Lower East Side, used first by the bohemian radicals, known as Beats, who fled there from the high rents of the previous generation's countercultural paradise, Greenwich

Village, then by real estate agents who liked the implied link to that now-pricey enclave (x-xi).

As some former slums began to gain a certain cachet, the term *ghetto* began a new phase of existence. Michael Dear and Jennifer Wolch have argued that the deinstitutionalization of people with physical, intellectual or mental health disabilities in the 1960s led to "service dependent population ghettoes" in many North American cities. In the classic economic terms of supply and demand, a supply of established low-cost rental accommodation, preferably close to established support networks, meets a demand of increasing migration to these sites, through formal referral and in the absence of other options. But the lack of options is no accident; it is the result of political choices made by people with more power, which govern the extremely limited choices of those with little power. In Marxist terms, the development of these ghettoes represents the meeting, not of neutral forces of supply and demand, but of particular social processes and evolving spatial forms (Dear and Wolch 1987, preface, 8-9). Dear and Wolch use Parkdale, along with east downtown Toronto, as a case study of the development of such a ghetto.

The idea of a ghetto based on discrimination not by race or religion but by disability does have precedents. New York's Bowery was the city's "last stop on the way down" for alcoholics and chronically ill men from the early twentieth century onwards (Sante 1991, 14). This area, like Seattle's Skid Row (originally where inland logs were rolled down to seagoing vessels; Ford 1994, 65) lent its name to other streets of extreme poverty. Boweries and skid rows are usually associated with single men in poor health who have no long-term housing options other than leftover buildings, many of them in substandard condition.

Paul Groth (1994, 10) documents the largely hidden history of residential hotels, which have been characterized as the homes of those who are "friendless, isolated, needy, disabled, marginal, on welfare, psychiatric, alcoholics or drug addicts, drifters or transients, elderly men or welfare mothers with three kids," but which offer a range of conditions and options. He posits that the growth of homelessness in the United States is at least in part a function of the wholesale destruction of these options (twenty-three thousand units lost in Chicago alone between 1973 and 1984), just when the need for them was increasing. Poor single women had even fewer options than men did. Boarding houses were a significant source of income and housing for single women (as can be seen in various negative descriptions of landladies cited in the literature on slums), but institutionalization always loomed as a threat for women too old or too ill to pay the rent, or for women whose strategies for coping with poverty were judged immoral. However, as former slums began to be marketed to the middle class, inevitable tensions arose between the increasingly impoverished and marginalized inhabitants of boarding houses and the renovators.

The post-World War Two period is usually remembered as the time when mass suburbanization was enabled by mass corporate production of Levittowns and their successors. Perhaps in reaction to the majority, the growing counterculture in the United States began to speak with contempt of suburbia (contempt towards suburbia has a much longer history in Britain and Australia, possibly because mass suburbanization had already occurred in large cities by the beginning of the twentieth century). Hugh Hefner's *Playboy* magazine carved out a consumer niche from 1953 onwards by vociferously rejecting the suburban values embodied by suburban wives. Instead, Hefner proclaimed his bohemian central city values in the first issue of the magazine: "We like our apartment ... we like mixing up cocktails and an hors d'oeuvre or two, putting a little mood music on the phonograph and inviting in a female acquaintance for a quiet discussion on Picasso, Nietzsche, jazz, sex" (cited in Ehrenreich 1983, 44). Barbara Ehrenreich contrasts this vision of bachelor paradise with that of the Beat authors, such as Kerouac, who extolled "the underworld and underclass invisible from the corporate 'crystal palace' or suburban dream homes." Yet these masculine rebels agreed on some points: love of jazz and black culture in general (at least in the abstract), and disdain for the nuclear family and its supposed home in the suburbs (55-56). Then, in *The Feminine Mystique* of 1963, another unlikely ally joined in, the suburban wife herself. The housewives described by Betty Friedan may have suffered from "the problem without a name," but the problem's place was clear: the suburban periphery of the city.

The 1960s were a time of immense social change. Women entered the paid workforce in growing numbers. Heterosexuals tended to marry later, divorce more often, and have fewer children. The increase in woman-led households, with and without children, increased the demand for child care, public transit, restaurants, and proximate work. People lived longer and lived alone for longer periods. A broader base of migrants brought new tastes and new housing needs, especially in Canada and Australia, which were unaccustomed to high levels of non-European immigration. Alternatives to the nuclear heterosexual family began to be openly discussed, with singles using bars and restaurants for sexual searching. The 1960s were also a time of rapid economic change, with central city industries languishing while jobs in corporate business, education, the arts, and the public and non-profit sectors grew rapidly. Many industrial and service workers followed their jobs to the periphery of the city, while growing numbers of the new middle class followed corporate, government, media, cultural, and academic jobs into the central city. As suburbs continued to grow, housing prices and transportation costs increased to a point at which they were in many cases higher than the costs of central city housing (Beauregard 1986; Ley 1996, 8; Smith 1996, 52). As innovation and creativity were posited as the motors of growth in an information economy, a bohemian index used by Richard Florida (2002) has been positively correlated to urban wealth. People – artists, immigrants, sexual outsiders – once considered peripheral or even threatening to mainstream society have become central to economic growth in the beginning of the twenty-first century, and the places where they live have correspondingly become admired.

During the early 1960s, the term *gentrification* first appeared, invented by a London sociologist, Ruth Glass. The *Oxford American Dictionary* defined it as "the movement of middle-class families into urban areas, causing property values to increase and having the secondary effect of driving out poorer families" (cited by Smith and Williams 1986, 1). *Gentrification* is an odd and perhaps deceptive term. The first people to renovate houses in poor or working-class neighbourhoods and former industrial areas are often artists, single parents, and other people on the margins of the middle class; they are hardly gentry (D. Rose 1984; Zukin 1989). But the term stuck with most critical commentators because it contains the ideas of displacement and potential class conflict, as opposed to the purely positive *revitalization*.

Gentrification has an ideology, a set of beliefs that seem diametrically opposed to the consensus that had grown over the previous hundred years. Central city neighbourhoods are not bad places to live or metaphors for the failures of industrial capitalism. It is moral and healthy, not immoral and unhealthy, to be able to walk or commute quickly to work and shopping (assuming that work is in an office, not a smoke-spewing factory). Old houses are beautiful, not obsolete. Families belong in the city. Children should play on the street (that is, the sidewalk). Diversity is good, not dangerous or evil. Rehabilitating older housing and walking are part and parcel of the ecological movement that began in the 1960s: reuse and save, not consume and destroy (Allen 1984).

In a deeper way, pro-urbanism and pro-suburbanism share essential elements. They both represent utopian quests for community. They both refer to a simplistic vision of the past: the urban ideal is the dense, polyethnic, centralized urban village of the railway age, rather than the suburban ideal of the traditional rural village (Allen 1984). And of course, every utopia needs its dystopia. The virtues of the central city are now contrasted with the vilified periphery. By the 1980s, central city housing was not cheaper than suburban housing, at least in Canada. Central neigh-bourhoods were "being selected *despite* cost disadvantages compared with the suburbs." The suburbs, however, were associated with "negative val-ues" that these consumers wished to avoid: standardization, homogeniza-tion, blandness, conformism, conservatism, patriarchy, "straightness" (Ley 1996, 205).

Jon Caulfield's interviews with gentrifiers in central Toronto reveal a remarkable dependence on stereotypes of suburbs and suburbanites. One respondent had internalized the lessons of the *Feminine Mystique:* "I'm of a generation that equated going to the suburbs with putting my head down, having many babies and never thinking again for the rest of my life." A single woman equated suburbs with "couple life." A third respon-dent was apparently immune to the contradiction in the following state-ment: "People who move to the suburbs are pulverized by a dominant culture that defines what the normal, acceptable lifestyle is ... for us to go and live in a suburb would be, in our circle, abnormal" (Caulfield 1994, 189). A book co-written by the renowned "new urbanist" architects Andres Duany and Elizabeth Plater-Zyberk confidently asserts that in a landscape of "cookie cutter houses" and "mindlessly curving cul-de-sacs," "you would not be welcome ... not that you would ever have reason to visit its monot-onous moonscape" (Duany, Plater-Zyberk, and Speck 2000, x).

At some point in the late twentieth century, for some writers at least, the suburb had become foreign and menacing, like nineteenth-century descriptions of central city slums or fourteenth-century descriptions of the hostile places outside the city wall. As in the days of Chaucer, the unwary urban explorer could become trapped in greenery and dead ends, where environmental thieves and robbers lurk in their fearsome McMan-sion residences.

Was the central city so different from the suburbs? And if so, how did it differ? In 1961, the residents' association in Cincinnati's Clifton, the late-nineteenth-century suburb turned declining central city neighbour-hood, began to advocate for the preservation of what it called an "in town suburb" (Miller 2001, 68). The Clifton Town Meeting began to organize house tours of historic properties, advocate for more recreational space, and oppose any attempts to tear down older buildings (86-118). Clifton was successful in marketing itself to professors from nearby educational institutions. But despite the liberal intentions of the residents' association, there were continuing tensions over residential segregation, particularly fear of encroachment from a nearby black community: "Negroes next door no cause for panic," read a panicky-sounding 1960s community newspa-per headline (81, 131). In Clifton, at least, gentrification involved a return to the original suburban marketing strategy, albeit with a new, slightly more diversified twist.

Demand-side changes in taste were sweetened by the supply side: institutional mortgage providers reinvesting in the central city, governments offering rehabilitation grants, developers seeking new grounds for profit, and hyperbolic real estate agents. Peter Williams, in a 1978 study of gentrification in Islington, London, speaks of the role of financial institutions in supporting neighbourhood change. Since the late nineteenth century, the majority of the housing in Islington had been owned by absentee landlords, who sold to other absentee landlords at low prices: usually ten times the generally low annual rent for the property. Despite rent controls, rental property was considered a suitable investment, and sales were not frequent: approximately ten sales per year over a large area. Only one estate agent specialized in Islington (73).

In the late 1950s, three changes rapidly raised house prices and home-ownership rates in Islington. The first was a change in borough housing policies: the local government now wished to support investment in houses and, accordingly, decontrolled rents in 1957. The second was an increase in immigrants, many of whom were forced to buy property because of discrimination in the rental housing market. The third was an increase in demand from middle-class homebuyers, actively encouraged by a new generation of estate agents who scented profit in what was then called the "Chelseafication" of Islington (P. Williams 1978, 73-78). The architecture of older houses was aesthetically pleasing to both consumers and agents, but they also correctly assumed that neighbourhood house prices were rising. The number of properties on the market rose from 45 in 1965 to 114 in 1969 and 323 in 1972; sale prices increased from an average of £2,750 in 1959 to £7,154 in 1969 and £19,392 in 1972. Institutional lenders were increasingly inclined to lend larger sums, as the investments proved sound (74).

The example of Islington seems to support Neil Smith's influential rent gap theory (1978), which was based on the early work of Harvey (1973). According to the theory, gentrification occurs because housing suppliers note places where actual rent falls below potential rent, and markets them accordingly. The state supports profits made on the commodity of housing by directly subsidizing renovators and by indirect measures such as the abolition of rent controls. But Beauregard, among others, argues that the rent gap theory is overly simplistic. According to him, the potential for gentrification is not simply equal to a rent gap: "capital cannot annihilate space," gentrifiers are not just yuppies, and gentrification is rarely simple in form, cause, or effect (Beauregard 1990, 856).

Beauregard (1990, 857-71) offers case studies of four Philadelphia neighbourhoods to illustrate the "chaos and complexity of gentrification." City government was heavily implicated in the process of revitalizing Society Hill in the 1950s and 1960s, subsidizing the construction of new luxury housing to replace demolished "blighted" structures, renovating older housing itself for resale, and providing loans to owners for rehabilitation. This urban renewal success story has been used by many writers as a classic example of the rent gap in action, as well as a model of government-directed gentrification (Smith 1978; Teaford 1990, 115-17). Another neighbourhood, Spring Garden, rapidly gentrified in only one portion, where a hospital was converted to luxury apartments using heritage tax credits. Here the process was developer-driven, with some government assistance. Newcomers and the working-class Hispanic community formed a common front to combat drug activity (Beauregard 1990, 864-66). A third neighbourhood, the Northern Liberties, was developed in mixed land uses during the 1860s. A century later, there had been considerable population decline, and some of the abandoned buildings were rehabilitated by artists. This in turn led to some new residential construction (again using tax credits), but change was slow. A fourth community, Fishtown, had not gentrified during the 1980s despite its proximity to other gentrifying neighbourhoods and the new virtue of centrality (866-70).

Some older industrial cities, like Manchester and Detroit, lack the excess capital to drive investment in wholesale gentrification (Ley 1996, 81). There, gentrification looks like "islands of renewal in seas of decay," in Brian Berry's phrase (1985). But in many other cities, the marketing of the central city to lure both middle-class settlers and tourist dollars has been in place since the 1960s, with profound impacts on local government politics, taxation, and spending. Anglo-American central cities now begin to resemble seas of renewal with small islands of decay ( Wyly and Hammel 1999).

In the meantime, suburbs are changing. Industrial jobs that moved out of the central city in the postwar era have now moved out of the region. New immigrants often settle directly in outer suburbs, which are often the only places with affordable housing. Along with the visible signs of a new economy, such as industrial parks and superstores, there is a hidden army of suburban workers, primarily women and visible minorities, struggling within an invisible economy (see, e.g., Baxandall and Ewen 2000). David Ley may have been correct when he predicted in 1984, "With the revitalization of the past decade, sections of the post-industrial city have begun a transformation from the home of the labouring classes toward a zone of privilege reminiscent of the innermost ring in Sjoberg's model of the preindustrial city. If present trends continue, the social geography of the nineteenth-century industrial city may even appear to urban scholars of the future as a temporary interlude to a more historically persistent pattern of higher-status segregation adjacent to the downtown core" (Ley 1996, 201). It is also possible that future cities will be the multinucleated sprawling conglomeration of central and edge cities posited by the LA school (Dear 2002). What is certain is that the rhetoric of suburbs and slums has shifted yet again.

## Conclusion: The Case Study in Theoretical Context

This chapter has focused on the importance of changing images of place to the growth and differentiation of Anglo-American cities over the past two centuries. Explanations that focus solely on investment factors such as the cost of land or the probability of profit do not provide a complete account of such changes. Nor do explanations that focus on ideological constructs such as housing tastes. Instead, changing perceptions of places are based on both economic transformations *and* the culturally based desires and fears of those with the power of residential choice.

Toronto fits the larger pattern of Anglo-American urban development. Although US and Canadian cities have significant differences in governance and values, these are no more significant than the differences between big and small cities, between the northeast and southwest United States, or between particular cities like Montreal and Toronto. In short, I agree with Harris (1996) and Doucet and Weaver (1991) in placing Toronto within a North American context, and also in making comparisons with Australian and British urban development. I disagree with the particularist approach of Jim Lemon (1996, 287), who states that, in Toronto, the "city that works," "Except for Parkdale, talk of vulnerable, declining, and even blighted neighbourhoods, which were ubiquitous in the 1940s, fell by the wayside by 1975." On the contrary, Parkdale is not terribly unusual, whether within the Toronto context or internationally. In Toronto, Parkdale can be and has been compared to Regent Park and Alexandra Park, two central city public housing projects with considerable gentrification at their edges, and with St. James Town, a mostly privately owned group of high-rise apartments that provides poor living conditions for first-generation immigrants within a neighbourhood with increasing cachet for the new middle class.

As Fishman (1987), Rybczynski (1995), Hall (1998), and many others point out, ideas about urban problems and their solutions disseminated quickly through an international network even before the creation of the planning profession in the early twentieth century. The impact of London's 1851 Industrial Exhibition and Chicago's 1893 Columbian Exhibition on ideas about cities cannot be overemphasized. In addition, local newspapers reported problems and progress in other cities; many urban reformers and writers travelled widely; designs for model houses were carried in national magazines; and, of course, Canada and Australia's nineteenth-century elite were usually no more than one generation removed from Britain.

An important asymmetry between suburbs and slums was that slums were almost entirely described by outsiders, who presented themselves to the rest of "us" (middle-class society) as intrepid explorers and knowledgeable experts on the problems of "them." The straightforward subject/object relationship between writers on slums and slum inhabitants in turn led to easy stereotypes. In contrast, nineteenth-century suburbs were described, at least in North America and Australia, by people who lived in and promoted suburbs. Then, beginning in Greenwich Village and the West End of London in the early twentieth century, the voice of progress began to shift from periphery to centre. Political power may still be retained in the sprawling suburbs of North America and Australia, but that power is resented and derided by an increasingly powerful central city intellectual elite. This intellectual elite denigrates postwar suburbs just as their suburban predecessors condemned slums.

The ideal of proximate access with psychological distance became associated with development at the periphery of the industrial city by the mid-nineteenth century. Nineteenth-century suburbs were intended to inject some of the social stability and family values of village life into a rapidly changing urban system, while providing the best of the modern world. The virtues of suburbs were contrasted with the vices of central city slums. As demand grew for centrally located housing, many places that were once suburbs became engulfed within the central city. Densities in these areas increased, as did ethnic and social signs of difference from the norm. This process of decline, or becoming a slum, became codified in theory, although there were many different kinds of central city neighbourhoods, just as there were many different kinds of peripheral neighbourhoods. Residential intensification, the subdivision of units and properties, became feared as the harbinger of decline.

As successful cities grew outwards, however, there came a point at which proximate access to the central city became problematic for some people living on the periphery. Moreover, in contrast to the dominant concentric zone theory, central city housing demand often remained high for higher-income households in some neighbourhoods, as well as for the industrial poor. When industries moved to the periphery while knowledge-economy jobs grew in the central city (a process which, like suburbanization, is sometimes erroneously assumed to have started after World War Two), housing suppliers faced a new set of demand factors. Demand became rationalized by reversing theory and values to support central city housing choices. The central city became the "village," the place that epitomized positive postmodern societal values of diversity and liveability; in contrast, the suburbs were trapped in values of the past, namely boring homogeneity and excessive energy consumption. The city was revitalized while suburbs were increasingly seen as devitalized. Although actual housing and neighbourhood patterns and process are always more complex than prevalent theories, in the new rhetoric of urban space, the central city is the moral core and the suburbs the rotten cancerous growth. The dream of "a good place to live" remains as alive as ever.

# 2

# The Flowery Suburb: Parkdale's Development, 1875-1912

Halfway up the stairs
Isn't up,
And isn't down.
It isn't in the nursery,
It isn't in the town.
And all sorts of funny thoughts
Run round my head:
"It isn't really
Anywhere!
It's somewhere else
Instead!"

– A.A. Milne, "Halfway Down"

## Inventing the Flowery Suburb

Saturday, 17 May 1879, "was a red letter day in the western, or, as it has now been christened, the 'Floral' suburb of Parkdale" (*Globe*, 19 May 1879). The Village Improvement Association, made up of prominent families in the newly incorporated municipality, organized a tree planting ceremony. This was no formal political gesture with a spade. Fifty saplings, donated by the village's reeve, nursery owner John Gray, were muscled into the hard spring ground along eight streets by an estimated six hundred men, women, and children. Even if the figure is exaggerated, a large proportion of Parkdale's residents participated in this exercise. Afterwards, the crowd repaired to the grove owned by a lawyer named Maynard, to indulge in well-deserved lemonade and cake while listening to local musicians. A speech made by Reeve Gray on this occasion referred to Parkdale as the Floral Suburb. The name stuck: Parkdale continued to be called the Flowery Suburb well into the twentieth century, and the phrase was recycled in the 1970s to refer to the neighbourhood's past glory.

The tree-planting ceremony was a great success in achieving its underlying goal: to present an image of progress, natural health, and moral virtue to potential purchasers of property. The *Mail*'s correspondent, well lubricated with sarcasm if not liquor at the teetotal event, provided an extended summary of "Parkdale's Progress" in his coverage of the tree-planting day. He began by giving the vital statistics of this "village of very aristocratic pretensions, suburban to Toronto": a population in four figures, with four trains a day stopping on their way downtown, as well as steamship connections, and land increasing in value "within the past few years from $75 to $800 and $1000 an acre." Then he turned to a curious sexual metaphor to describe the past battles between those who wished the suburb annexed to Toronto and those who had successfully incorporated Parkdale as a separate municipality: "Toronto sought on divers occasions to become possessed of her, but she turned coldly from the blandishments of her too experienced lover, whose perfidy is proverbial, and gathering her spotless skirts closer about her, drew further away from the proposed new housekeeping arrangements." Clearly enjoying this metaphor, the correspondent continued, "Adopting the maxim that 'A virtuous mind in a fair body is like a fine picture in a good light,' she became austere, proud and chaste. Ostracized the saloon-keepers, frowned on negro minstrels, erected several churches, established a pound, built a school house, decorated her walls with placards of church meetings, tea parties, temperance socials, sacred concerts, and theological lectures, and became pious in good style" (*Mail,* 19 May 1879).

The newspaper reporter was somewhat backhandedly praising the new community for qualities other than its setting, although he also mentioned "the high ground off the lakeshore" and the "fine views." Nor was proximity to Toronto or rising land prices Parkdale's primary draw for potential buyers. Rather, an image of sylvan purity was being projected to newspaper readers. The Village of Parkdale was to be a place of innocent amusements and moral advancement, physically adjacent to the rapidly expanding industrial city, but as separate as possible when it came to governance and social norms. The conflict between Parkdale as a place morally distinct from Toronto and Parkdale as a place to profitably purchase land persisted throughout the period of the suburb's development.

The use of a chaste female to symbolize the nascent village was no coincidence. Christopher Armstrong and Viv Nelles (1977, 1-2) argue that Toronto in the late nineteenth century was a "slightly British version of a North American city," looking and acting like "one hundred other aspiring commercial cities on the continent." As in US and Australian cities, middle-class suburban space was being promoted on the basis of two related domestic ideals. One, argued predominantly by men, sought to confine wives and daughters to residential communities in order to protect them from the moral and physical dangers of the central city. The other ideal, argued by both sexes, affirmed the importance of home in providing a "platform for shared values," a basis for the "domestic education" of the next generation, and a possible suburban basis for a more humane city (Marsh 1990, 7). The difference was one of emphasis: protection on the one hand, hidden power on the other. Both domestic ideals sought to counterbalance what was seen as a corrupt and unhealthy central city. Those in Parkdale who had opposed annexation by Toronto in 1878 had used the threat of unchecked liquor licensing as a basis of their drive to incorporate a separate municipality (*Globe,* 5 July 1878), and, as will be seen, Parkdale Council took several steps in its first years to promote public health and morality. Parkdale was not being promoted merely as an extension of urban space into the periphery. It was intended to exemplify what was, for Toronto, a new kind of space: a suburb where the values of middle-class women and children would predominate, an extension of the safe domestic sphere.

Throughout the summer of 1879, news items reinforced this message almost daily. On August 18, the *Globe* reported that "certain parties in the 'model village' play croquet on Sundays, and their pious fellow-villagers are indignant thereat." Two days later, the paper covered a civic holiday picnic held at Beaty's Grove to honour that prominent Parkdale landowner for donating part of his property for the extension of King Street West to Roncesvalles Avenue. After the picnic, there were wholesome entertainments such as races, dancing, and, finally, hymns sung around a bonfire. Even when a violent incident occurred in what was "usually a quiet suburb of Toronto," as reported on September 27, the *Globe* made sure that readers knew that "the gang of roughs" who assaulted Parkdale hotelkeeper Robert Moore in a drunken brawl were "residents of Brockton," the Irish working-class community to the north of the Flowery Suburb.

Yet the 1878 *Might's Directory,* the earliest source we have for Parkdale's class composition, indicates that half of Parkdale's pioneering households were working class (see also Laycock and Myrvold 1991, 14), and there were occasional hints in the newspapers that Parkdale was being settled by people who were interested in issues other than Sunday croquet. On 25 September 1879, the *Mail* reported that "employees of the Massey Manufacturing Company have been making unsuccessful house-hunting expeditions through the village." Two months later, the *Globe* carried the salutary tale of a railwayman who had bought a lot in Parkdale and was subsequently killed in a workplace accident. His wife and family were now "well provided for," thanks to his investment (10 November 1879). In the 1881 assessment, the most common occupation of the 216 household heads in Parkdale was "railwayman." With related titles such as "conductor," "switchman," "porter," "railway foreman," "yardman," and "station master," there were an even dozen. In addition, several of the six "engineers" listed may have been locomotive drivers. Two trunkmakers, two moulders, and various other "labourers" were presumably employed by the budding industrial conglomeration just east of the suburb's boundaries (see Map 1), and there were at least two guards employed by the women's and men's prisons also in that precinct. In all, a little over one-third of household heads could be classified as working class. One-quarter were self-employed small businessmen: tailors, travelling agents for manufacturers, owners of dry goods stores, saloon or boarding-house keepers. The remainder included equal numbers of clerical and business/professional workers (11 percent each), along with those classified as unwaged (mainly widows and other female household heads; Figure 2.1).

In contrast to the domestic ideal of the suburb as home to virtuous women and children unsullied by commercial connections, approximately 70 "abandoned" women and girls, "the most unhealthy of their sex" (Mulvaney 1884, 67), were incarcerated in Parkdale's Magdalen Asylum for Fallen Women by 1879. There were a further 150 women and girls in the Mercer Reformatory for Women just east of the suburb, and significant numbers of poor and "immoral" women in two other nearby institutions: the Home for Incurables within Parkdale and the Provincial Lunatic Asylum just east of Parkdale (Splane 1971, 181-82, 223). A little fewer than 10 percent of Parkdale households were headed by women (mostly widows) in 1881 and 1891, and many married women as well as widows were actively involved in the development of Parkdale, as landowners and lenders.

Moreover, after initial opposition, Parkdale's Village Council allowed and even subsidized the growth of industry within its boundaries (Laycock and Myrvold 1991, 13). In contrast to the continuing rhetoric of "aristocratic pretensions" in the "model village," Parkdale was developing into a mixed-land-use and mixed-income community, with a variety of household structures, at the periphery of the city. Why, then, was there a large and growing gap between the way that Parkdale was described and its socio-economic and housing conditions? Could the middle-class domestic ideal of the Flowery Suburb be compatible with a growing industrial working-class reality? Was Parkdale really so different from the rest of Toronto, and if so, how? The answers to these questions begin with a discussion of Parkdale's location within Toronto.

## The Context for Parkdale's Development

The British colonial settlement of Toronto was in its eighth decade when Parkdale was first subdivided into lots and promoted. Although the Humber River, whose mouth is just west of Parkdale, was used as a portage shortcut by the Huron, Seneca, and Mississauga First Nations, the area that is now Toronto had no long-term Aboriginal or European permanent

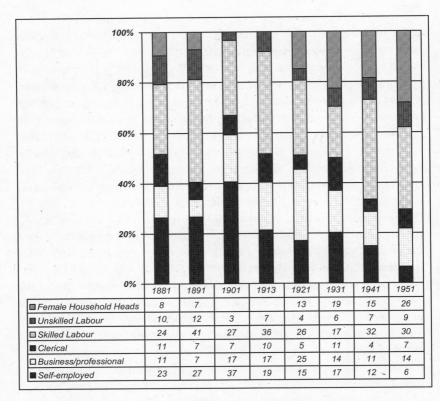

| | 1881 | 1891 | 1901 | 1913 | 1921 | 1931 | 1941 | 1951 |
|---|---|---|---|---|---|---|---|---|
| ▨ Female Household Heads | 8 | 7 | | | 13 | 19 | 15 | 26 |
| ▨ Unskilled Labour | 10 | 12 | 3 | 7 | 4 | 6 | 7 | 9 |
| ▢ Skilled Labour | 24 | 41 | 27 | 36 | 26 | 17 | 32 | 30 |
| ▉ Clerical | 11 | 7 | 7 | 10 | 5 | 11 | 4 | 7 |
| ▢ Business/professional | 11 | 7 | 17 | 17 | 25 | 14 | 11 | 14 |
| ▉ Self-employed | 23 | 27 | 37 | 19 | 15 | 17 | 12 | 6 |

*Figure 2.1.*   Employment of household head, Parkdale, 1881-1951
*Note:* There are no figures for female household heads in the 1901 or 1913
assessment samples.
*Sources:* Parkdale Council 1881; City of Toronto Assessment Rolls, 1891 sample; Harris 1992. Graph created by Ric Hamilton, McMaster University.

settlement during the two hundred years before the American Revolutionary War of 1776-1783. Two French forts were built during the early eighteenth century, the second (Fort Rouille) just east of Parkdale in what are now the grounds of the Canadian National Exhibition, but they were soon abandoned. The war brought tens of thousands of British Loyalist, or Tory, refugees north of the border, settlers whom the powers in London were anxious to retain and reward. By 1791, there was a new province of Upper Canada, separate in culture and governance from predominantly francophone and Catholic Lower Canada. After a prolonged argument about the capital for the new province, colonial administrators were reluctantly dragged away in 1793 from charming but indefensible Niagara, on the US border, to a more secure but marshy settlement immediately dubbed Muddy York (Careless 1984, 9-10, 14).

The first lieutenant governor of Upper Canada, John Graves Simcoe, was responsible for laying out the grid that still dominates Toronto's street pattern. Beyond the eight-block-square town plan, thirty-two hundred-acre "park lots" were granted to recalcitrant officials as a reward for moving to Toronto. The lots stretched north of what is now Queen Street to Bloor Street, one concession line (a little over a mile) to the north, and from the Don River three concession lines west to what is now Lansdowne Avenue in Parkdale. West of Lansdowne, the lots doubled in size to become "farm lots." The choice waterfront land south of Queen, stretching west from the tiny town to what is now Dufferin Street, was set aside for a thousand-acre Garrison Reserve including a new fort. West of the reserve and south of Queen Street, the remaining land was divided into "broken lots." None of the original owners of the lots in what is now Parkdale lived on their land (Lundell 1997, 10-12; Laycock and Myrvold 1991, 7).

Created as an administrative capital and military outpost, the Town of York began its growth as a commercial centre in the early 1800s. Like Chicago, its site was uninspiring but its location within the North American continent was excellent. The "Toronto passage" portage up to Georgian Bay provided a shortcut between the upper and lower Great Lakes, and construction began almost immediately on Yonge Street, which would connect the town to the first navigable river at Holland Landing (Glazebrook 1971, 35). Toronto's harbour could also act as a transshipment point between Britain and fertile farms to the west and southwest. By 1800, an old Aboriginal trail, renamed Dundas Street, had been surveyed and cleared. Six years later, a second westward road, now Queen Street West (and its extension, Lakeshore Road), was opened, but it tended towards flooding and was thus less popular than the more northerly route of Dundas Street (Careless 1984, 43; Laycock and Myrvold 1991, 7-8; Reeves 1992a, 45). The Don River's deep ravine impeded development to the east of the city, with the exception of the Queen Street East corridor, until the early twentieth century.

By 1834, when the Town of York became the City of Toronto, some of the owners of lots west of the city's boundaries began considering future development. Of these landowners, none is more remarkable than John George Howard. Today, Howard is remembered locally as the philanthropic old man in a Santa Claus beard who donated High Park, which became the basis of central Toronto's largest green space, to the city. His home in High Park, Colborne Lodge, is open to the public, and a highly sentimentalized version of his life is provided there. We hear about his happy domestic life with his wife, Jemima, unfortunately unblessed with children, and his peaceful retirement days spent sketching and acting as park ranger. This version of Howard's life underestimates his impact on the city and overestimates his benevolence. Howard was a deeply disturbed man who suffered all his life from what would probably be diagnosed today as manic depression. He had three children with a mistress while imprisoning his wife in Colborne Lodge and attempting to commit her to the Provincial Lunatic Asylum, which he had designed. He was also Toronto's chief architect and surveyor for over twenty years, whose ideas on urban landscaping and suburban design parallel those of Frederick Law Olmsted. As the man responsible for High Park and the asylum, two places intimately connected with the wax and wane of Parkdale's image, his life deserves closer examination (Martyn 1980, 116-20; Hudson 2000).

Howard was born, the child of an unwed mother, in a small village north of London in 1803. In his autobiography, he concocts a genealogy claiming descent from a noble Scottish family, the Howards, but he was originally named Corby after his home village. At fifteen, he joined the navy and learned surveying at sea. He later apprenticed with a series of land surveyors and married Jemima Meikle, the daughter of one of his masters, when he was twenty-four. Soon after, he followed his wife's family to Upper Canada. After a difficult first winter, Howard found work as drawing master at Upper Canada College, which led to architectural contracts with students' families. In 1834, he was hired by Toronto's first mayor, William Lyon Mackenzie, as city engineer and surveyor (Howard 1883; Martyn 1980).

Toronto was then still a small provincial capital. However, Howard was a visionary thinker who subscribed to London journals and was up-to-date with the latest trends in city building. He almost immediately bought a picturesque farm lot overlooking Humber Bay and began enjoining friends to buy adjacent lots. His dream was a suburb of villas in a park setting, a more rustic North American version of Regent's Park in London. Twice in the 1840s and 1850s, he advertised five-acre lots within his property as Ontario Park, a "suburban retreat for professional and business men in the City ... with a fine view of the lake," and even built a villa, Sunnyside, on speculation (Martyn 1980, 116; Reeves 1992a, 50). But, in this as in many other matters, Howard was too far ahead of his time. The lots did not sell, and the first buyer of Sunnyside defaulted on his mortgage. Howard also laid out Jarvis Street, Toronto's first "exclusive" address, for Samuel Jarvis, and probably worked on the first plan of subdivision for what later became the wealthy suburb of Rosedale, for Samuel's cousin William Jarvis. Both the Ontario Park and Rosedale subdivisions featured winding irregular streets, in stark contrast to the grid plans of most of Howard's contemporaries. Howard's most successful curvilinear "subdivision" in Toronto was St. James' Cemetery, just west of the Don River, designed in 1845. These lots found immediate customers.

In 1840, Howard began work on what became a thirty-year enterprise to build North America's largest lunatic asylum, managing every detail, from a separate water intake pipe from Lake Ontario to a complicated set of stairwells linking the wards, which were organized by gender and severity of illness. The asylum's construction was caught in endless delays, and Howard's grand plan was never fully realized. Another frustrating experience was his design for a waterfront esplanade in 1852, which was neglected in favour of a Grand Trunk Railway–sponsored plan that made public access to the waterfront unsafe and unpleasant (Goheen 2001). By 1856, the strain of unpaid bills from the Jarvis family, too many unfulfilled contracts, and maintaining two households caught up with Howard. He had a nervous breakdown (or, as a contemporary historian put it, "his weary brain called out for rest") that led to his early retirement at the age of fifty-two (Franklin 1998a; see also Morris 2000; Robinson 1885, 78; Reeves 1992a, 50).

In the late 1840s, Toronto received its first substantial wave of economic refugees, Irish fleeing the 1845-1849 potato famine. Many of these immigrants found work clearing lumber off the O'Hara estate, which by 1850 comprised a park lot and two farm lots, totalling five hundred acres, to the west of Toronto's city limits. Walter O'Hara, an Anglo-Irish Catholic, had served in the Peninsular War before becoming a colonel in the Upper Canada Militia (his battle experiences in Spain are commemorated in the exotic Parkdale street names of Roncesvalles and Sorauren). More concretely, he encouraged the creation of Toronto's first industrial suburb, Brockton, centred on the first westbound toll gate beyond Toronto along Dundas Street. By the early 1870s, Brockton had two ropewalks, several abattoirs and lumberyards, a basketmaker, and three taverns close to the toll gate. It also had a strong Catholic character, one of the few parts of Toronto with a minority culture identity in the overwhelmingly Protestant "Belfast of the North" (Patterson, McDougall, and Levin 1986). Map 4, of Toronto and its suburbs in 1860, shows the western suburb of Brockton, and the curvilinear subdivision of Rose Park (Rosedale) next to the northern suburb of Yorkville. Most lots in the future Parkdale (labelled as the western half of Brockton in this map) are as yet unsubdivided, and bear the names of landowners Gwynne, Dunn, and McDonell.

While Brockton developed west of the city's boundary, the military Garrison Reserve east of what would become Parkdale was filling up as well. After the US invasion and burning of York during the War of 1812,[1] the military function of the reserve lands had gradually waned, and the

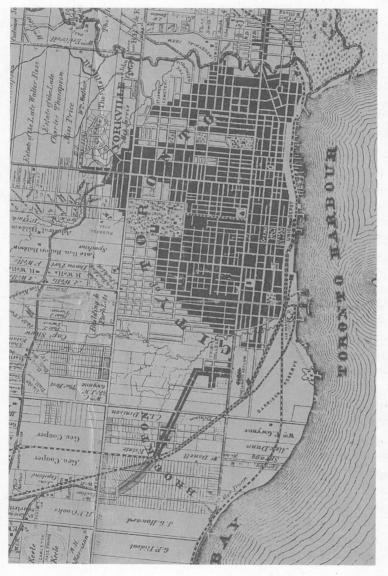

*Map 4.* Toronto and suburbs, 1860. Brockton refers to the entire area west of the city, including the Dunn, Gwynne, and McDonell estates that will be subdivided to create Parkdale. Note the suburb of Yorkville directly north of the built-up city, with the curvilinear subdivision of "Rose Park" (Rosedale) immediately to the northwest.

*Source:* Tremaine's Map of the County of York, Canada West (City of Toronto Archives MO 0004-1).

government began selling off plots for other uses. First and foremost came the railways: the Northern Railway (originally the Ontario, Simcoe and Huron) to Georgian Bay in 1853; the Great Western Railway to Hamilton, Detroit, and points west two years later; the Grand Trunk Railway to Guelph and western Ontario in 1858; and the Credit Valley and Toronto, Grey and Bruce Railways, also serving western Ontario, by 1879. Four of these railways divided Brockton and what would become Parkdale as they turned northward west of the city; the Great Western Railway continued west along the waterfront. At least two of the railways had shunting and works yards close to the Queen-Dufferin intersection, and all had stations within Parkdale. By 1879, the intersection was also served by a "Queen and Parkdale" horse tram, which by 1887 was extended west to High Park. A King Street tram reached Parkdale by 1883 (Careless 1984, 74; Laycock and Myrvold 1991, 23-24).

Two hundred acres set aside for farming at the Lunatic Asylum (the inmates were expected to earn their keep) were sectioned off for other institutional uses: the Central Prison, which began construction in 1871, and the Mercer Reformatory for Women and Girls in 1878 (Splane 1971, 166-68). The Government of Ontario had rotated its annual agricultural fair between several cities from the 1840s onwards, but the City of Toronto began to bid for a permanent site in 1858, when it constructed a replica Crystal Palace in the Garrison Reserve. By 1879, an annual Toronto Industrial Exhibition, open the three weeks before Labour Day, was established at a permanent site just east of Parkdale. The first fair was attended by 102,000 people, and by the turn of the century, annual attendance was close to half a million. The Toronto Industrial Exhibition, which changed its name to the Canadian National Exhibition in 1903, was eventually seen as a mixed blessing to Parkdale. While providing a year-round landscaped green space adjacent to the community, and a tremendous late-August economic boost to shop and hotel keepers, the fair also brought vehicle and pedestrian congestion that made the Queen-Dufferin intersection close to impassable for three weeks. Streetcars and trains were overcrowded, and there was considerable rowdyism, drunkenness, pickpocketing, prostitution, and theft, much of it centred at North Parkdale train station, where two special constables were kept busy during the fair. Several female residents of Parkdale were picked up by the police for "vagrancy" (prostitution) during exhibitions in the 1880s and 1890s (Walden 1997, 20, 32, 48-57).

Industries were attracted to the Garrison Reserve by the proximity of five railways, as well as municipal tax subsidies. Hart Massey's agricultural machinery company relocated from Newcastle, Ontario, in 1879. By 1884, the four-storey factory had four hundred workers, and by 1891, a series of mergers had made the Massey Company Toronto's largest employer, with over seven hundred workers. John Inglis' machinery factory employed eighty employees after 1882, and John Abell's implements factory employed close to two hundred after 1886 (Careless 1984, 112; Gad 1994). While Toronto had provided 11 percent of Ontario's industrial jobs in 1870, by 1910, it was the location of 27 percent of all industrial employment, much of it centred in the former Garrison Reserve and radiating northwest along the rail lines (Walden 1997, 8; Careless 1984, 181).[2]

Although the vicinity of Parkdale was rapidly filling with institutions, industry, and growing rail and road traffic to the north and east, there were countervailing influences to the south and west. The land that became Parkdale included the only undeveloped waterfront lots within easy access of downtown Toronto. And Howard, after his early retirement, decided to become the beneficiary of Toronto's first municipal pension plan. He negotiated the sale of his two-hundred-acre lot to the City of Toronto as a municipal park, in return for a $1,200 annuity and the right to live in his Colborne Lodge estate and act as park ranger until his death. He also attached restrictions to the use of the land, stipulating that no "drinking booth, alehouse, saloon or tavern" be located on the property and that it be "kept select for the wives and children of mechanics, and the working classes generally, also the Sunday School children and the different charities' picnics." This must have seemed like an excellent deal to the city when council voted on and accepted the agreement in 1873. Howard was seventy years old at the time, and seemed to be in frail physical and emotional health. But he lived on for another seventeen years, by which time the city had paid him over $20,000. The city paid less than $15,000 to add the two-hundred-acre Ridout estate to High Park in 1876, with no conditions attached. Still, High Park became an immediate boon to a growing city without large open spaces, especially after 1878, when the Great Western Railway began to run inexpensive excursion trains on Saturday afternoons and holidays (Reeves 1992a, 50).

An 1878 map of the southwestern portion of York County (Map 5) shows these potentially conflicting sources for growth in the vicinity of Parkdale (which by now had been given that name). On the one hand, the new Exhibition Grounds to the east, High Park to the west, and the waterfront to the south offered green space and the potential for pleasant walks and prospects. The railways and horse cars provided easy commuting opportunities to downtown jobs for the middle class. On the other hand, the railway yards, industries, lunatic asylum, and prisons, while providing

*Map 5.* Toronto's western suburbs, 1878. The eastern portion of Parkdale has been subdivided into urban lots. Note the Provincial Lunatic Asylum, Central Prison, Steel Works, and New Exhibition Grounds to the east of the new suburb, and High Park to the west.
*Source:* Canniff 1968.

working-class employment opportunities, would be considered unpleasant neighbours by a middle-class clientele. However, Parkdale lots could be sold to middle-class commuters and industrial walk-to-workers, and to a certain extent, they were marketed to both.

## Marketing Parkdale

As Toronto entered the second half of the nineteenth century, its social geography resembled that of many North American cities of the time: a finely scaled jumble of commercial and industrial uses, with residences for all classes spread across the developed area. There were some elite blocks, like Bay Street and Wellington Square, but they were adjacent to labourers' cottages, industries, and rail tracks. Ethnic segregation was limited to poor Catholics (mostly of Irish origin) living in the central area later called the Ward, north of Queen Street between University Avenue and Yonge Street, with other settlements in the marshy eastern periphery (later called Cabbagetown) and Brockton. The small black community, mostly refugees from slavery in the United States, were concentrated on one downtown block of York Street, just west of elegant Bay Street. Unlike most North American cities, Toronto remained over 75 percent Protestant and over 90 percent British in origin until well into the twentieth century, which meant that Toronto had a somewhat different context for ethnic, religious, and racial segregation than had cities like New York, Montreal, Winnipeg, Boston, and Chicago (Goheen 1970, 84-115; Piva 1979, 11; Careless 1984, 89-94, 200-202).

By the 1860s, the northern portions of several streets – including Jarvis Street, St. George Avenue, and Queen's Park Crescent – were being subdivided by their park lot owners into large lots for sale to the growing commercial elite. Yorkville, just north of the city limits along Yonge Street, became Toronto's first incorporated suburb in 1853. Unlike Brockton, which did not attain its own government until 1883, Yorkville had a mixture of self-employed craftspeople, shopkeepers, labourers, and clerks working locally, and a few merchants and professionals commuting by the omnibus service provided along Yonge Street after 1849. Again unlike in Brockton, the developers of Yorkville promoted their suburban lots to the middle class, advertising the "pure and healthy air" that would presumably be found one and a half miles (two kilometres) north of, and uphill from, downtown (Hutcheson 1978, 3). Suburban boosterism worked: the population of Yorkville grew from eight hundred in 1853 to over five thousand in 1881, with an increasing proportion of middle-class commuters (1-3). Yorkville, however, was never a "high-class" suburb, as contended by Goheen (1970, 73). It continued to mix industry, commerce, and various sizes of houses in the fine-grained pattern of the central city.

Places further afield took note. By the mid-1850s, the village of Maple, twenty miles (thirty kilometres) north of Toronto, was promoting itself as a half-hour railway commute from the city, with lower taxes and cheap firewood (Glazebrook 1971, 104). Residential development began to enjoy regular boom and bust cycles: a boom in housing construction during the

1850s was followed by a bust due to oversupply in the 1860s. Another boom in the late 1860s was followed by a worldwide recession in the mid-1870s. The late 1870s saw a third boom that lasted through the 1880s in Toronto, only to screech to a halt in the early 1890s during the worst global economic recession before the 1930s (Ganton 1982; Doucet and Weaver 1991). The tendency to re-subdivide and rebrand unsuccessfully marketed lots, already noted in the previous chapter, was found in Toronto as well. Lots unsuccessfully offered to "genteel residents" would eventually be advertised as suitable for "mechanics and others," with auctions moved to the evening to accommodate wage-earners' hours (Ganton 1982, 212).

In 1851, three-quarters of what would become Parkdale was under cultivation, and during the next two decades, subdivision plans for the entire area were registered (Laycock and Myrvold 1991, 9). Ganton (1982, 203), who has analyzed the process of subdivision in late-nineteenth-century Toronto, calls these lots "transitional": two-to-fifteen-acre lots that were intended to be sold to land speculators or market gardeners, rather than to be built up immediately. The deaths of three of the area's principal property owners, Walter O'Hara, William Gwynne, and Alexander Dunn, between 1868 and 1875 provided the opportunity for their widows and children to subdivide their land into small urban lots and market the area as a suburb (205; Laycock and Myrvold 1991, 10-11).

A subject that has received little attention in the literature on suburban development is the importance of widows and other female inheritors to the subdivision and home financing process in the nineteenth and early twentieth centuries.[3] A woman who inherited property and money tended to search for investments that would minimize the gap between the annual income of a wage-earning man and the much smaller interest she could receive on capital after his death. While subdivision and mortgage loans were somewhat risky endeavours, they were less risky and more respectable than other options, such as loans to new businesses. A network of property-handling agencies had sprung up in North America by the 1870s that acted as intermediaries between women and orphans' capital on the one side, and land developers, home builders, and individual buyers on the other (Doucet and Weaver 1991, 78).

The biggest landowner in Parkdale from 1875 until her death in 1910 was Eliza (Nell) Gwynne, sole surviving child of one of Parkdale's original settlers. In 1875, immediately after the death of her father, Nell Gwynne and the O'Hara family ( Walter O'Hara had died in 1874) were approached by a land developer named William Innes Mackenzie, who became known as the "Father of Parkdale" (Laycock and Myrvold 1991, 10). Mackenzie had enjoyed a very chequered career up to that point, not atypical of the lives of nineteenth-century businessmen. Born in Scotland in 1824, he migrated to Hamilton, Canada, in 1848. As an 1886 *Cyclopedia of Canadian Biography* discreetly put it, he held "several other positions" in New York, Mobile, and other North American cities before returning to Great Britain as financial manager of an ill-fated railway speculation company. After that bankruptcy, he ended up in Yorkville in 1874, where he found several wealthy backers to support a new company with the grand name Toronto House Building Association (G. Rose 1886, 50-51). The THBA purchased the southern twenty acres of the O'Hara estate in 1875 and the northern thirty acres of the Gwynne estate the following year, and immediately registered subdivision plans for an eight-block area immediately north and south of Queen Street and west of the city limits.

It seems likely that the association gave the area the name of Parkdale sometime in 1875 or 1876 (Laycock and Myrvold 1991, 10). Unlike many subdivisions in Toronto (Rosedale, Seaton Village, Brockton), Parkdale was not named after a landowner or an estate. Nor was it a colloquial name, like Cabbagetown. Rather, the name Parkdale seems to have been purpose-built for marketing. Rosedale was already associated with Toronto's elite, and High Park was becoming a popular spot for picnics and other natural pursuits. By 1883, the area just east of the Don River had changed its name from Riverside to Riverdale. Of sixteen Chicago-area subdivisions advertised by Samuel Gross in 1885, mostly for lower-middle- and working-class buyers, six have *park* in their names and two have *dale* (Ward 1998, 134). The name Parkdale was thus a combination of two important signifiers in late-nineteenth-century suburban culture, both suggesting natural beauty and remoteness from the sights and smells of the city.

A sample of the promotional material produced to advertise Parkdale lots can be found in 1881's *Parkdale Register,* which summarizes the history of the area to that date and provides sketches of its most notable citizens. Located only three miles west of Toronto's city hall, "The site is higher than that of the major portion of Toronto, and is exceedingly picturesque, being surrounded by a landscape that possesses all the varying attractions afforded by the beautiful Lake Ontario, and the diversified scenery of an undulating expanse of fertile country, wooded, watered, cultivated, and adorned with attractive homes." The streets were described as "regular, kept in good repair, and ornamented with young trees." The climate was modified by lake breezes, which meant that the area was "not subject to malarial influences and is uncommonly healthy." The real estate market was "exceedingly active," due to the "steadily increasing desire of those whose avocations require them to spend much of their time amid the bustle of Toronto, of providing themselves with a quiet home in an agreeable locality." The "unpretentious homes" of the "working and middle

classes" were "neat and comfortable," showing evidence of the wise residents' "thrift and prosperity" (1-5). The *Register* suggests that the primary
target for advertising was commuting businessmen, while recognizing that
others might be attracted to Parkdale.

Apart from a name that clearly differentiated the development from
Brockton, there were other preconditions for the settlement of Parkdale.
In November 1875, the THBA organized local landowners to "be assessed
for the purpose of constructing a sidewalk on the north side of Queen
Street from the city limits to Sunnyside," and York Township subsequently
granted $200 and levied $800 for a half-mile of wooden sidewalk. The late
1870s also saw petitions to York Township to grade roads along Roncesvalles, Jameson, Elm Grove, Gwynne, O'Hara, and King, to erect a cattle
guard across the Great Western Railway junction with Jameson, and to
provide a schoolhouse on Lansdowne. The City of Toronto constructed a
sidewalk on Dufferin from Queen Street to the Exhibition grounds, and
sidewalks were provided by York Township along a further five Parkdale
streets in 1878 (Laycock and Myrvold 1991, 10; York Township, Minutes,
1874-1878). Construction of an Anglican church began in 1877, and a
Methodist church followed in 1878, with the Presbyterians close behind
in 1879 (Laycock and Myrvold 1991, 12).

Across North America, the late 1870s witnessed a frenzy of speculative
land flipping in suburbs, although actual building activity was slow
(Doucet and Weaver 1991, 43). Land registry records for Parkdale indicate
that this trend was true for Toronto as well. Plan 387, for a portion of the
north side of Queen Street, was registered by the THBA in 1875. Lots 4
to 6, between O'Hara and West Lodge (one of the six sample blocks in
this study), were immediately sold to a man named Duckworth for $1,667,
with a mortgage provided by the vendors (who advertised themselves as
a "Building, Loan, and Savings Society") for all but $400. Four years later,
the mortgage was discharged when Duckworth sold the three lots to a real
estate dealer named John Laxton for $1,900 cash. Laxton almost imme-
diately re-subdivided and sold less than half of the property to a man
named Woods for $1,325. Woods, however, did not build on his land until
1886. Similarly, Sophie Dunn, widow of Alexander, sold lot 61, plan 333
(the entire east side of Dowling Avenue south of King Street, another sample block) to Robert Gooch, a real estate agent, for $1,903 in 1873, with
a vendor mortgage of $950. Gooch immediately resold this lot and one
other to Goldwyn Smith for $3,318, although he did not discharge his
mortgage to Sophie Dunn until 1883. Three years and two sales later, lot
61 was repurchased by Robert Gooch for $6,000, triple what he had orig-
inally paid, although there was still no house on the property.

Some row houses were erected during the late 1870s, for quick resale, in the southeast portion of Parkdale, just south of Queen Street. These were purchased by some wealthy people as an investment and temporary home while more elaborate villas were being built. For instance, legal publisher Charles Frankish was constructing a mansion on Dowling Avenue by the lakeshore (later occupied by his business partner Robert Carswell), but in 1881 he lived in a modest row house on Elm Grove Avenue, alongside two carpenters, a bookbinder, and two prison guards sharing a house (Parkdale Council 1881; Land Registry Records).

Land speculation was breathlessly reported by newspapers, which benefited from real estate advertisement revenue and also considered high land prices a sign of municipal progress. The *Mail* reported on 9 July 1879 that "the mania for Parkdale lots has subsided." Two months later, it announced a bounce-back: "More lots in Parkdale have been sold in the last fortnight than during the whole of the preceding months"; and three days later added, "Lots are selling rapidly in Parkdale, and there are scarcely any vacant houses" (2 and 5 September 1879). In 1882, the newspaper positively crowed: "The [Parkdale] property which was bought from Mr. Farrell last week for $10,000 has been sold again for $14,000. Can this be beaten in Winnipeg?" (4 March 1882). Suburban news items included sales of lots and announcements of auctions, and, then as today, news of the business of house selling seemed to transform itself effortlessly into shilling the product.

Despite the fact that there were fewer than a thousand residents in Parkdale in 1878, a hot political debate was being waged over the future of this suddenly valuable property. In June, two separate delegations from Parkdale presented petitions to York Township Council, one requesting Parkdale's incorporation as a village, the other asking that it not be incorporated but continue to be governed by the county. At the same time, Toronto alderman Richard Denison, who owned land and held office in both Toronto and York Township, presented a motion asking for the city's boundaries to be extended from Dufferin westward to the Humber River (Laycock and Myrvold 1991, 12). The *Globe,* which favoured annexation, pointed out the absurdity of having an independent village between the city and its new municipal park, and thundered in an editorial: "We cannot allow ourselves to be girdled around with incorporated villages, whose presence may by and bye cause annoyance by absurd restrictions, and disease by neglect of ordinary sanitary precautions" (27 June 1878). Parkdalians who favoured incorporation turned these moral and physical health arguments around, saying that Toronto's tap water tasted like "purgatory and death united ... a miasmic liquid," and that Toronto's city government was notorious for its corruption, especially in the granting of liquor licences (*Parkdale Gazette and Brockton Advocate*, 8 September 1881). Denison argued that the balkanization of Toronto into many separate municipalities would threaten the city's rivalry with Montreal for commercial supremacy, while a letter to the *Globe* pointed out that the lack of metropolitan government had done London no harm (*Globe*, 29 June and 5 July 1878). The *Evening Telegram*, which maintained neutrality on the question of annexation versus incorporation, focused on the underlying issue of taxation for municipal services. On "one side of the issue," "Parkdale is to all intents and purposes, except those of taxation, a part of the city now," and it was unfair for businessmen to "enjoy all the advantages" of living in a city without "contributing to its cost." On the "other side," property owners had the right to "protect against municipal extravagance and jobbery" so prevalent in Toronto (27 June 1878).

Parkdale's fate was ultimately decided not by businessmen and property owners, but by some of its most marginalized residents. After a preliminary census found fewer than the 750 residents required for incorporation, a tribe of gypsies was allegedly bribed to become temporary citizens.[4] Alderman Denison also charged that signatures were collected of those "who were not really inhabitants," such as "mechanics from Toronto who were working there temporarily" and residents of "the Roman Catholic institution," that is, the Magdalen Asylum for Fallen Women, which had been established at O'Hara's old estate of West Lodge in 1876 (*Globe*, 29 June 1878). While early marketing strategies focused on the middle class, Parkdale became an independent municipality as of 1 January 1879 thanks to the kinds of institutionalized and insecurely housed people who would be seen as unwelcome intruders one hundred years later.

## Disputes over Character: Parkdale as an Independent Municipality, 1879-1888

Throughout Parkdale's ten years as an independent municipality, tensions between what I will term "pro-development" and "slow-growth" forces helped shape the neighbourhood's physical form and social composition. Each side of the debate promulgated an image of Parkdale's character. The pro-development forces viewed Parkdale as the expanding edge of a growing city, with inexpensive housing opportunities for all. They would be ideologically aligned with the "big tent" suburban promoters described in Chapter 1. The slow-growth forces wanted physical and moral exclusivity in the suburb, by maintaining an identity distinct from and morally and economically superior to Toronto's. Dolores Hayden's history of American suburbs (2003) speaks of exclusive "picturesque enclaves" being developed from the 1850s onwards, with more working-class "streetcar build-outs" the predominant form of suburban growth by the 1870s. In Parkdale, we see in microcosm the conflict between these two different visions of suburb.

These conflicts within Parkdale also reflected political tensions within Toronto. In local politics, the late nineteenth century was characterized by an ongoing battle between "boosters" and "cutters." The boosters were an unlikely coalition of businessmen at the top of the heap and work-ingmen at the bottom, for whom new housing developments, civic work contracts, and tax rebates for railway promoters and industries meant revenues and jobs, respectively. The cutters were ratepayers who wanted some limits on municipal expenditures, even if it resulted in slower growth for the city (Magnusson 1983b, 98).

As well, Parkdale's local governance reflected progressive discourses from further abroad that were developing during the 1870s and 1880s. From the United Kingdom came the "gospel of civic improvement," originally developed by Joseph Chamberlain in Birmingham. This movement held that civic authorities needed to provide and own their city's water, sewage, and gasworks, as well as to control education, health, and welfare, in order to prevent disease, promote efficient growth, and preserve the moral and physical health of all citizens. From the United States came the munici-pal reform movement, moving away from the cronyism and corruption of previous city governments towards a more open and impartial form of democracy (Magnusson 1983a, 13-14).

In the public arguments leading to incorporation, a letter from "a res-ident of Parkdale" accused the pro-annexation movement of being led by a few absentee "speculators, each owning from 5-10 acres of land in that section, and who have not the slightest interest in the place further than to increase the value of their property"; they would "leave the purchasers of the building lots to pay the taxes." In contrast, this resident had gone to the expense of sinking a well and outhouse, and did not "want or need city water or drains" (*Globe,* 28 June 1878). Another letter to the *Evening Telegram* (29 June 1878) complained about the city spending hundreds of thousands of dollars landscaping the Exhibition Grounds while Queen Street West was in a pitiful condition; Parkdalians would not be caught in this spendthrift trap. Pro-incorporation forces were thus arguing that Parkdale could be managed by its sensible middle-class homeowners, who would live in a semi-rural environment without need of municipal ser-vices. Some city dwellers, including the editor of the *Globe,* believed the combination of few services and low taxes would attract an entirely dif-ferent class of residents. As a letter from "a Toronto Ratepayer" argued, Parkdalians should be left to their own devices: "There they will have rail-way facilities, easy access to the city, cheap land, and not be disfiguring our streets with their modest dwellings ... If mechanics or men of modest means wish to purchase property within the limits of their purse, let them go" (*Evening Telegram,* 8 July 1878).

By the time of the village's first election, held on 6 January 1879, "two parties" were identified in coverage of political meetings. One ticket, led by Charles Frankish, the legal publisher, Thomas Abbs, a former tenant farmer who had just opened up a grocery store on Queen Street, and several others, was opposed to "speculation and extravagance"; they were the low-tax, low-service, sell-lots-quickly party. The other, led by Colonel Gray, the nurseryman, and Joseph Norwich, a Queen Street butcher and large landowner in northwest Parkdale, were slow-growth advocates, wishing to hold on to their land and make improvements until wealthy people were willing to buy large lots for estates. There were both political and religious differences between the parties. Frankish and, more particularly, future town clerk John MacLachlan were nonconformist pro-temperance liberal Grits typical of the new commercial elite in Toronto. Gray was a Tory Anglican, representative of the old Toronto elite. The THBA's Mackenzie, who, of course, epitomized the pro-development forces, accused Gray's party at a public meeting of not being suitable to govern, because "they kept large tracts from people and paid low [non-residential] taxes"; the crowd responded with a loud "hear, hear" (*Globe,* 25 November 1878). Nevertheless, the slow-growth Tories won the first village election.

There was a council consensus on several progressive government proposals. The first was a frontage tax, by which a majority of residents on a street would petition for sidewalk or street improvements, to be paid by themselves using a special levy. This special assessment system, which Robin Einhorn (1991) claims was pioneered in Chicago during the 1870s, met with approval by the *Globe* (28 December 1878), which otherwise had little good to say about the suburban municipality's governance. At the first meeting of the village council, on 20 January 1879, a medical officer of health was appointed. This was exceptionally forward-thinking, since the City of Toronto only got around to appointing a public health officer four years later, at which point it was the first city in Ontario to do so (MacDougall 1990, 10).[5] Parkdale's school board also proved to be ahead of its time on education issues. By 1878, Parkdale residents on the York Township School Board had taken the township to court in order to obtain funds for adequate facilities at the public school, and Parkdale School was expanded at local taxpayer expense twice more during the next six years. In 1883, the York Township Model School was located there, with twenty-eight teachers in training, and by 1886, it housed one of the first kindergarten classes in Canada, along with a full gymnasium, steam heat, and the latest in school equipment. An additional elementary school, Queen Victoria, and Toronto's second high school had opened by the time Parkdale was annexed in 1889 (Laycock and Myrvold 1991, 44-45). A Mechanic's Institute, or public library, had been formed by 1881, with a board that included ministers from the three largest denominations (Presbyterian, Methodist, and Anglican). One hundred people paid the dollar annual fee to gain access to almost two thousand volumes and twenty periodicals. Parkdale Council subsidized the institute, as well as an art school founded in 1888 with a predominantly adult membership of eighty-seven (46, 56).

The council, meeting biweekly, pursued other measures which it believed would contribute to good living conditions for all classes. One of the first bylaws prohibited domestic animals running at large, a measure aimed not only at residents keeping pigs, cows, and poultry, but also at cattle drovers from west of the city who brought their cattle along Queen Street to be slaughtered in Toronto. Amusingly, the medical officer of health's own cow was almost immediately impounded and released from the village pound only after a stiff fine (Parkdale Council, Minutes, 6 August 1879). Bylaws to provide night soil removal and regular crackdowns on butcher shops, slaughterhouses, stagnant gutters, and dysfunctional "earth closets" also assisted public health. Water and sewer work contracts were awarded. Trees were planted by the municipality, mostly supplied by Reeve Gray, who also sold trees and plants to the city for use at the Exhibition Grounds, Riverdale Park, and University Street (*Mail*, 11 May 1882). Residents of working-class streets seized on the Flowery Suburb imagery, with petitions to change the name of Greig Street to Elm Grove and Marion Street to Maple Grove.

More controversial were the growing number of morals-related bylaws being passed by the village council. Bylaw 18, adopted in May 1879, made it illegal to give intoxicating drink to a child, an apprentice, an insane person, or a servant if forbidden by his or her employer; to circulate indecent prints or placards; to use profane language; to appear on the street intoxicated or to behave in a disorderly manner; to keep a house of ill-fame or to harbour "bad characters"; to gamble; or to expose oneself near a public highway or other public place. Parkdale Council sent a deputation to Toronto City Council to argue against the construction of the Gladstone Hotel across the Dufferin tracks, and prohibited the sale of "intoxicating liquors" in the municipality. Several months later, this bylaw was flouted when the Union Hotel obtained a licence from the village council to serve liquor, and two local grocers secured licences to sell it (*Empire*, 21 June 1879), although Parkdale still considered itself stricter than Toronto when it came to the issuance of liquor licences. There were regular crackdowns on public swimming in Lake Ontario, especially on the Sabbath (*Mail*, 9 July 1880, 8 July 1882). The municipality also tried to limit peddlers by making them purchase a fifteen-dollar licence, but immediately faced a mutiny by female residents, who threatened to buy their coal-oil and other goods in Toronto if they could not be delivered to their doors (*Empire*, 10 June 1879).

Industries seeking sites in Parkdale faced a seemingly contradictory attitude from the council. In December 1879, Harris and Crowhurst's sheet metal factory on the west side of Dufferin Street was producing portable houses for export to Australia (*Globe*, 13 December 1879). A month later, the *Mail* (10 January 1880) reported that a cotton manufacturing company had asked the village council for tax relief in return for locating in the municipality, but Parkdale was the "last place to procure a bonus. Its residents desire nothing but 'flowers and a rural home' – as one of the councillors poetically puts it." A glucose factory was refused permits twice in 1882, before being given a permit to operate in the subsequent year (*Mail*, 16 June, 4 July, and 27 July 1882).

In January 1883, the annual election finally produced a majority for the pro-development party. By April, Parkdale had repealed all of its previous "dangerous trade and nuisance bylaws" and began to openly compete for industries with Toronto. The Gutta Percha Rubber Company, a Canadian branch plant of an American firm, was granted a ten-year tax exemption, a special water rate, and free gas. In return, over one hundred jobs were provided, mostly to local residents. The Toronto Stove Manufacturing Company, also employing about a hundred men, erected a factory on a five-acre Dufferin Street lot in return for a similar arrangement. Several lumber companies were permitted to use steam power for their mills. Ironically, Gray, the leader of the slow-growth forces, was a major beneficiary of this change in policy. He sold his nine-acre nursery adjacent to the tracks for industrial use in the mid-1880s, making a considerable profit (Laycock and Myrvold 1991, 52-53, 42). Parkdale residents were also employed in large numbers at the Ontario Bolt Company west of High Park, which opened in 1883 and employed five hundred people by the end of the decade (Careless 1991, 112). On 3 January 1884, when the Bolt Company's special train, carrying sixty workers from central Toronto, crashed, killing twenty-four passengers, the *Globe* reported that Parkdale Council held an emergency meeting and raised $158 for a widows' and orphans' fund, although there were no Parkdale fatalities (presumably because the Parkdale employees walked to work; Franklin 1988b).

The slow-growth party was also ineffective in its occasional attempts to control working-class housing, equating row houses with the tenements of New York and Edinburgh. Although there was "much excitement" about an early bylaw barring roughcast houses within the developed portion of Parkdale, no houses were charged with contravening the code (*Globe,* 4 and 22 August 1879). Similarly, it was reported that "Parkdalers are alarmed at the suggestion made by [the *Globe*] that small tenement houses be built in the suburb. It is contended that nothing would tend more to retard the prosperity of the village," yet row house construction continued apace (*Mail,* 5 April 1881). Complaints about "Mrs. Virtue's tenements" at the 5 January 1881 council meeting did not stop their construction. John

*Figure 2.2.*   Working-class "tenements": Melbourne Place, built c. 1883, photographed 1955. The inscription on the back of the photograph reads, "The narrowest street in Toronto."
*Source:* City of Toronto archives, Fonds 1244, series 460.

Coatsworth, one of the busiest builders of both high-end and low-end houses in the suburb, upset neighbours with three row house developments in 1882. Trenton Terrace off Cowan and Melbourne Place near Queen and Dufferin were built (Figure 2.2), but the third, planned for the lakeshore on Dunn Avenue, appears to have been blocked by an injunction taken out by neighbours. This may have been related to deed restrictions placed by Nell Gwynne, the original landowner, who continued to live in her villa and take an active role in Parkdale politics until her death in 1910 (*Globe,* 30 January 1882; *Mail,* 6 and 11 March 1882).

Despite the *Mail's* breezy assurance that "this savvy municipality is evidently quite competent to take care of itself" (24 February 1880), Parkdale Council found itself shouldering an untenable debt load as the years went on. In 1880, it attempted to resolve a long debate with York County Council over the removal of tolls along Queen Street by extending King Street westward to the intersection with Roncesvalles, effectively detouring around the toll. York Council responded by moving its toll gate to the new intersection (Laycock and Myrvold 1991, 16). In 1882, Parkdale Council took on debentures for $130,000, or nearly $100 per inhabitant, to expand the village waterworks and provide "more complete drainage than any other village or city in the dominion" (*Globe,* 7 June 1882; *Mail,* 3 June and 28 July 1882). In 1885, Parkdale became a town, and the number of council members increased from five to seventeen. Street maintenance was a constant drain on revenues during winter and summer. The municipality's newfangled horse-drawn snowplough collapsed during the first storm in the winter of 1879, and the *Mail* claimed in 1882 that "the 'Flowery Suburb' has streets choked with weeds" (*Mail,* 27 December 1879, 31 July 1882).

The project that brought Parkdale close to bankruptcy and led to its annexation by Toronto was an underpass, or subway as it was then called, under the rail tracks at Queen and Dufferin. A safe passage across the four railroad lines was essential for the commercial and residential growth of the municipality. Gray's own father had been killed by a train in January 1878, and hundreds of items in the newspapers testify to the dangers to both pedestrians and carts. To give some typical examples, a teamster named Strothers carrying a load of bricks narrowly escaped death when his cart got stuck at the crossing (*Mail,* 4 January 1878), an unnamed "gentleman" got his foot stuck in the tracks and came close to losing it (*Mail,* 23 January 1882), and a Toronto, Grey and Bruce train derailed at the Queen Street crossing, fortunately causing no fatalities but backing up traffic for hours (*Mail,* 20 June 1882). As the contemporary observer Mulvaney put it in 1884 (257), "The want of such a provision for public safety [as a subway or bridge] has led to many accidents, and has hitherto depreciated the value of Parkdale real estate, as parents are unwilling to expose their children to such a very serious risk."

From 1879 onwards, Parkdale Council sent regular deputations to Ottawa to pressure railroad companies to pay for adequate safety devices. The companies responded by occasionally assigning a man to direct traffic at the intersection. In 1883, the province passed a bill empowering Parkdale and Toronto, along with the railroad companies, to make an agreement for a subway. The legislation cautioned that Toronto and Parkdale had to mutually agree on how costs would be divided and paid, but when Toronto backed out of the agreement, Parkdale forged ahead even though two-thirds of the proposed subway was within city limits. When the subway finally opened in 1885, at a cost of about $20,000 to Parkdale, residents found the passage unlit, muddy, and smelly. Many continued to risk the dangers of the overland route rather than risk the "dreadful hole," also known as the "mudway" (Laycock and Myrvold 1991, 20-22; *Mail*, 8 January 1889).

Pressure for annexation increased in both Parkdale and Toronto when Brockton became part of the city, along with Yorkville and Riverdale, in 1883-84. In January 1885, Parkdale ratepayers voted to join Toronto by a large margin, but negotiations foundered once the city was apprised of Parkdale's debt load. The following year, the clerk-treasurer was fired for being "addicted to drink" (an assessment that would be obvious to anyone trying to read Parkdale's handwritten minutes from 1884 onwards). By 1888, Parkdale was entirely surrounded by the city, and the province ordered another vote on annexation (Laycock and Myrvold 1991, 31-32). Once again, annexation was "the only topic in the Flowery Suburb" (*Mail*, 20 October 1888), and arguments for and against it echoed those made ten years previously.

Those in favour of keeping Parkdale a separate municipality argued that Parkdale Council had kept taxes low, provided clean water and a pleasant living environment, and guarded against the city's bad influences. These anti-annexation forces called themselves the Citizens' Protective Association, and their mottos included "Save our Streets and Waterfront" and "Vote for Home Rule and the Town Pump" (*World*, 16 October 1888; *Parkdale Gazette*, 27 October 1888). One letter writer from Parkdale claimed he paid $65 annually for his sixty-foot lot on a street "sidewalked, sewered, and block-paved," while a friend just across the subway in Toronto paid more for a twenty-four-foot frontage with inferior services, and was closer to "a great big institution where Ontario provides light and heat, amongst other things, for at least one thousand poor demented unfortunates," meaning the Lunatic Asylum (*World*, 16 October 1888). Parkdale had schools, sewers, and a separate water supply, and was ready for a population five or six times its present size, at which point per capita debt would decrease (*Mail*, 22 October 1888). The municipality was also entirely free of "low groceries and houses of ill-repute." In contrast, Toronto had turned its beautiful waterfront into "a sewage pond." The only people in favour of annexation were large owners of vacant lots: "men who have never lived, nor intend to live, within two or three miles of our midst," who wanted to dispose of their lots during the land sale boom that they hoped would follow annexation (*World*, 13 October 1888).

Those in favour of annexation painted quite another picture of Parkdale's governance. According to them, Parkdale Council was a nest of "Boodlers, Town Pap-Suckers, Stick-in-the-Muds, Ward Heelers," et cetera, whose doings set a new standard for corruption and incompetence (*Mail*, 26 October 1888). Exhibit A was the subway. Parkdale citizens had paid five times more than they would have if they had been part of the city, and three years after construction, it already needed considerable repairs and widening (*World*, 24 October 1888). The pro-annexation forces claimed that debt, mostly due to the subway, was $123 per head in Parkdale, twice the debt load of Torontonians. Parkdale schools were overcrowded, and the social and physical infrastructure in general was in need of immediate improvement. Annexation would also allow better competition with other suburbs (*Mail*, 13 October 1888). For instance, "land is still cheap in Rosedale," a portion of which had been annexed in 1887, while taxes had trebled in Parkdale since incorporation (*Mail*, 24 October 1888). The *World*, an inexpensive tabloid popular with workers, nailed its pro-annexation colours to the mast early in the debate. It did not scruple to make up letters to the editor supporting its stand, such as an obviously fictitious missive from "the Honourable John de Barnacle" (perhaps a caricature of John Gray) bewailing the possible loss of patronage if Parkdale was annexed: "How could I get a hundred dollars or two for myself and a contract now and then for my friends?" (*World*, 20 November 1888). Allegations of corruption seemed to be confirmed in the waning days of the independent municipality when Parkdale School Board purchased a site for a third public school, on Fern Avenue, from the father of the chairman of the board, at twice market value (*Mail*, 13 March 1889).

The leaders of both sides in the debate were local real estate agents. When Isaac Lennox, of the Citizens' Protective Association, claimed at a public meeting that the annexation movement was led by "land sharks," W.H.P. Clement retorted that "housebuilding companies had done a great deal for the town in its infancy" (*Mail*, 24 October 1888). Despite middle-class leadership, and unlike during the 1878 incorporation debate, both pro- and anti-annexation forces made explicit appeals to working-class freeholders. The *World* printed two suspiciously similar letters from "A Workman" and "A Carpenter" before the vote. The first writer said he had initially opposed annexation, but was increasingly worried about future tax increases should the municipality remain separate. Annexation would be an inducement to builders, which would result in "more work to be done by men like me, and instead of having to pay streetcar fare to our work, as we have to now, we will have plenty of work at home" (27 September 1888). The second letter repeated many phrases from the first, telling of a changed mind on the vote because Parkdale Council was made up of those with "swell houses" (13 October 1888).

The anti-annexation *Mail*, in contrast, reported, "Small householders, who have not any real estate to dispose of, seem to be against a matrimonial arrangement on any terms" (10 October 1888). J.J. Ward, a Parkdale councillor and merchant tailor who was a leader in the labour movement, claimed at several public meetings that Parkdale provided good cheap houses, whereas in Toronto, "You can't show me a house ... with a $6 [monthly] rent" (*Mail*, 18 October 1888). The pro-annexation forces played into the hands of the Citizens' Protective Association when A.F.G. Gianelli, the Italian vice-consul who lived in a large villa on Jameson Avenue, said at a public meeting, "Parkdale's isolation prevents many well-to-do people, who would otherwise go to live there, from going to a place that they think is a place for mechanics only" (*World*, 16 October 1888). H.H. Cook, Parkdale's member of Parliament and an opponent of annexation, immediately responded that "he wanted Mr. Gianelli to understand, in connection with his sneers about the town's inhabitants being principally mechanics, that he was not going to introduce any of his ancient aristocratic views in this democratic country. A mechanic was as good as any man, and they were thoroughly substantial citizens" (*Mail*, 18 October 1888). Gianelli was forced to back down with the time-honoured excuse that his remarks were misrepresented, and that "mechanics are a vital element in every country" (*Mail*, 24 October 1888).

On Saturday, 27 October 1888, the day of the vote, the *World* abandoned its veneer of interest in its working-class Parkdale residents when it advertised for all absentee landlords to show up in Parkdale: "A cab at 9 ½ Adelaide Street, the Annexation Committee room, will take you out to Parkdale to record your vote for Union and Progress ... You have a vote in every ward in which you are upon the voter's list." The ward breakdown of the final result shows that small householders near the rail tracks voted against annexation while landowners in the larger, less developed areas voted for the motion. Mechanics seemed to be in favour of home rule and the town pump. Without 464 absentee landholders (of a total of 1,128 votes), the anti-annexation forces would have won, as the *World* admitted immediately after the vote (29 October 1888). Parkdale ceased to exist as a municipality on 1 January 1889, exactly ten years after it had incorporated.

The ten-year life of Parkdale as an independent municipality provides a counter-example to the usual stereotypes of politically independent suburbs existing to protect middle-class people's property values by excluding non-residential uses and poor people. As both Kenneth Jackson (1985, 147-50) and Dolores Hayden (2003) point out in the US context, the late nineteenth century was a transitional point between big tent and exclusive suburbs, suburbs that sought growth at any cost and suburbs that marketed themselves with race, ethnic, or class distinctions to maintain high property values. Although political power was held by small businessmen in Parkdale, both commuters and people whose primary business interests were there, the net impact of early political decisions resulted in the suburb being a low-cost haven for working-class homeowners and renters. Land was cheap, social services were extensive, and access to jobs across the rail tracks and within the municipality was good to begin with, and better by the end of the 1880s. Although Parkdale was the fastest-growing suburb in the greater Toronto area during the early 1880s (*Might's Directory* 1881), large tracts of land in the west and north remained undeveloped at the time it was annexed by Toronto. Again counterintuitively, Parkdale was a suburb where the wealthy predominated only after annexation by the city, during the worldwide recession of the 1890s.

### Boom, Bust, and Echo: Social and Housing Conditions in Parkdale, 1880-1913

The 1880s saw a real estate boom across Toronto, fuelled by job and population growth. Industrial employees and payroll doubled in the decade, thanks in part to protective tariffs enacted by the federal government, and the city's population more than doubled, to almost 200,000 people, between the 1881 and 1891 censuses (Careless 1984, 200, tables 1 and 4). Toronto was at the forefront of innovations: Eaton's mail order catalogue was launched at the Industrial Exhibition in 1884, and the following year an invention with even more influence, the electric streetcar, was first displayed there (112-13). Good times and a high demand for skilled workers led to labour activism. A January 1886 strike at the Massey factory fizzled out after labour spokesmen were fired and the police called in, but a strike by horse tram drivers two months later met with considerably more public sympathy and eventual management concessions, even though commuters from Parkdale were temporarily inconvenienced (D. Morton 1973, 43-45; see also Kealey 1980).

Parkdale's housing construction in the late 1880s had favoured working-class homeownership. The proportion of skilled labourers in the suburb had increased from 24 percent in 1881 to 41 percent in 1891, and over half of these skilled labourers owned their homes, double the rate for Toronto as a whole (the average homeownership rate in Toronto was 27 percent in 1899, according to Harris 1996, xii; Parkdale Council 1881; City of Toronto Assessment Rolls 1891). Robert Libby was born in 1881 and lived on Callender Street for close to ninety years. In his audiotaped reminiscences, written up in community newspapers in the 1970s, he tells of how his father, a blacksmith working for the Canadian Pacific Railway, bought one of two semi-detached houses built by Walter Wilcox, the yard master, in 1883, with Wilcox occupying the other house. While his oral memoir is not entirely clear on the point, the CPR seems to have assisted Robert Libby Sr. with home financing, by part payment with a land grant outside Toronto. When Libby sold that land, he had enough cash for a down payment on the house. While Wilcox moved to West Toronto Junction in 1890, following the relocation of the CPR shop (see below), the Libby family decided to stay in their Parkdale home. Eventually young Robert followed in his father's footsteps and worked for the CPR for several years.[6]

Although large landowners like Nell Gwynne and Joseph Norwich, and real estate companies like the Hamilton firm of Fuller and Plumb, still held the majority of undeveloped Parkdale land in the early 1880s, many people followed the entrepreneurial path of Wilcox, and built one house to live in along with an adjacent house for rent or sale. According to the 1881 assessment rolls, a twenty-five-year-old bricklayer named William Westcott lived in one row house and owned another on Lansdowne Avenue, each assessed at $900, along with two fifty-foot lots assessed at $400 each. Udney Walker, a bookkeeper and member of Parkdale Council, owned three houses on the same street, assessed at between $650 and $750. Even in the first years of Parkdale, lower-income homeowners rented out part of their houses to help pay the mortgage. Thus, in 1881, Gilbert Harkly, a guard at the Central Prison, had as a lodger on Elm Grove Avenue Michael Wood, a fellow prison guard, while Mrs. Rawcliffe, a grocer on Queen Street, had an engineer named James Tout living above her store (Parkdale Council 1881).

Working-class residents felt immediate negative impacts when Parkdale was annexed by the City of Toronto in 1889. The Mechanic's Institute, whose operation had been subsidized by Parkdale Council, agreed to transfer all of its books and furniture to the Toronto Public Library on condition that a branch be opened in Parkdale. The promised library branch did not appear until 1964. For the intervening seventy-five years, South Parkdalians had to make do with the Queen Street library a half-mile (one kilometre) east of Dufferin Street, although North Parkdale was closer to the handsome High Park branch on Roncesvalles Avenue built in 1910 (Laycock and Myrvold 1991, 56-57). It could also be argued that annexing Parkdale was a bad deal for the City of Toronto. The annexation of Parkdale was cited as one of the reasons that the city was in a debt crisis by the early 1890s, and Parkdale was the last major suburban annexation for over fifteen years (C. Clark 1898, 1-2). The much-lauded Parkdale waterworks were judged inadequate by the city, and their land, on the shore of Lake Ontario just west of Roncesvalles, was sold for industrial use in 1893, much to the displeasure of residents banding together under the name Parkdale Advancement Association, who wanted the lakeshore property developed as swimming baths (City of Toronto Council, Minutes, 8 and 22 May 1893).[7]

In 1891, the City of Toronto went back on another of its annexation promises, to keep political representation for the suburb on City Council. The doubling of the city's size during the 1883-1889 wave of annexations had led to an unwieldy system of thirteen wards, each with three aldermen. Now, Toronto was hit by the fever for administrative reform already apparent in big cities like Chicago (Einhorn 1991), New York (Lubove 1962), and London (Briggs 1993). Six new wards were created, long narrow north-south strips that sliced across class, ethnic, and religious lines. Although the new ward system was intended to break up political machines, the new ward system eventually ensured political domination of older working-class areas south of Bloor by newer suburbs north of Bloor (Armstrong and Nelles 1977, 68). Parkdale was swallowed up in Ward 6, which stretched from Dovercourt Road (east of Dufferin) to west of High Park. With minor modifications, this ward system stayed in place until the late 1960s.

The suburb could no longer offer inducements to local employers. By 1889, the four railways that made up Parkdale's northeastern boundary had been amalgamated into two: Canadian Pacific and Grand Trunk. In October of that year, CPR was offered considerable inducements by the new Town of West Toronto Junction, including ten years of tax abatement, free water, and a bridge over the tracks, to move its rail yards from the corner of Queen and Dufferin to Dundas and Keele (*Mail*, 25 October 1889). Although historical geographer Gunter Gad (2004) contends that the yards moved only in 1907, street directories and oral histories suggest that railroad workers immediately moved to the new industrial suburb.

And then Parkdale, like the rest of Toronto, was hit by a worldwide recession. There was concern about a coming crash in Parkdale land values by early 1889, when the *Mail* warned that "if annexation does not occur before 1890, many speculators will be caught" (2 February 1889). But despite annexation, land registry records show that some speculators were spectacularly caught out over the next few years. A set of four modest row houses on Gwynne Avenue, numbers 61-67, sold for $4,450 in 1889 and were resold for $3,450 a little over a year later. On Queen Street, a newly constructed commercial building at numbers 1418-20 was purchased in early 1890 by a butcher named Richard Hayes, who sold his house on Dowling Avenue in order to finance the deal. The purchase price was $8,700, with a $4,000 mortgage provided by an individual surnamed Thomas. Within a year, Hayes had borrowed a total of $9,220 from the Synod of the Diocese of Saskatchewan, with his property as collateral. The synod took over the property in 1894 and managed it until a 1913 sale to the long-time lessee Munro and Son, druggists, for $2,850. One newly constructed detached villa, 109 Dowling, sold for $10,000 in October 1891 and only $7,000 in December 1892. An even grander villa on the corner of Dowling and King was mortgaged for $13,000 when it was sold at a considerable loss in September 1890 for $10,000 to Anderson Ruffin Abbott, who was not only Canada's first black doctor but the son of one of Toronto's foremost real estate speculators. Abbott in turn sold the house to Henry Anthes in 1903 for $5,500, writing to his lawyer: "I think the sooner we get rid of the Dowling Avenue property altogether the better" (Abbott 1880-1905, vol. 2). The contemporary observer C.S. Clark (1898, 2) named as principal victims of the depression "widows and orphans, whose money was advanced through the agency of some rascally lawyer upon worthless second mortgages," as well as borrowers who sank all their savings into land speculation.

Estates for the wealthy constituted virtually the only Toronto building activity in the early 1890s, when Parkdale was described as "the only place where there are any real estate" transactions (*Telegram*, 28 November 1894). The period 1890-1921 was Parkdale's heyday as a home for the rich. The proportion of business owners and managers in Parkdale rose from 3 percent in 1881 and 1 percent in 1891 to 17 percent in 1901 and 1913, to 25 percent in 1921. The raw numbers are even more startling: there were 6 household heads out of a total population of 1,000 who could be classified as wealthy businessmen in 1881, 10 in 1891 (when Parkdale's population was 6,000), over 300 in 1901 (by which time Parkdale's population was 11,000), and over 500 wealthy businessmen in a total population of 15,000 by 1913 (Parkdale Council 1881; City of Toronto Assessment Rolls 1891-1913). Benjamin Westwood, a fishing tackle manufacturer, moved from the Annex to a new mansion at the foot of Jameson Avenue in 1890.

Its assessed value was $18,608 (Figure 2.3). He was joined by George Magann, a railway contractor, who built an adjacent mansion with an assessed value of $17,050 in the same year. The 1881 *Parkdale Register* had listed a few doctors and lawyers and many self-employed businessmen among its worthies. But when G. Mercer Adam's *Toronto Old and New* was published in late 1891, the new Parkdale mansions of a considerable number of business magnates adorned its pages: people like Sturgeon Stewart, managing director of the Eno Steam Generator Company, who owned a villa called Glen Zephyr on Dowling, and Richard Thorne, a folding bed manufacturer. In 1911, a book called *Greater Toronto and the Men Who Made It* included dozens of others, including the presidents of the Steel and Radiation Company, Dominion Radiator, Canadian Pipe and Steel, Gold Medal Furniture, and two piano manufacturing companies, along with a couple of bank presidents. Interlocking memberships in Parkdale Methodist or Presbyterian churches, the Masons, and several charitable enterprises cemented relations among the wealthy members of the community.

For the wealthy, Parkdale could indeed provide an ideal place to live, combining easy access to the city via railway or streetcar with a pastoral lifestyle. The novelist Mazo de la Roche, who lived as a child with her

*Figure 2.3.* The year-old lakeside mansion of the Westwoods, 1890, with the privately owned boardwalk in the foreground and the Clark estate visible behind the Westwood mansion
*Source:* Adam 1891.

grandparents on Dunn Avenue at the end of the nineteenth century, recalled "her first real home" as "one of five that stood on a tree-shaded street that ended in a kind of wooden terrace with seats, overlooking the lake." Along with the boardwalk, provided by owners of the lakeside lots, she could see boathouses from which rowers and sailors would emerge on warm summer evenings, protected by a breakwater crib built by Parkdale Council. Behind her, there were "fields of tall feathery grass and daisies" (cited in Gatenby 1999, 251).

But even throughout this period, Parkdale remained a mixed suburb. It liked to compare itself with Rosedale, but whereas in 1913 half of household heads in Rosedale were businessmen or professionals with only 13 percent listing themselves as clerks, skilled working class, or labourers, Parkdale had as many skilled wage earners as self-employed businessmen and professionals (36 percent each), and more clerical workers than the Toronto average. A more accurate comparison could be made with the Annex, the area bounded by Bloor, Dupont and the northern CPR rail tracks, Bathurst Street, and Avenue Road (see Map 1). Developed, like Parkdale, between the late 1870s and World War One, the Annex's first housing had been modest working-class houses on its eastern and western edges. During the 1890s depression, mansions and villas for the wealthy sprung up along Walmer and Admiral Roads, and on St. George Street north of Bloor. There was residential segregation, but it was on a block-by-block scale. Scions of Toronto society, like the Gooderhams and the Eatons, lived a few blocks away from industries and industrial workers (Lemon 1986, 7).

Sometimes the social distance in Parkdale was even more close-grained. Toronto was transfixed in late 1894 by the murder of Frank Westwood, the eighteen-year-old son of the fishing tackle magnate mentioned above. Clara Ford, a thirty-three-year-old "mulatto tailoress" who sometimes dressed in men's clothes, was arrested six weeks later for the crime. It transpired that Ford, along with her mother and teenaged daughter, had lived next door to the Westwood family for three years, in a shed behind the adjacent house. (Their household shows up on no assessment or directory records.) The considerable newspaper coverage of the crime quotes a number of lodgers living in the immediate vicinity, indicating that several houses in the area had been converted to multiple-occupancy residences, which again is not reflected in available records. Ford's initial defence was that Westwood had tried to rape her in a lakeside boathouse, the culmination of years of harassment. This defence was dropped before the trial in favour of a safer strategy that portrayed Ford as an ignorant "girl" coerced into a false confession, but the case leaves behind the strong impression that social harmony in Parkdale may have had large fissures.[8]

The Westwood murder highlights the difficulty in reconstructing class and ethnic difference, and possible conflict, in Parkdale. *Parkdale: A Centennial History* categorically stated in 1978 that there were no ethnic minority communities in Parkdale before World War Two (Parkdale Centennial Research Committee 1978, 54). But there certainly were minority culture individuals. In 1891, there were at least three black households in Parkdale, ranging from the wealthy Abbotts in their new villa to the impoverished women in the Ford shack three blocks away. The existence of a possible third black household comes from a suburban crime report: Alfred Lewis, a "negro" who kept a small lunch counter near the subway stair, was fined fifty dollars and court costs, or three months in jail, for selling liquor without a licence (*Mail*, 12 December 1888). In 1901, Jewish households included a well-to-do piano salesman, Maurice Cohen, whose family lived in a Dowling Avenue villa until the 1950s, the blacksmith Kinkenbloomer on Queen Street, and Harry Rosenthal, boatman at the Dufferin Street dock. A number of Irish names are also scattered throughout the suburb. To judge from church construction and religions of prominent men, Presbyterians and Methodists were more numerous and richer than Anglicans and Catholics (the latter did not have a church or school in Parkdale until 1902, over two decades later than the Protestant congregations). Both Robert Libby and Ethel Abel mention in their oral histories that gypsies or tinkers occasionally camped in Parkdale in the waning years of the nineteenth century, although it is unclear whether they mean Romany or Irish immigrants (Toronto between the Wars 1971-1972; Abel 1971). The number of roomers and boarders is probably underestimated in directories and assessments, since sometimes a lodger shows up in one but not the other for the same year. To state the obvious, a lot more information is available about wealthy, majority-culture men in the late nineteenth century than about those marginalized by gender, ethnicity, or income. Parkdale seems to have its share of people who could be considered "different," but these people may not have formed recognizable communities. It is impossible to know the extent to which minority-culture individuals felt at home in Parkdale, let alone make a comparison with experiences across Toronto.

As was typical for fringe areas, the business of development employed many Parkdalians throughout the 1880-1913 period. The 1881 assessment shows twenty-six household heads, or 12 percent of the total, working in the construction trades, including ten carpenters, seven builders, two bricklayers, and a plasterer. The proportion had risen to 14 percent by 1891, and even in 1913, 9 percent of household heads worked in the construction trades (Parkdale Council 1881; City of Toronto Assessment Rolls

1891-1913). As early as 1878, a local benefit raised fifty dollars for the family of resident Alex Lawson, injured in the construction of the Industrial Exhibition (*Mail,* 13 November 1878). Three years later, the *Mail* reported 175 men, many presumably local, working on the construction of Parkdale's sewer system (27 March 1882). The recession of the early 1890s hit these workers especially hard. B.A. Lillie, another long-time Parkdale resident, tells of how a bricklayer named Caulfield, laid off in the early 1890s, borrowed forty dollars from Cook, the local MP, to buy a cow, which was pastured in the fields around his home at the undeveloped corner of Sorauren and Garden. His sons delivered the milk, priced at three cents a pint and five cents a quart. Eventually, the business became successful enough for him to buy land on Roncesvalles for what then seemed like the outrageous price of thirty dollars per frontage foot. His grandson became a director at Borden Milk, a large firm (Lillie 1971b). Others, of course, were not so enterprising or fortunate, and there are many stories of hardship during this era.

One of the most intriguing is the tale of Ethel Abel, a well-known neighbourhood resident who lived in the same house on Cowan for over eighty years. Abel's reminiscences were published in neighbourhood newspapers and the *Toronto Star,* and repeated in planning reports in the 1970s and 1980s, as Parkdale's history became of interest to a new generation of residents (see Chapter 4). For instance, the 1983 "Neighbourhood Plan Proposals: South Parkdale" cites her as saying, "Our neighbours were mainly professional people, lawyers, doctors, retired academics and so on," to support the contention that Parkdale was an upper-middle-class residential suburb from development to the mid-twentieth century (City of Toronto Planning and Development Department 1983, 21). But her three hours of audiotaped oral memoirs suggest a different version of her early life than do directory and assessment records. Abel's father owned a Yonge Street tailor shop until 1893 or 1894, when the business went bankrupt. At that point, through the intervention of an MPP known to the family, he became the head tailor at the Central Prison, and the family moved to a house in Parkdale. While head tailor at the prison might be considered a relatively comfortable civil service job, it was still a considerable social step down from owning a business. The 1898 *Might's Directory* lists the family's immediate neighbours as four men working for the CPR, two travelling salesmen, a lineman for Bell Telephone, and a telephone operator at a hotel, hardly "mainly professional people." By the turn of the century, the family was renting out at least part of their twelve-room house, which by the 1930s had become a full boarding house. Rather than a story of residential stability and middle-class affluence, as it was used, Abel's narrative can be seen as an example of the lengths to which some Parkdale families went in preserving an image of stability and affluence in the face of downward mobility.

One of Ethel Abel's immediate neighbours was the Parker family, representative of the sixty or so Parkdale households supported by travelling salesmen by 1891. Parkdale was an ideal residence for itinerant sales agents due to its location on the railways radiating out to western Ontario. Mr. Parker, an immigrant from England, was a commercial traveller for ladies' wear, and would be gone for three months at a time, according to his daughter Dorothy Goddard (Toronto between the Wars 1971-1972). By 1912, the family had done well enough to move down Cowan Avenue to the lakeside, where their house was surrounded by fruit trees. Here we do find an example of upward mobility.

The presence of institutions near and around Parkdale provided a distinctive ambiance, as well as job opportunities. In the early years, the Lunatic Asylum, whose dome was "visible for 30 miles distant" even in 1923, and the Central Prison-Mercer Reformatory conglomeration, "a gloomy pile of grey stone" with "high walled precincts and grated windows," would have dominated views eastward to the city (Middleton 1923, 642; Mulvaney 1884, 54). Ethel Abel recalled sending laundry out to the Magdalen Asylum on West Lodge, while Robert Libby would sometimes watch convicts being marched to the Central Prison along Queen Street (Toronto between the Wars 1971-1972). Escapees from the Lunatic Asylum and the Central Prison regularly used Parkdale as a shortcut to the western edge of the city and possible freedom. For example, on 20 March 1882, the *Mail* reported that "Guard King, who last week so gallantly recaptured the two negroes who tried to escape from the Central Prison, is a resident of this village, and therefore knew the locality well." Parkdale residents even felt a certain sense of entitlement to jobs at the institutions: "Residents feel somewhat sore at the appointment of a stranger to the position of resident engineer to the Mercer Female Reformatory" (*Mail*, 27 December 1879).

The period 1906 to 1913 saw an echo of Parkdale's 1880s housing boom. This was the period during which the neighbourhood's remaining undeveloped land by the lakeside, towards the western edge of Parkdale, and along the east-west streets off Roncesvalles, were built up. The primary market was lower-middle-class workers seeking inexpensive housing within an acceptable walking distance to work. Although land prices did not double or treble the way they had in the 1880s, speculation and house building did seem to bring steady profit, to judge from land registry records of one subdivision, plan 287. This subdivision, part of which eventually became Galley Avenue, was registered by Walter O'Hara in 1868 as two-acre transitional lots. Lot 20 was sold to the McLean family for $484.50, with a vendor mortgage of $323. One of the McLean daughters, Fanny Wright, borrowed heavily on the property during the 1890s recession, which led to foreclosure by the real estate firm of Mossom Boyd in 1896. The land speculator Ritchie (who also flipped properties on Queen Street) successfully gambled that the land would increase in value, buying lot 20 for $2,000 in 1902 and reselling it to a builder named Walker for $7,000 in 1910. Walker built eleven houses on the north side of Galley in the spring of 1911, borrowing $2,000 per house for construction costs. Most of the capital came from a male lender, although two women also provided loans (Land Registry Records).

The design of the houses reflected a new era of relative affluence for industrial and clerical workers (Figure 2.4). Unlike the two-bedroom row houses on Gwynne Avenue, similar to those pictured in Figure 2.2, which were built for rental purposes in the early 1880s, the Galley houses were larger four- and five-bedroom semi-detached houses. Both Galley and Gwynne properties had eighteen-foot frontages, but the Galley lots extended back 133 feet, as opposed to 87 feet on Gwynne. There were also indoor toilets on Galley and, by the mid-1920s, a rear lane to allow car parking, while the Gwynne row houses were constructed with outdoor privies and backed onto the row houses on Melbourne Place. By the fall of 1911, all of the Galley houses had been sold for between $3,700 and $4,000 each, while Gwynne houses were being sold for half that price. Walker offered several of the homeowners seven-year vendor mortgages ranging from $900 to $2,000, although two transactions were cash sales and one purchaser obtained a mortgage from another individual. To judge from the land registry records, Walker made a modest deferred profit from building the Galley houses.

Although the supposed division between working-class North Parkdale and middle-class South Parkdale began to be written about in the 1906-1913 period, purchasers of 44-54 Galley included as much of a mix of occupations as did those who lived south of Queen Street: a manager at a downtown factory, an optician, a real estate agent who used his home as an office, a post office clerk, a checker for the Grand Trunk Railway, a teamster, and two widows. Most were in their late twenties or early thirties. One of the widows and a "gentleman" rented out their houses: to a superintendent in a nearby factory and to another GTR worker, respectively. The real estate agent had a clerk as a lodger (Land Registry Records; City of Toronto Assessment Rolls 1913). With the exception of the real estate agent, who sold within the year for a profit (and who had received a slight discount on his house price from Walker, probably because he was responsible for handling the other sales), the houses remained in the same hands for an average of twenty-five years. It was only in the late 1910s and into the 1940s, after the end of Parkdale's initial development that we begin to see this kind of residential stability.

### The Image of Parkdale to 1912: "Neatly Shaven Lawns and Owners"

During Parkdale's life as an independent municipality, contemporary books and newspapers sometimes acknowledged Parkdale's land use and social mix, but they focused on its affluence and difference from the central city. The first book I have found to mention Parkdale is the 1878 *Illustrated Atlas of the County of York*, where it is described as a "pleasant new suburb" (Canniff 1968). An 1884 book described it as "one of the pleasantest of our suburbs ... rapidly being filled up with handsome private residences and villas" (Mulvaney 1884, 257). A history of Toronto the following year called Parkdale "beautifully situated, overlooking the lake shore," with "a number of handsome villa residences," although it also

*Figure 2.4.* Middle-class houses on Garden Avenue, built c. 1912, photographed June 1972. These are similar to the houses on Galley Avenue. Written on the back is "His Great Grandfather John F. Rogers lived here 1913."
*Source:* Baldwin Room, Toronto Reference Library, Toronto Streets series, 979-42-3.

*Figure 2.5.*   Commercial Parkdale: a postcard of Queen Street West, looking east from Roncesvalles, c. 1918.
*Source:* Baldwin Room, Toronto Reference Library, Toronto Streets series, T 14029.

acknowledged that "of late, manufacturing enterprise has been developed, and the population is increasing rapidly" (Robinson 1885, 86-87). For the twenty years after annexation to Toronto, Parkdale continued to be described as a wealthy and somehow special suburb. Photographs of handsome villas were reproduced in descriptions of Toronto, scenes of "Queen Street West, Parkdale" and leafy avenues such as Cowan and Dunn were available as postcards (Figure 2.5), and praise of the area and its people abounded in publications intended for well-to-do residents and tourists.

Writers, both the promotional and the presumably more objective, sometimes twisted the facts in order to present an uncomplicated image. In a book published by the *Mail* newspaper in 1891, G.M. Adam claimed that the "recently annexed suburban villages of Parkdale and Brockton" were now "a vast network of streets and avenues, with handsome villas or rows of continuous houses" (54), although less than half of the lots were as yet developed. A tourist guide produced by the Toronto Street Railway Company in 1894 said of its King Street line, "This line passes through Parkdale, one of the most charming of Toronto's residential sections ... Business men find it delightfully convenient to drop work and worry for an hour or so in the day to enjoy the refreshing stimulant of a trolley trip to the suburbs" (30, 45). Fifteen years later, a similar guide produced by the Dominion Coach Line (1910, 40) invited tourists to "glide into the charms of Parkdale, the delightful retreat of Toronto's wealthy and aristocratic people." Yet, from what we know about residents' workplaces, over half of Parkdale household heads during that period were able to walk to work in nearby industries and institutions, and probably could not have afforded daily streetcar fares.

The apotheosis of Parkdale as middle-class suburban dream come true was published in 1912, at the conclusion of a newspaper article describing "The Temperament of Toronto Streets":

> Lastly, South Parkdale. Small, trim houses on small, trim lots, with neatly-shaven lawns and owners ... The windows are abnormally clean here ... Some Rosedalians think that Parkdale is the place where you get off the [street] car to enter the Exhibition. So it was once. Now it is a compact community which preserves many of the older and more pleasantly informal amenities of Canadian life. People drop in on each other there. The men call each other, many of them, by their first names. The ladies have travel clubs and socials, and enjoyable gatherings, where the mystic symbols –"RSVP"– are not in evidence ... The residents seem to live within their means, and at a guess I should say the savings accounts in Parkdale banks are something enormous ... it seems that these good people have reasonable and moderate views ... Can a street reflect anything better? (*Globe*, 6 February 1912)

This description returns to the ideal of the Flowery Suburb as described in 1878: clean, safe, thrifty, somehow chaste in its values and aspirations. If we take this image at face value, then indeed we are left with a stable area, one that remained moderately wealthy and residential throughout its development at the periphery of Toronto. Parkdale's upscale image fit into the concentric zone model that was already part of the understanding of North American cities at the turn of the century. Its social geography was supposedly a contrast to the central city's heterogeneous jumble of land uses, its way of life superior to what the older city had to offer. It was simultaneously modern in its architecture, design, and services, and pleasantly old-fashioned in its customs and outlook.

When we look closely at the imperfect records of directories, assessment rolls, land registry books, and oral memoirs, however, a more complex picture emerges. This "other" Parkdale's development was also influenced by its location at what was then the periphery of the central city. But there were two more factors at work. Industrial and residential expansion along railway lines and Queen Street, with later infill, suggest the kind of sectoral growth hypothesized by Hoyt (1970; 1939, chap. 4), with Parkdale acting as an extension to the industrial wedge that originated in the Garrison Reserve and eventually encompassed West Toronto Junction, Mount Dennis, and Weston along the northwestern rail lines, and Mimico and New Toronto to the west. Parkdale's development was also influenced by its waterfront location. In the late nineteenth century, the waterfront lots were considered choice locations for mansions and villas, although the presence of shacks and lodgers is also revealed by the Westwood murder. But the traffic congestion problem at the Queen and Dufferin intersection foreshadows the central importance that an efficient waterfront roadway would assume in the future, with the construction of the Gardiner Expressway.

The dominant image of Parkdale during its initial development, promulgated by newspapers and promotional materials of the time, and repeated in newspapers and planning reports a hundred years later, was of a stable, residential, middle-class model suburb. It was supposed to be a simpler place than the central city, not quite nursery but not quite town, a separate sphere of "flowers and a rural home." The evidence of housing and social conditions suggests a far more complex and conflicted place, where providers and inhabitants of cheap housing for industrial workers sparked other developers and residents' concerns about "tenement housing" lived in by "mechanics." Initially, Parkdale attracted more industrial workers than middle-class commuters. At the eve of World War One, fifty years after John Howard attempted to attract homebuyers to the area with promises of a "suburban retreat for professional and business men in the City," Parkdale had finally attracted a proportionately large number of rich businessmen and professionals. Even then, it was as much a working-class industrial suburb as a middle-class commuter haven. By that time, however, Toronto was growing outwards, Parkdale's lots were filling up with buildings and households, and developers were moving on to greener pastures. Parkdale was about to undergo a radical change in image, one that seemed equally disconnected from its residents' lives.

# 3
# "Becoming a Serious Slum": Decline in Parkdale, 1913-1966

> First there is that golden age, the time of harmonious beginnings. Then ensues a period when the old days are forgotten and the golden age falls into neglect. Finally comes a time when we rediscover and seek to restore the world around us to something like its former beauty.
>
> But there has to be that interval of neglect, there has to be that discontinuity; it is religiously and artistically essential.
> – J.B. Jackson, *The Necessity for Ruins*

## From Suburb to Slum: "Parkdale's Housing Problem"

In 1934, Toronto celebrated its centennial as an incorporated city. The lieutenant governor of Ontario, Herbert Bruce, took the opportunity for a stirring call to action. At a centennial luncheon in the spring, he addressed a Board of Trade audience: "We have a great and beautiful city ... blessed by honest and efficient government ... but I fear ... [it] has acquired the inevitable 'slum districts' ... Would it not be a splendid thing to commemorate this, our hundredth civic year, by the creation of a large and noble plan ... that would mould this city more nearly to our heart's desire, a plan that would recognize the inalienable right of every man and woman and child to a decent and dignified and healthful environment?" (cited in Lemon 1985, 59).

Soon after the luncheon, Toronto City Council approved an enquiry into slum conditions, one of many prepared during the 1930s depression by municipal governments in Canada, the United Kingdom, the United States, and Australia (see Bacher 1993, 69-72; Howe 1994, 153). The Bruce Report, released in November 1934, relied on information prepared by the City of Toronto Department of Public Health and University of Toronto School of Social Work. It concluded that two thousand to three thousand dwellings were "unfit for a satisfactory family life," based on a standard of fitness that included adequate "shelter from elements; lighting, ventilation and heat; water and sewage; cooking and food storage; freedom from vermin" (Bruce 1934, 13-14). These substandard dwellings were mapped, and only six properties, less than 0.01 percent of the total number of unfit dwellings, were within Parkdale's traditional boundaries of Dufferin Street, the rail tracks, Wright Avenue, Roncesvalles Avenue, and Lake Ontario.

The report quickly moved on from the issue of substandard structures, however. When describing "those features of bad housing which are particularly injurious to health and decency," the first element was "overcrowding." According to the report, overcrowding is "usually associated with the practice of taking in boarders or roomers, often a financial necessity if rent is to be paid." Yet the apparent costs outweighed the benefit: "The breakdown of family life upon the introduction of another family into the dwelling unit is almost inevitable" (Bruce 1934, 34-35). Using the criterion of overcrowding instead of health or safety hazards, the report inveighed against

> the "bad areas" of Toronto [that] ... may be divided into three parts which exhibit rather different types of slum conditions. On the west, there is the old section of Parkdale ... Parkdale's housing problem is the result of the economic deterioration of what was formerly a prosperous district of quite large, substantial houses. Into these houses are now crowded a vastly greater number of families than the architects ever foresaw. Many of these families are of foreign origin. The presence of railroads and factories to the south increase the noise, traffic, and dirt. While it is the least undesirable of the three districts we are describing it is fast becoming a serious slum. (23)

The solution proposed by the Bruce Report was the wholesale clearance of areas identified as slums, and their replacement by more rationally planned and designed public housing projects. John Bacher (1993, 10), the historian of Canadian housing policy, calls the Bruce Report the "bible for social housing" in Canada. The showcase urban renewal project recommended in the Bruce Report, complete with housing footprint and new neighbourhood street plan, was completed twelve years later as North Regent Park, Canada's first public housing project.

The reaction to the report's description of Parkdale is as startling as the description itself: there was none. The considerable newspaper coverage that followed the publication of the Bruce Report contained heated debate about the costs of slum demolition and the merits of public housing investment. But there was no questioning, in editorials, letters, or the words of local politicians, of the characterization of areas described as slums. In the other two "bad areas," Cabbagetown and the Ward, the Bruce Report was the culmination of over forty years of newspaper and government reports calling the areas unhealthy, unsafe, and immoral. But Parkdale was different. From the late 1870s to the early 1910s, newspapers and books had described it as a model suburb, with a healthful physical environment, charming villas, and upstanding middle-class citizens. As late as 1912, twenty-two years before the Bruce Report, Parkdale was proclaimed to be the antithesis of slum living, a place of "neatly shaven lawns and owners." How did the neighbourhood fall so far, so fast? Were there major changes in housing or socio-economic conditions that might account for the former suburb's rapid perceptual decline in two decades? Was Parkdale really becoming a bad place to live? Why did no voices protest Parkdale being called a slum? What other factors contributed to the transformation of a modern model suburb "with very aristocratic pretensions" into a neighbourhood labelled as "becoming a serious slum"?

Assessment and land registry data show that to some degree, Parkdale did become less attractive to middle-class residents, and to investment money, after World War One. Location played a role in Parkdale's fall from grace. In the 1870s and 1880s, Parkdale was at the periphery of the built-up city. By the 1920s and 1930s, the former suburb had been engulfed by development to the north and west (see Map 1; Harris and Luymes 1990). Newer and more modern middle-class suburbs were commanding the lion's share of attention from newspapers. In 1924, the *Toronto Star* considered Rosedale, Forest Hill, and High Park to be the three neighbourhoods "where Toronto's wealth was greatest"; four years later, *Might's Directory* named these neighbourhoods along with the Beaches (five miles east of downtown), Moore Park (north of Rosedale), and the Humber District (northwest of Parkdale) as "matchless suburban residential districts" (cited in R. White 1993, 88, 187). Parkdale was now seen as part of the more anonymous older central city, with many of the problems endemic to formerly prosperous neighbourhoods in the inevitable stage of decline. Whereas there are hundreds of newspaper clippings about Parkdale's character between the late 1870s and the early 1910s, descriptions of Parkdale as a place with a distinct identity are rare between 1913 and 1969. And these references are almost always negative.

Location was only one factor in the decline of Parkdale's image. At the end of the nineteenth century, many observers recognized that supposedly well-to-do retreats like Parkdale and Rosedale were exceptions among the less prosperous suburbs springing up in the "goose pastures" just outside the boundaries of the developed city (C. Clark 1898, 2). The early twentieth century saw industrial and self-built suburbs being constructed in the periphery, along with a few exclusive developments for the elite. Rosedale maintained its reputation as an elite district throughout most of the twentieth century, even though it was considerably closer to downtown than Parkdale. More important than Parkdale's relative position within the metropolitan area was the twofold threat that it came to represent to

Toronto's development as a City of Homes, a phrase widely in use by the early twentieth century (Harris 1996, 86).

First, Parkdale became identified, in newspapers and government reports, with the moral danger of single women and men living in apartments and boarding houses. Whereas once Parkdale was praised for offering home-ownership opportunities to all classes, it was now derided for offering far too many rental opportunities to both sexes. Parkdale had once been described as a chaste young woman who spurned the advances of the promiscuous city, but now it was identified with potentially promiscuous modern women working outside the home, who at best were delaying marriage and at worst would be responsible for "race suicide." In the late nineteenth century, Parkdale had been at the forefront of Toronto's shift to working-class homeownership: half of the suburb's households were owners in 1891, as opposed to Toronto's average of a little over one in four (Figure 3.1; City of Toronto Assessment Rolls 1891, sample for assessment area 6.1; Harris 1996, 135). In the early twentieth century, Parkdale was again in the forefront of housing trends with a move to smaller flats in apartments and subdivided houses. But that was the wrong cutting edge for the time and place. Parkdale's middle-class detached houses, which when constructed were considered the acme of modern fashion and healthfulness, became criticized for being too large to be efficient as single-family homes without servants, and lacking in amenities such as attached garages. Of particular concern was the conversion of large villas to multiple-unit boarding houses and flats. Ironically, the streets in South Parkdale where wealth had been concentrated became the places where economic and social change seemed most rapid and harmful. Once Parkdale was considered a good place to live, with good people; now it was becoming a bad place to live, with housing forms that could make women and men go bad.

Second, Parkdale's access to the lakeside, once a selling point for the suburb's promoters, became seen as an impediment to the free movement of cars to a new generation of suburbs. Toronto's waterfront, and eventually the whole city, was being reconceived as an efficient organism with commercial, industrial, and recreational uses strictly segregated, yet joined by broad new highways. These plans had no place for a lakeside residential community so close to downtown. Parkdale lay in the path of a bigger and better vision of the city.

In the 1870s, developers had been quick to capitalize on innovations in technology, such as the growth of the railway and horse tram network, to promote Parkdale as a suburb. The independent municipality of Parkdale became the testing area for innovations in governance, such as

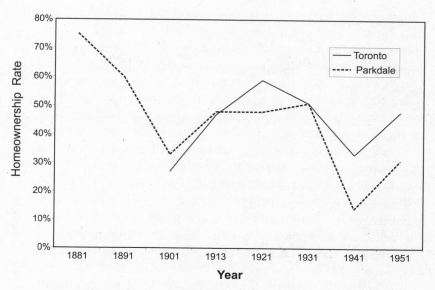

*Figure 3.1.* Homeownership rates, Parkdale and Toronto, 1881-1951
*Source:* Parkdale Council 1881; City of Toronto Assessment Rolls, 1891
sample; Harris 1992. Graph courtesy of Ric Hamilton, McMaster University.

segmented taxation (special assessments for street improvements) and employing a medical officer of health. Municipal bylaw and zoning controls over land use and housing development were attempted during the 1879-1889 period, but were ineffective. Innovations in house building and finance also emerged in Parkdale during the 1870s; the Toronto House Building Association exemplified the new large development and finance companies. Developers, builders, and real estate agents were intimately bound up in local politics and governance.

Similarly, the early 1910s were a time when technological change, in particular the growth of automobile ownership, merged with a growth in the scope and powers of local government to create the first real regional planning in Toronto. The city hired its first commissioner of works to coordinate civic improvements in 1912, and also developed a Social Services Commission to develop welfare policy. Warren Magnusson (1983b, 104) associates these two developments with the first move to comprehensive planning, which included in its remit "rationalizing land use in order to improve the efficiency of transportation, beautify the centre of the city, and enhance the quality of the environment in residential neighbourhoods." Bylaw and zoning controls were once again attempted, this time to great effect in some parts of Toronto, although not in Parkdale.

Developers continued to play major roles in urban politics, with mixed impacts on the neighbourhood. According to Christine Boyer (1983, 60), the early twentieth century was the era during which the ideal of "the city as a perfectly disciplined spatial order" took hold across North America, and Toronto's municipal government took an avid interest in the new spatial discipline of urban planning (Moore 1979). Parkdale's disorderly land use and social diversity, although present from the first, increasingly became seen as a sign of decline.

### The Turning Point of 1911-13:
### Apartment Houses Arrive in Parkdale

The two-year period from 1911 to 1913 saw the publication of two influential civic reports in Toronto, each the outcome of decades of advocacy. One report was an ambitious plan for Toronto's waterfront, which will be discussed in the next section. The other was Toronto's first municipal slum report, released by the new medical officer of health, Dr. Charles Hastings.

After a string of ineffective, politically appointed health officials, the choice of Hastings was the culmination of the city's recent successes in the public health field. In 1883, four years after the Village of Parkdale, the City of Toronto had appointed its first medical officer of health. Three years later, the city hosted the American Public Health Association annual conference. As of 1903, a diploma in public health was available at University of Toronto. In 1909, provincial legislation provided funding for local public health departments and ensured that the medical officer would report to a small appointed board of health, rather than directly to City Council (MacDougall 1990, 10-27).

Although on the verge of retirement at age fifty-eight when appointed in 1910, Hastings became a leader of powerful intellect and energy, one of two strong civil servants who effectively ran Toronto for the first third of the twentieth century (R.C. Harris, the commissioner of works, was the other). Hastings was a central figure in the public health movement in North America: he was a founder of the Canadian Public Health Association in 1910; an organizer of the Rockefeller Foundation's international public health education project, which sent students from around the world to do field work in Toronto; and the president of the American Public Health Association by 1918 (MacDougall 1990, 26). One of Hastings' preconditions for becoming medical officer of health was independence from City Council interference, although he reserved the right to advise the council. Lack of oversight by ward aldermen was ensured by creating eight public health divisions whose boundaries were unrelated to the seven City Council wards. Hastings immediately embarked on several campaigns:

ensuring clean milk, banning outdoor privies, and hiring female "municipal housekeepers" to teach "Canadian methods of sanitation" to new immigrants. His most ambitious campaign was for municipally funded suburban housing, such as was being developed in the United Kingdom (Spragge 1979). Hastings, who grew up in Edinburgh, was strongly influenced in his housing ideas by his early exposure to the deplorable housing conditions in the tenements of that city. Hastings replaced his department's annual reports with monthly reports read directly to City Council, written in the style of short sermons. Over half of the reports he delivered between 1910 and 1913 dealt with the evils of lodging, tenements, and overcrowding (City of Toronto Council, Minutes, 1910-1913; see also City of Toronto Board of Health ·1912-1914).

Hastings' slum report built on a subgenre of slum literature in Toronto. In 1884, G.P. Mulvaney's history of the city had spoken of some diseased "arteries of Toronto," with the worst being "that part of York Street [in the Ward] ... occupied by dingy and rotten wooden shanties, the dens of Jewish old clothes sellers and recipients for stolen goods" (44). As mentioned in Chapter 2, York Street was also the centre of the small black community and was the heart of the Ward, which was considered the most disreputable area in Toronto from the 1880s until the 1940s. Difference could still be constructed as problematic, even in a city whose inhabitants were 80 percent Protestant and 92 percent of British (Anglo-Celtic) origin (census figures for 1881, in Careless 1984, tables 7 and 8, 201-2).

In 1898, C.S. Clark's curious "social study," *Of Toronto the Good*, was published. Based on an address to the World Convention of the Women's Christian Temperance Union, which was held in Toronto in 1897, Clark combined a travelogue of vice (complete with addresses and ratings of bawdy houses) with social commentary on a wide range of topics, from real estate speculation to the essential immorality of women. Clark's theme was that Toronto held itself to a higher standard than other cities, while having the same problems as "every city in America." For instance, "a considerable number of people own their own houses, though the circumstances may be a questionable advantage ... [since] people of moderate means are compelled to let furnished rooms or take boarders" (frontispiece, 3). Although Toronto was at that point "free almost from cheap lodging houses," Clark expressed concern about the declining standards in boarding houses and inexpensive hotels. Of particular concern was the increase in women living alone. If a young lady was to rent a room above a store, put in a sewing machine, and call herself a seamstress, who was to know what other activities were going on in the evening? If an unmarried young man and young lady had adjacent rooms in a boarding house, perhaps with a door between them, the obvious result would be the ruination of that young lady, assuming of course that she was not a willing participant in the hanky-panky. The author himself had lived in many lodgings where the landlady's and servants' morals were "light" (101-4). The situation was exacerbated by Toronto rents being higher than those in the rest of Canada, while the supply of skilled labour exceeded demand. Noting an advertisement for a young lady bookkeeper or cashier, offering $2.50 to $3 a week, Clark comments, "after paying her board out of the above it may consistently be asked: was the young lady expected to prostitute herself to obtain money for her clothes?" (62). Aside from the "shaky, tumble-down houses" in the Ward, Clark identified "the extreme east end [i.e., Cabbagetown and the Queen-Broadview area] and west end east of Parkdale" as "the abode of poverty" (1-3).

According to Mariana Valverde (1991, 17), Clark's book was one of a series of turn-of-the-century articles and campaigns across Canada addressing subjects as seemingly diverse as Sunday observance, temperance, prostitution, divorce, illegitimacy, immigration from China and India, public education, suppression of obscene literature, rescue of fallen women, and shelters for women and children. What these campaigns had in common was a sense that urban society's rapid economic and social changes could best be addressed by the scientific application of Christian ideals to issues like city planning. For instance, overcrowding and the taking in of boarders were linked to sexual assault, especially of children. This was the so-called lodger evil. Nighttime inspections of houses were encouraged by Winnipeg's medical officer of health, to ensure that "innocent looking" couches were not being opened up as beds, and that children of opposite sex were not sleeping in the same bed (136-38). Alleyway housing needed to be torn down in order to bring in light and also surveillance. Self-styled "child saver" J.J. Kelso asked: "If there could be a drastic measure passed requiring every house in which human beings dwell to front on a 40 or 60 foot street, or else be pulled down, how long would drunkenness, vice and ignorance exist?" (47). Overcrowded housing was explicitly linked with immorality and criminality in a 1909 keynote address by the appropriately named Miss Charity Cook to the Canadian Conference on Charities and Corrections: "We are told we have no slum district in Toronto and know nothing about the tenement house; but we do know that there is a great deal of overcrowding ... I fear that Toronto is breeding a class of criminals" (cited in A. Rose 1958, 36).

Municipal intervention was an essential part of this campaign for civic moral improvement. Even if Toronto's housing conditions had little in common with the truly deleterious conditions in some parts of New York,

London, and Chicago, local government needed to destroy signs of incipient slums, such as multiple occupancy and laneway housing. Rather than better wages or better housing in the central city, local governments put their hope in charitable and civic "philanthropy plus 5 percent" schemes that would provide model worker housing in suburbs. In fact, the role of municipal government was to close off avenues of housing change other than single-family housing in the suburbs. The *Report of the Medical Officer of Health Dealing with the Recent Investigation of Slum Conditions in Toronto, Embodying Recommendations for the Amelioration of Same,* presented to Toronto City Council in 1911, built on these Canadian campaigns, which were similar to contemporary anti-slum campaigns in the United States, the United Kingdom, and Australia (Hastings 1911; see Mayne 1993; Peel 1995a; Peterson 2003). In turn, Hastings' report became the template for many future reports, including that of the Bruce Commission.

First, the problem needed to be identified. There was a widespread belief that Toronto had avoided the poor housing conditions experienced in European and older North American cities. Hastings disputed this, pointing to a changing understanding of slums: "Originally, the term was applied to low, boggy, back streets, inhabited by a poor, criminal population. The term as used here, however, applies for the most part to poor, unsanitary houses, overcrowded, insufficiently lighted, badly ventilated, with unsanitary and in many cases, filthy yards" (Hastings 1911, 3). Given these criteria, "There are few conditions found in the slums of European cities, or in the greater American cities that have not been revealed in Toronto, the difference being only one of degree, and the conditions of the lesser degree today, will, if not corrected, become those of a greater degree tomorrow" (4).

Second, the problem needed to be defined as one of housing type rather than physical housing conditions. After the introductory definition of *slum,* the report went on to emphasize not lighting, ventilation, or lack of indoor plumbing, but the persistence of "common lodging houses" lived in by immigrants whose "ideas of sanitation are not ours." Alarmingly, "our inspectors have some evidence that certain small hotels and old and roomy houses are about to undergo the dangerous transformation into foreign lodging houses." Equally alarmingly, "a total of 92 tenement houses," where "three or more families live independently ... may well make us stop and think of the necessity of some action along this line" (Hastings 1911, 8). When it came to recommendations, the first dealt with "the lodging house evil" and the second with "the tenement house problem." The need for indoor privies came sixth, developing an adequate water supply was eighth, and the ninth and final recommendation was to find some mechanism for dealing with "exorbitant rents" (17). The moral health of urban society, beset as it was by foreigners and changing social norms, was of greater import than its physical health. Decent housing was more important than affordable and adequate housing. The issue of "dangerous" housing types and uses was more pressing than actual housing conditions.

The third message of the report was that it reflected a growing social consensus, and that simple, widely agreed-upon solutions existed for the identified problems. The report assured readers that demolishing unfit lodging houses would meet with approval from landlords: "In Birmingham, during a similar campaign, it was known that 73 percent of landlords were strongly in favour if it," while slum dwellers would happily move to suburban garden cities, if provided (Hastings 1911, 18). With a strong housing bylaw banning tenements and lodging houses, suburban garden cities, and proper city planning, Toronto could avoid the curse of slums.

Hastings' slum report did not specifically mention Parkdale, since its focus was the downtown area. However, the report had strong indirect impacts. Until the turn of the century, Parkdale's homeownership rate had been considerably higher than in the rest of Toronto. Now, cheap homes were being built throughout a new set of suburbs. By 1913, Parkdale's homeownership rate, 48 percent, was the same as the Toronto average. The last undeveloped streets in North Parkdale had been built out into new homes during the 1906-1913 construction boom, and were mostly bought rather than rented, as we have seen on Galley Avenue. Eight years later, Toronto's homeownership rate was just under 60 percent, one of the highest figures in North America, while Parkdale's rate had remained at 48 percent (Harris 1992).

Meanwhile, a new housing form was developing in South Parkdale. By 1913, some of Parkdale's large villas were beginning to be subdivided into two or three flats, and some of the large lots that had remained undeveloped became the sites of small apartment buildings. For instance, on Dowling Avenue, two 44-by-143-foot lots that had been the subject of foreclosure in the 1890s were bought cheaply by a developer named George Chapman in 1906. Five years later, at the height of a citywide building boom, he built four triplexes on the site. These apartment buildings were immediately bought as investment properties by the Hutchins brothers, who initially rented the flats to businessmen and clerks (Land Registry Records; City of Toronto Assessment Rolls 1913, 1921).

Richard Dennis, who has written about Toronto's first apartment boom, points out that the first apartment buildings in Toronto, built at the turn of the twentieth century, were luxury flats intended for upper-middle-class bachelors and childless couples. Like purpose-built apartments for the rich in Paris, New York, and Chicago, the designs of these apartment buildings included rooms or suites for servants, and sometimes communal dining rooms or other shared housekeeping facilities. They were located in high-status areas with large lots, such as Jarvis Street and the Annex. In 1909, twenty-three apartment buildings were listed in *Might's Directory*. In the years from 1910 to 1913, the number of apartment houses increased by 108, and in 1914 alone, 78 new apartment buildings were listed. While there was a shift to smaller projects with more modest efficiency apartments, the builders continued to locate their apartments in high-status areas, including Parkdale. By 1915, Parkdale contained ten large (twenty or more unit) apartment buildings, one-third of Toronto's total, mostly on the commercial streets of Queen and King (Figure 3.2). Another twenty-two smaller apartment buildings, three- or six-suite purpose-built flats like those on Dowling Avenue, or conversions of Victorian villas, had also been developed within Parkdale (Dennis 1989, 9-10, 16; 1998, figures 1-3, 23).

*Figure 3.2.* The Parkdale Mansions apartment building, Dowling Avenue at King Street West, built c. 1915, photographed 1972. Note the older villa next door, a prime candidate for subdivision into flats in the 1910s, then single-room-occupancy units in the 1970s.
*Source:* Baldwin Room, Toronto Reference Library, Toronto Streets series, 979-42-9.

In retrospect, it is hard to comprehend the moral panic occasioned by these apartment buildings. The apartments were well designed, built with high-quality materials and up-to-date plumbing, housed mostly clerical and sales staff, and either filled in vacant lots or preserved the facades of existing villas. They were near streetcar connections and close to workplaces. Yet newspapers and local ratepayers reacted with horror and indignation to these new apartment buildings, which they labelled with the all-purpose negative term *tenements,* previously applied to row houses in the 1880s. Government action was called for to stop the spreading cancer.

Throughout the spring of 1912, the *Globe* ran a series of increasingly alarming editorials on these new apartment buildings, drawing upon the rhetoric of Hastings' slum report. The first one began: "There is going to be a tenement house boom in the spring. Dozens of structures are contemplated that will occupy practically the entire space on which they are to stand ... Toronto must look to her building laws or she will be over-run, as San Francisco has been, with a plague of disease-breeding tenements" (5 March 1912). A month later, the newspaper warned that although "promoters of these tenements may seek to disguise them under the name of apartment houses," they were still the same evil entity (*Globe,* 4 April 1912). As pressure mounted for City Hall to pass a bylaw banning apartments on all but a few commercial streets, the *Globe* maintained that tenements "inevitably lower the housing standard" while artificially inflating central city land values. If apartment construction became more profitable for developers than building self-contained houses, Toronto would inevitably drift towards becoming a "city of stunted children and of unhappy adults. Its morals will suffer as well as its health" (27 April 1912). Finally, the day before the council vote, the *Globe* gave Torontonians another cautionary comparison to consider: Chicago, where "within less than a square mile ... 65,000 people live in... tenement conditions," with "thousands of children old before their time, grey-blooded, weak limbed, unfit," facing "the ruination of all the finer modesties of boys and girls whose very life necessities crowd them out of narrow tenement confines into the open street." This would be the physical and moral "human product" that would arise if "City Hall allows selfish or ignorant individuals to speculate unchecked" (3 May 1912).

While this heated rhetoric raged on, Parkdale was the site of the two most publicized battles over apartment house construction in early 1912. A developer named Solomon King ran into neighbours' opposition when he proposed a five-storey apartment house built out to the lot line at the corner of Jameson and King. Residents of Jameson's villas convinced City Council to buy a ten-foot setback from the developer, at which point he successfully applied to build on another storey (Dennis 1989, 31). In another case, residents of Maynard Avenue contested a six-suite apartment house on the grounds that the old Parkdale Village bylaws prohibited "dangerous, noisy or offensive trades or businesses." This dispute wound its way to the Supreme Court of Canada over the next three years, before being dismissed (*Star*, 1 May 1912; Dennis 2000, 269).

Given the newspaper coverage arising from the slum report and ratepayer outrage surrounding the issue, it is hardly surprising that in May 1912, after negotiating for the power from the provincial government, the motion to ban apartment houses and garages from all but a few commercial streets was unanimously adopted by Toronto City Council. Politicians pronounced that apartment houses were "breeders of slums," "chicken coops," and more damaging to property values "than any institution in the city" (Dennis 1989, 36-37). Yet in the two years following the bylaw's enactment, apartment house construction actually increased in Toronto, with dozens of developers applying for exemptions to the bylaws, or situating their buildings at the corner of a commercial and a residential street and then stealthily expanding along the residential corridor. Exemptions were generally granted along downtown streets, where the decline and demolition of older houses was considered inevitable. In the northern suburbs, like Rosedale and Forest Hill, exemptions were generally denied. Parkdale was the only part of the city in which exemptions were allowed and denied in equal numbers.

One reason for this mixed record was the character of Parkdale's local elite. While ratepayers' associations in Rosedale, Forest Hill, and the Annex were led by upper-middle-class professionals and manufacturers wholeheartedly opposed to any non-residential use, Parkdale's neighbourhood leadership had always included a large number of real estate agents, local developers, and mortgage financiers, as discussed in the previous chapter. Parkdale and Rosedale were often considered rivals in the 1880-1912 period, but they had little in common. Unlike Parkdale, located along railway and streetcar lines and close to a booming industrial conglomeration, Rosedale, with property holders grouped around a ravine well east of the commercial artery Yonge Street, had been fairly impervious to subdivision pressures during the 1870s and 1880s. In the late 1870s, southeastern Rosedale was still in the hands of only four landowners. In the 1890s, when there was significant building activity during a recession, the relatively few wealthy homeowners saw no reason to deviate from initial subdivisions of one house per acre. By 1905, Rosedale had formed the first ratepayers' association in Toronto, which pressured the city to zone out any non-residential use, from corner stores to manufacturing (Crawford 2000). Similarly, The

Annex Ratepayers Association, active from the early 1910s, set their boundaries to exclude poorer streets and wrote scores of letters to City Council
opposing garages and apartments (Lemon 1986, 14-16; City of Toronto
Board of Control 1912).

In contrast, when the South Parkdale Ratepayers' Association formed in
1912, it was to oppose the conversion of an old mansion to institutional
use (see next section), and very few letters opposing apartments or stores
were written under the association's letterhead. Parkdale's resident apartment developers provided mutual support by signing each other's petitions
for exemption from the apartment bylaws. For instance, W.B. Charlton lived
in Parkdale while being involved in sixteen applications to build small apartment buildings, although he moved further west to High Park in 1914. J.J.
Walsh, who advertised himself as an "estate broker and valuator: estates
managed, rents collected, property bought sold or exchanged; money and
loans on farm and city properties," was involved in over fifty apartment
building permits across the city while living in Parkdale. H.H. Williams, a
former resident of Parkdale, was a leader in Forest Hill's fight to keep out
apartment buildings, while developing and managing several buildings in
his old neighbourhood (Dennis 1989, 23-24). His brothers-in-law, the Bryces,
while not directly involved in apartment construction, owned or part-owned
seventy-seven rental houses and twenty-four vacant lots across the city, as
well as a lumberyard that serviced apartment developers, two factories, and
a roller-skating rink in Parkdale (Dennis 1987, 33).

Letters and petitions sent to City Council in 1912 and 1913 shed light
on the evolving politics of restrictive zoning. The residents' association of
High Park, the neighbourhood immediately west of Parkdale, opposed a
drugstore at the corner of Keele and the Queensway because any kind of
commercial establishment in this residential district would establish a dangerous precedent. In contrast, Yorkville residents sent two petitions about
one apartment building, one in favour and the other against. The owner
of the lot on which the apartment building was proposed pleaded with
City Council that it was "impossible for me to erect a first class residence
owing to the close proximity of car barns, a public library, livery stables,
etc" (City of Toronto Board of Control 1912, 1913). In Parkdale, the secretary of the South Parkdale Ratepayers' Association objected to the erec-
tion of an apartment building on King Street between Dufferin and
Cowan, since "any departure from the by-law will have the result that
sooner or later stores and factories will be erected in the present residential district." Yet within two blocks, there were sheet metal and radiator
factories, at least three commercial properties, and the bank where the

letter writer worked (letter from W.A. Stratton, 6 February, in City of Toronto Board of Control 1913). In more than one instance, an initial effort to establish a commercial establishment on a Parkdale street corner led to a compromise whereby the developer built an apartment building (probably his initial intent). For example, a proposed store at the north-west corner of King and Dowling was opposed by local residents in August 1912. A few months later, the same neighbours signed a petition to allow an apartment building, with specified materials and unit sizes, as the lesser of two evils (see Figure 3.2). Coming as they do at the start of the 1913 recession, the letters give a strong impression of fear among property own-ers that anything less than the perfection of single-family residences in the area would spoil the resale value of their houses and be the first step on a slippery slope to decline. But given the limited choices open to South Parkdale property owners in these letters, a purely single-family residen-tial neighbourhood may have already been considered an ideal past hope.

## The Lakeshore's Drive to Modernity

While new suburbs with more modern ideas on housing and neighbour-hood planning were springing up to the north and west of Parkdale, the lake-shore to the south was rapidly becoming engulfed in Toronto's drive towards modernity. Parkdale had one of the few stretches of non-industrialized shoreline in the developed portion of Toronto. Access to the lake was blocked by a rail line crossed by only four Parkdale streets, and the shore-line was without a natural beach. However, this did not stop members of the public from swimming there, to the often expressed displeasure of nearby landowners (Figure 3.3). Rowing and yacht clubs had joined the private boathouses along Parkdale's lakefront by the first decade of the century. At the southwestern border of Parkdale, where Queen Street turned into Lakeshore Road (see Map 2), a conglomeration of establish-ments – the Ocean House Hotel, Mrs. Meyer's restaurant, Duck's Marina – served as a small resort community in the 1890s. In 1894, the year after the Chicago World's Fair and its groundbreaking Midway Plaisance, both the Toronto Industrial Exhibition and several businesses along Lakeshore Road installed merry-go-rounds and other rides. By the turn of the cen-tury, Toronto's Easter Parade was held along the wooden esplanade built by owners of the large lakefront estates, a custom that remained a high-light of Toronto's social season until the 1950s (Filey 1996, 40-60; Reeves 1992a, 59). In 1906, the city purchased forty acres of undeveloped lakeshore land at the eastern edge of Parkdale in order to expand the Exhi-bition grounds (Parkdale Liberty Economic Development Committee 2000).

The lakeshore filled transportation, as well as recreational, needs. The intersection of Lakeshore Road and Queen Street was, by the turn of the century, the main western entrance into the city, and the bottleneck where the Grand Trunk Railway crossed the intersection had become as chaotic as the corner of Queen and Dufferin Streets had been twenty years earlier (Figure 3.4). As early as 1877, "A number of gentlemen who are owners of vacant land on the lakeshore, between the Garrison Common and the Humber contemplate the construction thereon of an esplanade, boulevard and carriage drive with an ample breadth ... block-paved, and planted with trees, and otherwise beautified" (*Evening Telegram,* 12 January 1878). A system of central city boulevards, including a lakeshore boulevard, was suggested by a civic booster group ten years later, again with Chicago as a model: "The first care of [an American] city after it has once entered upon a career of prosperity and growth, is to make itself 'smart' and attractive ... Chicago, for instance, a city built upon the site of a swamp, had no natural attractions to begin with, and yet every visitor to it now comes

*Figure 3.3.*   The lakeshore at Dowling Avenue, looking west, c. 1897.
Parkdale's lakeshore was rocky, and separated from the rest of the suburb by the Great Western Rail tracks. Despite these disadvantages, the area just west of this point was a popular swimming beach.
*Source:* Baldwin Room, Toronto Reference Library, Old Toronto series, 975-20-13.

away filled with admiration for its magnificent boulevard" (*Mail,* 24 October 1897). In 1906, the Ontario Association of Architects repeated the call for a "circumambient line of parkways." Toronto's parks commissioner also cited American examples when in 1910 he called for "a complete circuit of the city," and plans proposed in 1909 by the Civic Guild and in 1911 by its successor the Civic Improvement Committee all advocated a city-wide lakeshore route (Reeves 1992b, 46-56).

Wayne Reeves, who has written extensively on waterfront plans, calls this a "rich imagining" of Toronto's lakefront, where City Beautiful thought on a regional scale came at the expense of existing communities. With planning dominated by a small coterie of interrelated professionals, individual personalities mattered, and so did the merger of public and private interests (Reeves 1992b, 98-99). Nowhere was this more apparent than during the first years of the Toronto Harbour Commission (THC). In 1911, Toronto voters approved the reorganization of the old Toronto Harbour Trust into a new reform-minded commission. The THC, consisting of three members appointed by City Council, one member appointed by the

*Figure 3.4.*   The busy intersection of King Street, Queen Street, Roncesvalles Avenue, and Lakeshore Road, looking southwest, c. 1908. Robert and Minnie Libby and their three oldest children are in the foreground (see Chapter 2), carefully crossing the Grand Trunk rail tracks. They are dressed in their Sunday best. Perhaps they have just returned from a stroll along the lakeshore. Robert looks back anxiously at an automobile on Lakeshore Road as the police officer directs traffic. In the background is an advertisement for a new lakeside subdivision.
*Source:* City of Toronto Archives, William James Series, Fonds 1244, Item 245.

federal government, and one member provided by the Toronto Board of Trade, was granted authority over all 2,026 acres of the city's Lake Ontario shoreline, from Victoria Park Road on the east to the Humber River on the west. The first commissioners included two prominent businessmen associated with the reforming impulses of the Board of Trade, two long-time city aldermen (one representing Ward 6, which included Parkdale) who had been members of the discredited Harbour Trust, and, in the role of swing vote, the man who became the THC's most visible member for the next decade: Robert Home Smith, a lawyer and property developer then in his early thirties (65-67).

A long-term waterfront development strategy was the first order of business for the THC. E.L. Cousins, a resident of Parkdale, was hired as the THC's chief engineer, and Frederick Law Olmsted Jr., son of the famous park and suburb designer, was given a contract to assist him in developing this plan. Cousins was already well acquainted with the problems and prospects of the waterfront. In 1910, the young engineer had been hired to supervise the Grand Trunk Railway's grade separation project along Parkdale's lakeshore, which was intended to alleviate the traffic bottleneck at the intersection of Queen Street and Lakeshore Road. The City of Toronto then hired him as head of the Railroad and Special Works Department, where he lost his job within the year because of his vigorous promotion of an ambitious plan, proposed by Adam Beck of the new publicly owned Ontario Hydro Electric Commission, to integrate a province-wide radial electric railway system with Yonge and Queen Street rapid transit lines (Reeves 1992b, 47-50). At the THC, Cousins found his niche and presided over the most ambitious plan Toronto had yet seen.

Toronto's Waterfront Development Plan was unveiled in August 1913 (Toronto Harbour Commission 1913). It divided the city's waterfront into three sections. In the Eastern Section, substantial dredging would be required in order to modernize shipping facilities and expedite the expansion of industry. The Central Section, corresponding with Toronto's downtown, would see expanded commercial opportunities and new docks. In the Western Section and the Toronto Islands, new parklands and a grand amusement arcade and beach would be created to capitalize on the recreational potential of Lake Ontario, using four million tons of muck gathered from the dredging in the Eastern Section, topped with forty thousand cubic yards of topsoil harvested from a farm in Pickering purchased by the THC for that purpose. A lakeshore pleasure drive would link the new beach at Sunnyside with the Canadian National Exhibition and the Toronto Islands. A key feature of the waterfront plan was the strict separation of transportation functions. West of Parkdale, a new boardwalk along the waterfront would be joined by an expanded Lakeshore Boulevard to carry automobile traffic, a service road for trucks, and a streetcar track reservation. Land uses were also strictly segregated from east to west. The ideal of a purely recreational space, easily accessed by a new highway, would be accomplished by expropriating and demolishing close to two hundred Parkdale houses between the Grand Trunk rail line and the lake.

The plan met with universal acclaim by newspapers, politicians, and the general public, despite its costly $19 million price tag. The *Globe* overcame its usual suspicions of municipal fiscal irresponsibility and announced that the proposed plan would relieve Toronto's "torpor of hideousness," while the *Mail and Empire* acclaimed its suitable "magnificence." The waterfront plan was showcased during the Sixth National Conference on City Planning, which took place in Toronto in 1914, the first to be held outside the United States. A municipal referendum in January 1913 resulted in the necessary funds being added to the property tax assessment (Reeves 1992b, 67-74; 1992a, 13; Filey 1996, 49-50). At last, Toronto would compete in the City Beautiful sweepstakes. The founder of the movement, Daniel Burnham, had famously said: "Make no little plans." This vision for the waterfront was Toronto's first Big Plan to come to fruition.

It cannot be said, however, that the THC and its members were acting strictly out of altruism. Home Smith, who combined law, business, and politics in what a biographer describes as a "holy trinity" (Gunn 1990, 236), had been amassing more than three thousand acres west of the city for his Humber Valley development. According to Reeves (1992a, 43), "the scale, character, and marketing of the project were unprecedented, locally or nationally." A key component of this project, which was funded by magnates such as Lord Beaverbrook, was a trade-off with the city: Home Smith would donate the river valley bottom as a public park in return for annexation of the area and a municipally constructed Humber Boulevard. Lakeshore Boulevard would feed commuters directly into Humber Boulevard, which is at least part of the reason why Home Smith (who had advocated for a Lakeshore Boulevard when he was a member of the Civic Guild in the first decade of the century) made it such a priority for the THC. Home Smith and Cousins later collaborated on a plan for high-status apartments immediately north of Sunnyside, modelled on Chicago's Lincoln Park, which was never realized (Filey 1996, 79).

The City of Toronto almost immediately began buying properties along Parkdale's waterfront. Several large mansions had already fallen into disrepair. As far back as the recession of the early 1890s, Sunnyside villa had been sold for use as a Catholic boys' orphanage (later torn down as part of the development of St. Joseph's Hospital) and the sixteen-room Clark mansion (with the Ford shack in the back) had become a Salvation Army Rescue Home for Girls (*World,* 5 December 1892). In September 1913, the month after the Waterfront Plan was released, the City of Toronto bought the Dowling Avenue estate of former local MP H.H. Cook. Immediately, rumours flew that the property would be used as part of a plan to disperse the Provincial Lunatic Asylum into scattered sites around the city. J.J. Ward, the labour leader who had fought to keep Parkdale an independent municipality back in 1889, was among the residents who immediately formed the South Parkdale Ratepayers' Association to oppose any such plan. "South Parkdale is the oldest residential district in Canada," Ward fumed. "Objectionable businesses are not permitted to be established, and we certainly will not stand for an asylum." Another prominent resident raised the spectre of inmates of an asylum "interfering" with nearby bathers, while yet another compared the idea with opening a smallpox hospital in the heart of a residential area (*Star,* 9 and 10 September 1912). The *Star* shot back with an editorial against what would later be termed Nimbyism: "Whenever hospitals or fire halls or police stations are proposed, the people of the district come to Council with tears in their eyes, and say they don't want to be neighbours to these places. Yet they want them in the city somewhere – somewhere else ... Doubtless, an attempt will be made to locate the psychiatric hospital in the East end – from which deputants are either less frequent, or less influential, than from other parts of the city" (12 September 1912).

Both the outrage and reaction were soon irrelevant. By 1920, both the Cook and the adjacent Magann mansions had been demolished as the first step in turning Parkdale's residential waterfront into part of a grand municipal park with a boulevard running through it.[1] The gradual destruction of Parkdale's lakefront housing stock was considered a better outcome for the ratepayers' association than the use of its obsolete mansions as anything other than single-family homes.

## Attack of the Planning Reports, 1911-1934

On the eve of World War One, Parkdale was at the forefront of the social, political, and economic transformation of Toronto. Women, migrants from rural Canada, and, to a lesser extent, non-British immigrants were increasingly essential to the industrial, clerical, and sales workforce in Toronto. They were attracted to the efficiency apartments and converted flats found in Parkdale as well as downtown. Three separate interest groups – organized middle-class women, organized labour, and business leaders – were pushing local government in a more scientific and modern direction, and had strong opinions about the nature of future housing in Toronto. Over the next twenty years, these groups, along with academic experts and the media, would forge a consensus on "a good place to live" that would vilify the alternatives provided in the central city, which by now included Parkdale.

The theme of the measures proposed by the Toronto Local Council of Women to City Council in December 1911 was gender separation: separation of single women and men in housing, insane asylums, police courts, and prisons. A municipal Housing Committee, to be partly composed of women, should also endeavour to create "municipal lodging houses for the temporary accommodation of newly arrived immigrants, and also for the more permanent housing of single working men and (separately) of single working women as a means of counteracting the 'lodger evil'" (letter in City of Toronto Board of Control 1911). A 1915 "Report of the Social Survey Commission," led by the same organization, posited "overcrowding" and "economic want" as the primary causes of prostitution, with feeble-mindedness and immigration as secondary causal factors. Recommendations included caps on real estate speculation, especially in the suburbs, along with the construction of women's hotels and supervised boarding houses (City of Toronto Social Survey Commission 1915, 37-45).

Immediately before and during World War One, the Toronto District Labour Council was making recommendations for municipally funded family housing in the suburbs (correspondence entitled "The Housing of the Working Classes," undated, in City of Toronto Board of Control 1912). Concurrently, their sometime foe the Canadian Manufacturing Association was recommending model residences for factory employees in Toronto (*Labour Gazette,* November 1912). The Bureau of Municipal Research, created by civic-minded business leaders in 1915, advocated for stronger housing bylaws and suburban Garden Cities in their strongly titled report *What Is the Ward Going to Do with Toronto? A Report on Undesirable Living Conditions in One Section of the City of Toronto ... Which Are Spreading Rapidly to Other Districts,* co-written by Hastings and the new federal planning advisor Thomas Adams (Bureau of Municipal Research 1918). The city created a non-profit Toronto Housing Company in 1913, which built two small garden suburb developments in the east end of the city, but the units were mostly taken up by the same clerks and salespeople who were renting other apartment units, rather than by skilled labourers (Purdy 1997).

In the face of this growing consensus on the virtues of garden suburbs and the vices of any form of housing other than detached single-family homes, a somewhat dissenting opinion came from a City Council Housing Commission formed towards the end of the war. The Housing Commission condemned the fact that there were almost "eight new marriages for every new house" but promoted row houses and duplexes rather than detached new homes in the suburbs. While the "ideal condition would be that every family, large or small, had its own home, separate and distinct," the next best alternative was the remodelling of larger single-family residences into three-family apartment buildings, under "strict regulation" to avoid "slum conditions," at least "until broad constructive plans can be got under way." Businesswomen were looking for small apartments to avoid the "regrettable rooming house system" where "the temptations toward immorality" caused by young men and women living in the same house were "a source of grave danger." In contrast, "two or three girls or young women could get together and rent a suite" with a separate toilet and bath, along with a kitchen and room to receive friends. In short, "There will always be a 'Hub' population, and young and old couples and singles needed properly constructed apartment houses"; therefore, acceptable options should include converting "declining neglected property" into flats (City of Toronto Housing Commission 1918, 30-31). As Robert Beauregard (2003) has pointed out in the US context, there was always at least a hint of ambivalence in early-twentieth-century discourse on urban decline. Occasionally, as here, a report imagined a future beyond complete demolition for central city neighbourhoods .

After the war, the Ontario Housing Act of 1919 created a loan program to build suburban housing for returning servicemen. The five-year program was unsuccessful in terms of numbers, with only 6,200 homes supported, less than 15 percent of the estimated need. The loan program, like the Toronto Housing Company before it, tended to help regularly employed lower-middle-class male heads of household, rather than those most in need of affordable housing (Sendbuehler and Gilliland 1998). These tentative moves towards local and national housing policies were successful, however, in that they built up a national network of housing reformers: a national town-planning organization, accredited university programs, and professional journals, all with international linkages. The national network spread the belief that housing was "planning's raison d'etre" and that "planning was ... a Super Health Act ... the Science of the Environment ... a gospel of social regeneration ... that obviates the physical slum which breeds the moral one," in the words of a 1926 article in *Town Planning* magazine (cited 44).

After a near "total ... silence on housing issues from 1924-1932" at the national, provincial, and local levels (Bacher 1993, 62), the deepening economic crisis of the 1930s depression led to a new generation of housing reports in Toronto. Two years before the stock market crash of late 1929, the assessment commissioner reported that house prices were beginning to decline throughout the city, and expressed particular concern about "large old-fashioned homes" where "the high price of land and the necessity of spending a considerable sum in renovating the interior deter prospective purchasers. The result is that the owner has to ... dispose of the property at a sacrifice price, often for rooming house purposes" (City of Toronto Assessment Commissioner 1927, 6-8).

By 1931, 79 percent of Parkdale's housing stock was still single-family dwellings (Harris 1992), but the fact that one in five units was a flat or apartment did not sit well with some residents. There were complaints to City Council that several residences had become unlicensed guest houses displaying "room for rent" signs in their windows. The problem seemed especially acute along Jameson Avenue, the western end of King Street, and south of the tracks during the summertime, when crowds flocked to Sunnyside and the Canadian National Exhibition. Surely this commercial use of properties was contrary to the bylaw stating these streets were for residential use only? The issue was dragged back to City Council at least three times in 1931 and 1932 (City of Toronto Council, Minutes, 1931-1932). At first, council made an exception for doctors' and dentists' offices south of King Street. Then, when advised by the City Solicitor's Office that this bylaw would not hold up in court, the city barred all new signs. In the meantime, reported the *Globe*, a resident who had pushed for the initial bylaw had placed a sign in his own window requesting lodgers (19 April 1932). Along with some Parkdale residents, downtown hoteliers supported the bylaw, since the guest houses provided cheap competition. The local alderman, in contrast, was strongly against the bylaw, since "many people who have no other work were being desirous of taking in tourists ... to help maintain their properties" (*Telegram*, 8 February 1932), and "it would surprise you to know the number who are securing relief [welfare]" (*Globe*, 19 April 1932). In the meantime, the THC complained to City Council about the inflated prices some homeowners south of the rail tracks were asking as their properties were being slowly expropriated (*Telegram*, 5 May 1931).

The 1934 Bruce Report was the result of a committee that included Eric Arthur, a professor of architecture at University of Toronto who remained central in Toronto's planning initiatives until the 1960s, the Toronto Council of Women, and the Public Health Department. The Parkdale boundaries cited in the report were those of the public health district, everything south of Bloor Street, from Bathurst west to Sorauren (see Map 3). So when the Bruce Report compared the Yorkville rate of juvenile delinquency (7.9 per 10,000 population) with that of Parkdale (189 per 10,000; Bruce 1934, 35), it was really comparing all of north Toronto with all of west-central Toronto. The Bruce Report also signalled a shift from site-specific destruction of lodging houses and multi-unit housing to wholesale redevelopment of areas that were now thoroughly infiltrated with these "slum conditions." While Hastings' 1911 report had intended to prevent the creation of slum areas through inspections and bylaws, by 1934, the inadequacies of a purely reactive system were recognized. High land values in the central city meant that high-density housing was inevitable. It was the job of municipal government to acquire large tracts of land in order to build more modern and appropriate housing for low-income city dwellers.

Interspersed with the laudatory headlines announcing the report, like the *Evening Telegram*'s "Slum Demolition a Worth-While Endeavour," we find one voice raised in criticism, the Central Council of Ratepayers Associations, which found the planned public housing projects a recipe for segregating the poor (*Star,* 8 November 1934). But the ratepayers' associations, so vocal and seemingly powerful in the 1910s, were now dismissed in a headline as "Bodies of Little Influence / Sad Bunch of Old Women Piffling Away Time on Trifles" (*Mail and Empire,* 6 November 1934). Newspapers, in agreement with government reports, were thinking in bigger terms than mere neighbourhoods, and listening to more expert voices than those of mere residents.

## From "Beautiful Sunnyside" to "The Unemployed Man's Riviera": Housing and Social Conditions 1913-1951

In retrospect, it is easy to pinpoint the years 1911 to 1913 as the moment when Parkdale became cut off from its waterfront, and when concerns about multi-unit housing caused a sense of decline that the community was unable to turn around for the next sixty years. But if Parkdale was a community in decline at this point, the process was subtle, and largely unnoticed by residents for the next two decades.

Delayed by World War One, the waterfront development plans were completed on 28 June 1922, when the official opening of Sunnyside heralded the conclusion of this ambitious project. Newspapers that had enthusiastically greeted the original plans now swooned over the results. The front-page banner headline in the *Globe* the following day gives a sense of the tone: "Beautiful Sunnyside Beach, Front Doorway of Toronto, Is Officially Thrown Open – Aesthetic Dream of City History Makers-for Past Decade Resplendent Reality Today – Peep into the Future Grandeur Conjured by R. Home Smith, Chairman of the Harbour Commission, Man Largely Responsible for Making Vision of Past Come True."

The article not only flattered Sunnyside itself, with its combination of the "bizarre colourings of Ostend [and] the dreamy expanse of a Florida

Beach," but also praised its setting within Parkdale: "The approach from the lake as the yacht bearing the Harbour Commissioners' party rounded the contours of the shore from Dowling Avenue was one of novelty and delight ... appropriately set against a background of beautiful homes, luxuriant verdure, and exquisite landscape." The newspaper's linkage of Sunnyside and Parkdale as partners in prosperity was shared by the middle-class residents of the neighbourhood: "Following the toast to the king the proceedings were interrupted by a delegation from the Parkdale Business Men's Association. Speaking on behalf of that organization, Mr. Parker stated that he had been delegated to present a handsome basket of roses to one whom he might select as being a good friend of the district. That one being nominated as E.L. Cousins" (*Globe*, 29 June 1922).

The district did still seem to be a good place to buy commercial and residential property. Although there were not many property transactions in Parkdale in the late 1910s and early 1920s, those that occurred suggest healthy increases in property values. In my sample, one of the few Queen Street properties to shift ownership several times in this period, 1416 Queen Street West, was sold for $3,900 in 1893, $3,500 eight years later in 1901, and $3,300 in 1904. After renovations, the property sold for $4,400 in 1905, $6,450 in 1912, and an impressive $9,500 in 1927. Three doors over, number 1422 was sold for $8,250 in 1918 and $9,000 within two years. On Galley Avenue, one semi-detached house, initially sold for $3,800 in 1910, was resold in 1923 for $7,500, while the adjacent house increased in value from an initial price of $3,500 in 1910 to $6,500 in 1921. A villa on Dowling Avenue, sold in 1905 for $8,000, was resold in 1922 for double that price, to be torn down for an apartment building. A modest row house next to industries on Noble Street initially sold in 1890 for $1,050, then increased in value to $3,200 in 1924, albeit with a vendor mortgage for all but $500 (Land Registry Records). Comparable information on house price inflation in Toronto is limited until 1951, when the census began to record average house prices. But data on Canadian housing investment suggest that Parkdale mirrored larger trends: prices rising in the late 1900s until World War One, declining slightly during the war, and increasing throughout the 1920s, declining in the 1930s, then rising again after World War Two (Doucet and Weaver 1991; Ball and Wood 1999).

World War One accelerated a trend already noticeable in Parkdale, the neighbourhood's attraction for single women and widows. As both Michael Piva (1979, 39) and Carolyn Strange (1995, 176) have pointed out in the Toronto context, by the early twentieth century, inadequate "family wages" for male working-class household heads led many wives and daughters to work outside the home. The industries surrounding Parkdale hired mostly women during World War One and continued to hire women after the war (the Gutta Percha Rubber Company created a training film for its women workers with the encouraging title *Her Own Fault* in 1922; see Sobel and Meurer 1994, 43n). Parkdale also had a higher proportion of widows, spinsters, and other women heads of households than the rest of Toronto. (As discussed in the Introduction, assessment records did not provide any employment information on female heads of household, recording merely their marital status, not whether they were waged or unwaged.) On the 1921 assessment roll, women constituted 13 percent of household heads, as opposed to 10 percent in the rest of Toronto. Ten years later, the gap had increased: 19 percent of the household heads in Parkdale were listed as unwaged, as opposed to the Toronto average of 15 percent (Harris 1992). Single women tended to cluster in boarding houses run by other women, as well as sharing apartment flats. For instance, in 1931, women were household heads in half of the triplex units of 89-95 Dowling Avenue (City of Toronto Assessment Rolls 1931). Newspaper coverage of the 1924 murder of Martha Crooks, a widow running a rooming house on Jameson Avenue, reveals that the building housed mainly female roomers, including teachers at the high school across the street, except one room reserved for a man to "protect" the rest of the household. Unfortunately, a potential male tenant being interviewed was criminally insane and killed the landlady (*Star*, 25 January 1924).

One recent writer traces the origins of Queen Street West's eventual decline as a fashionable shopping area to the development of Lakeshore Boulevard in the 1920s (*Globe and Mail*, 4 August 1993). It is true that with the opening of Sunnyside Park and Lakeshore Boulevard, Queen Street ceased to be the main western entranceway to Toronto. But it is also true that Sunnyside attracted hordes of people to the western end of Parkdale in the summer, increasing commercial traffic along Queen and Roncesvalles. The old South Parkdale rail station had been moved to the Queen-King-Roncesvalles corner in 1912, and within the decade, there were four movie houses within six blocks of the intersection.[2] The Parkdale Curling Club at Queen and Cowan, built in 1898 by the local architect who also designed the central block of Canada's Parliament Building, was converted to the country's first indoor roller rink in 1906. By 1915, it had become the Pavlowa Dance Hall, famous for the soft drink served there, known as Honey Dew (Potts 1971). The suburb called "pleasantly old-fashioned" in 1912 was reinventing itself as the "amusement centre of the city" by the 1920s (phrase from Skeotch 1979). B.A. Lillie (1971a), remembering that era in the *Parkdale Citizen*, spoke with pride of "the longest hotel bar in town, complete with brass rails and swinging doors" at the Ocean House on Queen Street West, and Lakeview Mansions, also on Queen Street, advertising itself as "the largest apartment building in Toronto."

The 1910s and 1920s saw an increasing sense of difference between the older houses of South Parkdale and the newer and smaller houses north of Queen Street. In 1912, the local alderman complained about "fortunes [being made] in Parkdale bars"; the money coming "not from the people who lived in the good houses of South Parkdale ... [but] from the men with their dinner pails, passing by on their way to or from work" (*Globe*, 8 June 1912). Presumably, these factory workers with dinner pails hailed from north of Queen Street. However, a *Star Weekly* series that ran from 1916 to 1918 on the character of Toronto's public schools and their surrounding districts suggests that the locus of affluence and family formation had shifted from South Parkdale to the northwest. Parkdale School on Lansdowne, which served the northeastern corner of the neighbourhood along the rail tracks, was described as serving a "substantial industrial class, with only a very small foreign contingent." Its specialties were manual training and domestic science, well suited to the "industrious" students who worked on farms during the summer, sold and delivered newspapers after school, or worked in Queen Street stores on weekends (*Toronto Star*, 20 April 1918). Queen Victoria School, which served South Parkdale from the corner of Close and King, boasted a "uniformly high class" of residents, with "neither extreme wealth nor extreme poverty." But the building itself was now "undergoing gradual and inevitable deterioration" due to age (it was thirty years old at the time). "A few years ago," the article continued, "it was suggested that the big Parkdale school might be placed in the list of decadent institutions on the theory that the growth of Parkdale as a residential section had ended and that its houses would be occupied for the most part by older people, whose children had grown up, married, and were raising families in other parts of the city." But a new life had been granted by the development of duplexes and apartment buildings, where, according to the article, a new generation of children would presumably be found (*Toronto Star*, 2 February 1918). In this assumption, the article was incorrect. Assessment rolls from 1913, 1921, and 1931 indicate that the occupants of flats and apartments were mostly single people or older empty nesters. Meanwhile, the "original report" on Fern School, at the northwest edge of Parkdale, was "that the district bore none too good a reputation, but that day is long gone." Now it was "probably one of the best all-round school districts in the city," particularly west of Roncesvalles, where new houses were springing up rapidly. East of Roncesvalles, "the population is composed of a solid class of people who make their living for the most part in offices and warehouses" (*Toronto Star*, 3 March 1917). In other words, northwest Parkdale seemed to be on its way up, while South Parkdale was on its way down.

Unfortunately, due to ward boundaries, the assessment samples for the 1901-1951 period cut off eight blocks of northwest Parkdale, consisting mostly of houses constructed between 1906 and 1913. Although it could be argued that there was a general decline in the economic class of residents during this period, the decline was not straightforward or consistent (see Figure 2.1). The extremely high proportion of self-employed people (mostly small local businesspeople and salespeople) in Parkdale, 37 percent in 1901, decreased to 15 percent by 1921, but did not go below the Toronto average of 10-12 percent during this period. The proportion of Parkdale's household heads who were managerial or professional increased to 25 percent in 1921, well above the Toronto average of 15-17 percent. Even in 1941, by which time the proportion of managers and professionals had fallen to 11 percent, there were still a substantial number of middle-class residents in Parkdale. The proportion of skilled workers as household heads declined from the city average of 36 percent in 1913 to 17 percent in 1931. Then it increased again to 32 percent, as compared to the city average of 25 percent, during World War Two. The proportion of clerical workers tended to match the city average of 6-9 percent, with the exception of a relatively large 11 percent of Parkdale household heads in 1931. It is only in that infuriatingly vague category of "unwaged," dominated by women heads of household, that Parkdale consistently has a higher proportion than the city average. Across Toronto, the proportion of these unwaged household heads increased from 10 percent in 1921 to 22 percent in 1951. In Parkdale during the same period, the proportion also doubled, from 13 percent to 26 percent.

Assessment records depict a pattern of housing slowly filtering downward over time, from professionals and managers to clerks and salespeople in the bigger houses of South Parkdale, and from skilled workers to female heads of households in the growing number of flats and apartments. On Dowling Avenue, for instance, a house owned by a barrister in 1913 was rented by his son to a car cleaner in 1931. By 1951, it was owned by an absentee landlord and had been subdivided into four flats, lived in by a clerk, a salesman, an engineer, and a postal clerk. James Beaty's villa, occupied by his widow in 1913, had been subdivided into three flats by 1931, rented to a civil engineer, a designer, and a widow. In 1951, these three flats were rented to another widow, a barber, and a booker. On Empress Crescent, south of the tracks, one house rented by a clerk in 1913 was owned by a caretaker in 1931, and another house rented by a clerk in 1913 was owned by a compositor in 1931. None of the houses on Empress changed ownership after 1914, because they were under expropriation orders. There was also considerable stability in the houses on Galley, Gwynne, and Noble, with fewer than half the houses changing hands in the two decades, and the social composition remaining virtually unchanged (mixed on Galley, predominantly working class on Gwynne and Noble). Subdivision of houses increased slightly on Galley, and Queen Street business owners seemed slightly more likely to rent out the apartments over their shops than to live in them. The population of assessment area 6.1 increased from a little over 15,000 in 1913 to almost 19,000 in 1931 and over 21,000 in 1951, with most of the increase attributable to apartment construction and conversion of single-family houses to multiple units (Figure 3.5; City of Toronto Assessment Rolls 1913-1931).

Robert Libby, who continued to live in his family home on Callender Street after he married, was one resident who benefited from Parkdale's growth and intensification in the early twentieth century. He left the CPR rail yard at King and Dufferin in 1905 at the age of twenty-two, because

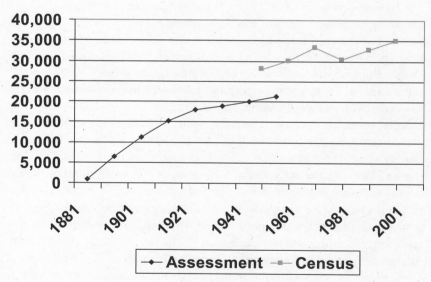

*Figure 3.5.* Population of Parkdale, 1881-2001
*Note:* Assessment area 6.1, used for 1901 to 1951 population figures, covers a smaller area than the 1879-1889 boundaries of Parkdale used for figures from 1951 on, when census tract information becomes available for that area.
*Sources:* Parkdale Council 1881; City of Toronto Assessment Rolls, 1891-1951; Census of Canada 1951-2001. Graph courtesy of Ric Hamilton, McMaster University.

he could get better wages working for J.J. Walsh, one of Parkdale's local developers, as a "jobbing carpenter." During World War One, he found work in a munitions factory and saved up enough to buy a second-hand piano for his six children (Toronto between the Wars 1971-1972). Young people also seemed to have little difficulty obtaining work. Albert Crosswell, whose father owned a grocery store on the corner of Rideau and Macdonell, was one of the industrious students mentioned in the 1918 Parkdale Public School article. He made deliveries to boarding houses on King, Dufferin, and Gwynne at lunch and after school during the war. On winter Saturdays, he would go sledding at High Park, and as he grew older, he enjoyed dancing at the Pavlowa on Queen Street and the Top Hat at Sunnyside (Oral History Project 1974-1978). Aubrey Bone, whose father worked for Russell Motorcars, delivered newspapers mornings and Saturdays. Ruth Ellis, whose father was a grocer, found a job that paid five dollars a week in a confectionery shop after she left school in the mid-1920s. Ethel Abel, daughter of a prison tailor, left a job at a bookstore that paid seven dollars a week during the same period, because they weren't paying her enough (Toronto between the Wars 1971-1972).

Although Parkdale was still overwhelmingly English and Scottish in origin, there were some signs of emergent ethnic diversity. By the end of the 1920s, the Queen Street sample block had a substantial number of resident shop owners of Jewish and Italian origin: Vincenzo Leo and Frank Delisi, fruiterers at 1406 and 1422, respectively; Samuel Weisberg the tobacconist at 1414; and Ida Geller and Gershon Ginsberg with ladieswear stores at 1424 and 1432 (Assessment Rolls 1931).

Rapid social change seems to have made Parkdale a fertile ground for prejudice during the brief life of the Ku Klux Klan of Kanada. The original Ku Klux Klan had been a short-lived southern US movement during the late 1860s. In the early 1920s, the notion of vigilante Protestant white people restoring order and purity enjoyed a resurgence in American cities of the north. The Ku Klux Klan of the 1920s was as much about greed as it was about racial and religious hatred. Ten-dollar membership cheques enriched the coffers of local organizers (K. Jackson 1967; Robin 1992, 2-5). According to a contemporary account, a Torontonian named Richard Cowan saw the "marvellous accession of wealth by the promoters" of the American Klan and decided to bring the movement home. In December 1924, Cowan signed an agreement in New York City with J.H. Hawkins, a seasoned Klan organizer who had been the Baltimore "Grand Dragon," and Lewis Fowler, a Baptist minister from Virginia. The contract focused on profit-sharing details rather than any philosophical content (Richards 1926). The three men returned to Toronto, and by early 1925, prominent members of the Orange Lodge were being telephoned about joining another "good Protestant organization" (*Star*, 9 February 1925). The *Toronto Star*, whose coverage was extensive and usually strongly supportive (a story headlined "Klan Issues Warning to Protect Children" uncritically repeated claims that "white children" were being lured into cars by "foreigners"; 28 July 1925), reported in February that the organization was applying for registration, with a $50,000 loan from the American Klan, and further alleged that a thousand members had already been initiated (12 and 16 February 1925). The principles of the Canadian Klan were said to be "to advance and protect the interests of white, Gentile, Protestant, Anglo-Saxon citizens of this Dominion by waging war against Roman Catholicism, Judaism, Negroes, the use of the French language in Canada, separate schools, and the immigration of foreigners" (Richards 1926). Throughout the spring and early summer, there were reports of crosses being burned in smaller Ontario towns, while secret meetings were supposedly being held in Toronto. Toronto membership was said to approach two thousand by June (*Star*, 4 June 1925).

On Friday, 7 August 1925, the first public demonstration by Toronto Klan members took place, starting at Queen and Lansdowne in the heart of Parkdale. At 11 p.m., over a dozen sedan cars, each packed with six people dressed in Klan regalia, left Parkdale Assembly Hall. The occupants of the cars included both men and women. They had removed their hoods, and the glow of the dome lights on their faces added to the "strange sight" as the sedans drove slowly eastward along Queen Street. At Spadina Avenue, the centre of the Jewish garment trade, the "parade" turned northwards, then east along Bloor. The sight unnerved many who were out that night, but the police claimed it was a "youth stunt" or a "masquerade." The Klan spokesman, Hawkins, said it was merely a "dress rehearsal" for larger demonstrations (*Star* and *Mail and Empire*, 8 August 1925). Two days later, a public meeting at the Parkdale Assembly Hall drew 160 people. The meeting was held to coincide with a march on Washington that was said to have drawn forty thousand US Klan members. According to the *Star*, whose headline was "Bolshevik Menace Threatens Canada," there were six white-robed, hooded figures on the dais, along with a "traditional fiery cross in background, an open bible lying upon a cushion with the Union Jack sewn upon the top of it, two great Union Jacks backstage, and another fluttering in the breeze created by an electric fan on the front left of the platform." Speakers' remarks focused on the threat from Eastern European immigrants, who were importing communism and threatening "our womanhood." Canada was in danger of losing its "Anglo-Saxon element." Although many of the crowd were said to be plainclothes policemen, the *Star* also noted that dozens of people signed membership cards before leaving (10 August 1925).

The meeting appears to have been the high-water mark for the Toronto Klan, just as the march on Washington was the high point for the American Klan of the 1920s. In October 1925, Hawkins was embroiled in a lawsuit with his former partners over unpaid salary, and by 1926 he had moved on to more fertile ground in Saskatchewan, where the Klan went on to influence the course of the 1928 provincial election (*Star*, 1 October 1925; Robin 1992). A rash of criminal incidents in rural Ontario, including arson at Catholic churches and extortion associated with Klan members, further tarnished the image of a kinder, gentler Canadian Klan. In March 1926, a turn-out of a dozen members to lay a wreath on the cenotaph at Toronto City Hall was labelled "weird rather than impressive" by their erstwhile supporters at the *Star* (5 March 1926).

The short life of the Toronto Klan mirrors the experience of many northern US cities, where, according to Kenneth Jackson, the Klan drew its strength from middle-class and skilled blue-collar workers who were concerned about rapid urban social change. The residences and professions of Toronto Klan members are hard to discover, given the short, secret life of the organization and absence of records. Cowan, for example, is called an "optometrist" in one report, but neither he nor Hawkins shows up in street directories of the period. The Canadian Communist newspaper, the *Worker*, claimed the Klan was the refuge of lawyers and "real estate sharks" (28 February 1925). The staging of the two demonstrations at Parkdale Assembly Hall could have simply been a function of a sympathetic or lackadaisical hall manager, rather than a local concentration of members. Nevertheless, Parkdale's demographics do match those of Chicago and Detroit neighbourhoods where the Klan was strongest: a high proportion of business, sales, and clerical employees and industry foremen, facing the threat of rapid neighbourhood transition (Jackson 1967, 108, 128).

The Klan flare-up suggests a difficult transition for newcomers to Canada who settled in Parkdale. The opposition in 1912 to a rumoured asylum by the lakeside points to a hardening of attitudes towards those Parkdale residents we know so little about, the institutionalized. In 1911, as part of the move towards modern and efficient governance, the City of Toronto created a Charities Commission to examine the private charities to which the city gave funds. The Monastery of Our Lady of Charity on West Lodge, formerly the Magdalen Asylum, housed 134 "delinquent females and feeble minded girls and women" who were there to be "reformed, or as explained by the sisters in charge, converted and protected." It also operated an industrial school for twenty-nine girls aged twelve to eighteen, who were admitted on three-year terms by parents, friends, police, or inspectors of prisons. These girls learned sewing, cooking, and housework. The Charities Commission approved of the $500 annual grant by the city, noting that "the inmates appear to be a contented, happy, lot ... [the premises] clean and bright, with rooms well ventilated" (City of Toronto 1912, 37-38). The commission was less impressed by the Toronto Home for Incurables on Dunn Avenue, which housed 166 mostly elderly inmates, many of them senile. They noted that the forty-year-old building needed repairs and, when built, had been expected to house 250 occupants. The hospital needed to find some way to increase revenues from its patients, or crowd more in, since the $11,760 annual grant was too much for the city to maintain (14-15).

The Central Prison had been replaced by industries in the late 1910s, although the Mercer Reformatory for Women remained until 1968 (*Globe and Mail*, 26 October 2002). The Queen Street Asylum was expected to follow in the prison's footsteps. In 1888, when a branch of the Provincial Lunatic Asylum had opened in suburban New Toronto, the City of Toronto had advocated with the province to close the main building on Queen Street West, since the presence of the asylum had hindered commercial and industrial growth in the area. The province replied that the asylum would eventually be removed, and in the meantime would only "give shelter to those afflicted who are more docile and perhaps to women patients alone" (*Mail*, 27 September 1888). In 1912, when another branch at Whitby opened, the province again promised to close the central asylum down, since it was now surrounded by noise and polluting industry instead of the rustic farm environs of Howard's initial vision (Dear and Wolch 1987, 87). In 1929, the property was sold to the Grand Trunk Railway, and five hundred patients were shipped to Whitby, but seven hundred patients remained in the overcrowded Ontario Hospital for the Insane, as the premises had been renamed. Few patients left the asylum. A 1931 newspaper article bragged of the "fine results in this tragic hospital," where 20 percent of those who entered would eventually be judged "cured" and "let out on probation" (*Toronto Star*, 27 August 1931).

James Lemon (1985, 65) identifies the publication of the Bruce Report with a turning point when the slum conditions in Cabbagetown, soon to be redeveloped as public housing, were "moving up to South Rosedale, to the Annex and out to South Parkdale." Although all parts of Toronto saw massive conversion of single-family houses into flats during the Depression and World War Two, including wealthy central city areas such as Rosedale, no part of Toronto changed as rapidly and as completely as Parkdale. Six percent of single-family dwellings (whether detached, semi-detached, or row houses), mostly larger villas in South Parkdale, had been converted to two- or three-unit flats in 1931, slightly below the Toronto average of 8 percent. Ten years later, 62 percent of single-family dwellings were subdivided into multiple households, almost twice the Toronto rate of 34 percent (Figure 3.6). This was in addition to the large proportion of purpose-built apartment buildings. As a function of the increase in tenants, along with an increase in absentee landlords, Parkdale's homeownership rate plummeted, from 51 percent in 1931 to 14 percent in 1941, considerably below the Toronto average of 33 percent (see Figure 3.1). Most of the new tenants were single people, which accounts for Parkdale's population only increasing by a little over a thousand people in those ten years, to 20,061. In comparison, Rosedale's homeownership rate slipped by a little over a third between 1931 and 1941, from 64 percent to 42 percent, and the number of subdivided houses increased from 23 percent to 38 percent, with the majority of new units accessory apartments. The Annex's homeownership rate decreased from 56 percent to 36 percent during the same period, while the number of subdivided houses went from 2 percent to 6 percent. Most of the subdivisions in the Annex created rooming houses, while other residential properties were converted to offices and university-related institutional uses (Lemon 1986, 17-18). In Rosedale and the Annex, subdivision could be rationalized as a temporary response to a housing and income crisis. Parkdale, in contrast, with its flats over stores on Queen, King, and Roncesvalles, residential hotels, apartment buildings large and small, rooming and boarding houses, villas converted into flats, and accessory apartments in the majority of houses, was indisputably a community of landlords and tenants in the City of Homes.

Richard Harris and Richard Dennis, who have written most extensively on rental options in Toronto during the first half of the twentieth century, agree that there was considerable social diversity amongst landlords and tenants, at least until the 1920s (Dennis 1987; Harris 1993). Widows ran rooming or boarding houses as a respectable form of income generation. Blue- and white-collar homebuyers took on lodgers as a way to help pay mortgages, which typically had a five-year term with quarterly interest instalments, and the principal payable at the end of the term. A higher rate of lodging in Canadian cities was correlated to higher levels of homeownership than was the case in American cities. Lodging also became attractive to both landlords and tenants during recessions and housing supply crises, when young singles and couples would also return to the family home, or two unrelated households would share rent or mortgage costs (known as "doubling up"). Thus *Might's Directory* indicates that 35 percent of Toronto households had lodgers in 1890, during a period of

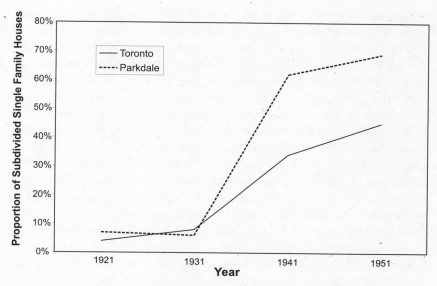

*Figure 3.6.* Proportion of subdivided single-family houses, Parkdale and Toronto, 1921-1951
*Source:* Parkdale Council 1881; City of Toronto Assessment Rolls, 1891 sample; Harris 1992. Graph courtesy of Ric Hamilton, McMaster University.

recession, but the rate was halved to 17 percent in 1897. The housing crisis of 1913 saw lodging rates of 37 percent, followed by a decline to 20 percent in 1925. By 1931, the lodging rate was back up to one in three. It peaked during the housing crisis of World War Two, then rapidly declined during the postwar suburban boom. Harris calls this phenomenon "the flexible house," and points out that the typical 1880-1913 Toronto house form, a narrow semi-detached house with two or three storeys and basement, was ideally suited for subdivision into two or three relatively separate units, although they were not purpose-built for multiple occupancy, as was the case in Boston, Montreal, and other North American cities (Harris 1994; 1996, 116-21).

Autobiographical material, which is admittedly fragmentary and possibly atypical, suggests that Parkdale housing continued to provide flexible alternatives for clerical and industrial workers, both owners and tenants, throughout the 1930s depression and into World War Two. For instance, Joseph Brunelle, born in rural Quebec in 1892, migrated to Toronto in his late teens. In 1915, he married Mary Ann Flood, the daughter of a fellow railway worker. Three years later, they purchased 84 Wright Avenue, a three-bedroom, two-storey row house in North Parkdale. Over the next few years, Joseph installed a new roof, an indoor toilet, and electricity, with the help of friends and family. A chicken coop and vegetable garden helped supplement Joseph's wages as a brakeman for the CPR. The Brunelles also rented out their second floor for twenty-five dollars a month. By the mid-1920s, the ground floor was rented out as well, as the Brunelles followed employment around Toronto. Joseph lists his jobs as bookkeeper with R.A. Lister, pot salesman, and, during the first years of the Depression, service station attendant. In 1931, he was offered a job as the "French correspondent" for Massey Harris. The family, which included fourteen children by then, moved back to 84 Wright. Joseph details the small economies by which the large family survived the Depression. He bought six dozen cracked or fertilized eggs three times a week from a co-worker at Massey Harris who lived on a farm; he walked the three miles to and from work each day; Mary Ann performed sewing wonders in preserving clothes from child to child. Joseph took pride in the fact that his wife never turned away anyone who knocked on their door and asked for food. The Brunelles lived at 84 Wright until 1965 (Brunelle 1972).

In 1930, Magdalena and Wilfred Eggleston, both making precarious wages as freelance writers, moved into a flat at 143 Dunn Avenue. They soon met and became friends with another struggling newlywed couple with literary aspirations, who rented the flat upstairs from them. Even though Raymond Knister had published his first novel to critical acclaim, his wife, Myrtle, needed to supplement the family income by working at a nearby textile factory. Wilfred later remembered: "I have some dim recollections of bill collectors hanging around and a brush with the bailiff when they were living above us" (cited in Gatenby 1999, 250). Alan Skeotch's father was born in Fergus, a small farming community in western Ontario. He moved to a farm in Saskatchewan in the 1920s, then, when farm prices fell, decided to seek his fortune in Toronto one winter in the early 1930s. His boots were stolen off his feet as he slept during the three-day train journey eastward. When the conductor announced Parkdale Station, he ran barefoot through the snow to the nearest hotel that offered cheap rooms. He lived next door to a bootlegger and across the hall from a prostitute, but it was a place to start looking for work (Skeotch 1979).

The Depression slashed Sunnyside's revenues, but people flocked to the free attractions throughout the 1930s and into the war years. It became known as the "unemployed man's Riviera." The Toronto Transit Commission offered free summertime service to any child holding a towel, and as many as twenty streetcars along seven routes were packed on weekends (Parkdale Centennial Research Committee 1978, 40-41). The Pavilion Restaurant at Sunnyside, one of the city's poshest restaurants during the

1920s, became the Club Top Hat in 1939, reputedly much less elegant (Filey 1996, 58). Sunnyside, along with Parkdale, had made the journey from splendour to shabbiness in a mere two decades.

## Urban Renewal Arrives in Parkdale, 1941-1966

World War Two precipitated a housing crisis in Toronto much more acute than the problems experienced during World War One. Workers, many of them female, flocked from the countryside to work in industries adjacent to Parkdale. For instance, the John Inglis Company just east of Parkdale hired over a thousand women to produce Bren guns, and opened the John Inglis Recreation Club in the old Parkdale Roller Skating Rink to help retain the lonely and homesick new recruits. Open from 8 a.m. to 11:30 p.m. on weekdays and weekends, the club offered dance lessons, friendship clubs, a snack bar, a library, and "safe, wholesome pastimes" such as beauty exercises and handicraft lessons. The most popular feature was the showers, and women preferred to spend their time in more exciting pursuits, such as outings to Sunnyside's Palais Royale dance hall (Sobel and Meurer 1994, 66-69).

The growing wartime housing crisis in Toronto precipitated a flurry of planning documents. Two municipal reports on housing conditions, as well as Toronto's first comprehensive zoning plan and first master plan, all appeared in 1942-43. The reports were compiled by many of the same housing reformers who had worked on the Bruce Report (A. Rose 1958, 1972). An attempt to raise $2 million in city bonds for public housing had foundered in 1937, when the Bureau of Municipal Research charged that dwellings marked for slum clearance were hardly slum properties and that enforcement of the Housing By-Law was forcing renovation of 1,700 dwellings at the owners' cost, as opposed to only six hundred new dwellings proposed in the plebiscite. As a less expensive measure, the bureau recommended renovating multiple-family dwellings rather than building new housing (*Evening Standard,* 29 November 1937). Undeterred, the 1942 report on housing conditions again conflated "overcrowding" with multiple occupancy. The fact that there were now far more family units than houses was a problem in itself, regardless of actual housing conditions. Despite recommending a temporary relaxation of bylaws to permit roomers (as had the similar report during World War One), the report emphasized the importance of a postwar housing construction program for new suburbs and rebuilt central city slums. It estimated that thirty thousand dwelling units in the central city would eventually have to be removed because of their decrepitude. They were damp and leaky, lacked central heating, or were verminous. Solutions short of demolition, such as further enforcement of the Housing By-Law or loans to owners to fix up their properties, were not considered (Arthur et al. 1942, 3-14). A 1930s home renovation program of the National Employment Commission had been evaluated by housing reformers as merely producing "rumpus rooms for the bourgeoisie" (cited in Bacher 1993, 96). Many older neighbourhoods, with their promiscuous mix of land uses, noise, car traffic, and other hazards, were simply judged beyond rehabilitation. By 1944, all of Parkdale was described as "declining," since subdivided housing was an "inevitable sign of decline" (Toronto Planning Board 1944, 15).

The end of the wartime and postwar housing crisis did not bring about a de-conversion of Parkdale's dwellings. Indeed, by 1951, seven in ten of Parkdale's former single-family dwellings had been converted to multiple housing units, and the area's population continued to rise. The (probably underestimated) population of assessment area 6.1 increased from a little under 19,000 in 1931 to 20,000 in 1941 and over 21,000 in 1951, and the 1951 census counted almost 28,000 inhabitants within the slightly larger historical boundaries of Parkdale (see Figure 3.5).[3] Although density was increasing, the neighbourhood could not be considered declining in terms of actual housing and social conditions. Homeownership began to increase again in Parkdale. The neighbourhood's class composition in 1951 resembled that of the rest of the City of Toronto, whose boundaries encompassed the affluent former suburbs of Rosedale and North Toronto as well as lower-income neighbourhoods. Parkdale's median household-head income was slightly lower than the census metropolitan area (CMA) figure in 1951, $2,457 versus $2,653, and the proportion of people earning less than $1,000 a year was higher in Parkdale than in Toronto region, but the population could hardly be characterized as low income. Fewer than 2 percent of Parkdale dwelling units were deficient in the base-level housing conditions of running water and furnace heating, as opposed to the average of 7 percent across the CMA. Fifteen percent of Parkdale households did not have exclusive use of a flush toilet, a slightly higher proportion than the CMA average of 13 percent, but unsurprising in an area with so many subdivided houses. A local economic downturn immediately after the war's end was probably due to war industry layoffs: "Delaying Factors in Industrial Readjustment," *Labour Gazette*, May 1946, describes difficulties in retooling plants for peacetime production as a factor leading to unemployment in Toronto and other cities. But by the 1950s, land registry records show large price increases for the first time since the 1880s, especially in the northwest corner of Parkdale, where a new Polish credit union provided mortgage funding for the neighbourhood's first substantial community of residents of non-British origin (Parkdale Centennial Research Committee 1978).

For instance, a two-unit property on Galley with an absentee landlord, which had sold for $7,500 in 1923, had declined in value by 1949 to the point that it was sold for $2,700 with no cash down. Eight years later, it was sold to a purchaser with a Polish surname for $7,200, again with no cash down, but with a mortgage provided by an institutional lender. The next year, 1958, it was sold to another purchaser with a Polish name for $9,000, who transferred the mortgage to St. Stanislaus' Credit Union, and by 1964, it had sold to a third Polish-surnamed purchaser for $16,500. A few doors down, a house that had sold in 1938 for $2,900 found a $4,300 sale price in 1948 and a $9,000 price, from a Polish purchaser who obtained a mortgage from St. Stanislaus, in 1961. By 1970, St. Stanislaus' Credit Union had held mortgages on half the houses in the Galley sample block face for at least part of the previous twenty years (Land Registry Records).

Even in South Parkdale, where institutional lenders were rare until the 1970s (Figure 3.7), house prices were beginning to exceed the average for Toronto and its suburbs. By 1961, the median house price (excluding apartment buildings) was $19,076 in Parkdale versus $17,301 in the census metropolitan area. A house on Dowling Avenue that had sold for $15,500 at the height of the market in 1927 sold for $13,000 in 1946, but soon increased in value to $36,000 by 1957. A house on Gwynne that had been repossessed by the agents of a private lender was sold under power of sale for $1,200 in 1940. By 1952, it had been purchased (by someone with an Eastern European surname) for $2,350 with a full vendor mortgage. Another house sold for $6,000 in 1953 and $9,500 in 1956; and a third house on the street sold for $2,200 in 1943, $8,500 in 1965, and $11,500 in 1969, all with full vendor mortgages. Even into the 1970s, one-third to one-half of sales in west Toronto (including Parkdale) involved vendor mortgages (Murdie 1986, 1991). To Robert Murdie, who has written on residential mortgage lending in Toronto during the postwar period, this does not indicate classic American redlining by institutional lenders. Rather, vendor mortgages had a long history in Toronto (as has already been seen in Parkdale), prolonged and exacerbated by mutual distrust between postwar immigrants and most mortgage lenders. Furthermore, Canadian banks were not permitted to provide mortgages until 1958, and even after legislation changed they were slow to enter the central city market. I would argue that contrary to Murdie's hypothesis, there was de facto redlining by some institutional lenders to individual homebuyers in central Toronto, including Parkdale, from the late 1940s into the 1970s. There may not have been maps and formulas, as in the United States, but federal government policy did guarantee loans for "limited dividend" new apartment developers and suburban new homebuyers, while doing next to nothing for central city renovators (Bacher 1993, 169). In Parkdale at least, most institutional lenders (the exception being the Polish and Ukrainian credit unions) ignored the needs of homebuyers until the strength of the central city homeownership trend became impossible to ignore in the late 1960s. However, the reluctance of mainstream institutional lenders to invest in Parkdale houses during the 1950s and 1960s seems to have had little or no effect on renovation or rapid price inflation during that period.

Although house prices were increasing in Parkdale by the 1950s and homeownership was growing, there had not been significant changes in class composition. The Polish immigrant homeowners on Galley were factory workers, labourers, and contractors, much like the tenants of British origin they had replaced. The Dowling Avenue apartment buildings, including two new buildings constructed in the late 1950s, still housed salespeople, bookkeepers, and accountants, with a high proportion of woman-led households.

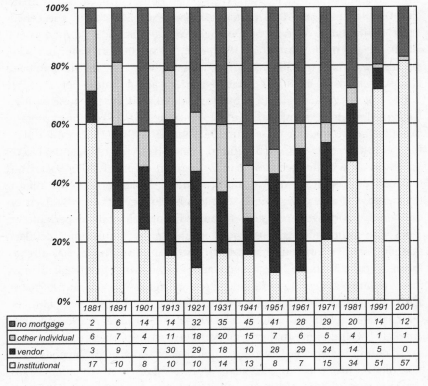

| | 1881 | 1891 | 1901 | 1913 | 1921 | 1931 | 1941 | 1951 | 1961 | 1971 | 1981 | 1991 | 2001 |
|---|---|---|---|---|---|---|---|---|---|---|---|---|---|
| ■ no mortgage | 2 | 6 | 14 | 14 | 32 | 35 | 45 | 41 | 28 | 29 | 20 | 14 | 12 |
| ▥ other individual | 6 | 7 | 4 | 11 | 18 | 20 | 15 | 7 | 6 | 5 | 4 | 1 | 1 |
| ■ vendor | 3 | 9 | 7 | 30 | 29 | 18 | 10 | 28 | 29 | 24 | 14 | 5 | 0 |
| □ institutional | 17 | 10 | 8 | 10 | 10 | 14 | 13 | 8 | 7 | 15 | 34 | 51 | 57 |

*Figure 3.7* Mortgage type in Parkdale, 1881-2001
*Source:* Land Registry Records, sample of six block faces by author. Graph courtesy of Ric Hamilton, McMaster University.

In the meantime, the idea of metropolitan government had arisen in the Toronto region, bringing with it recycled grand plans. The limits of the City of Toronto had remained essentially unchanged since annexations ended in 1912, but the edge of development extended far beyond this boundary. Most of the seventeen outlying municipalities went bankrupt during the 1930s, suggesting a need for metropolitan governance and cost sharing on roads and public transport. In 1942, the City of Toronto established a commission with the mandate to prepare a master plan for the entire region, including a green-belt system, metropolitan-wide zoning, a transportation plan that would include both expressways and public transport, and public housing (Reeves 1993, 1-10; A. Rose 1972). The 1943 Master Plan championed massive rebuilding in the central city in combination with a network of highways that would allow further decentralization of housing and industry. In the central city, "residential areas, generally, south of College Street have reached a point where age, obsolescence and actual physical dilapidation indicate that at no very distant date widespread demolition will become most desirable if not essential." These residential areas would be best replaced by massive public housing undertakings, since "haphazard rebuilding by private enterprise ... [will] never be a factor in arresting the processes of decentralization" (Toronto Planning Board 1943, unpaginated).

The first step in revitalization would be the adoption of a citywide zoning bylaw intended to replace the patchwork of restrictive bylaws regarding land uses. As we have seen in the example of apartment buildings, these restrictive bylaws had often been honoured in the breach. While large American cities had been developing comprehensive zoning plans since the early part of the century, Canada had been much slower in realizing the permissive as well as the restrictive powers inherent in zoning. As a result, most of central Toronto got zoned for multi-unit apartments in 1943, with the result that property values shot up in some central districts, although with no immediate impact in Parkdale (Moore 1979, 317-19). In Parkdale, the new zoning permitted conversion to group housing and multiple-dwelling houses (R3 zoning) on every lot north of Queen Street, with apartment house buildings (R4 zoning) permitted on most lots south of Queen Street, subject to a public meeting and planning approval. On the one hand, the new zoning was a welcome recognition, after thirty years of moral opprobrium, that many larger houses had become "obsolete, unsuitable, and unmarketable for single family use" (City of Toronto Independent Committee on Zoning 1942, 10). On the other hand, the combination of open zoning in the central city and extremely restrictive zoning (R1, or single-family use only) in most of north Toronto set the stage for a hierarchy of good neighbourhoods to be preserved and bad neighbourhoods to be destroyed. A *Globe and Mail* article from 1948 makes this distinction explicit: "Regardless of the conflicting estimates of need, provision of land within the city boundaries remains a primary consideration in solving the problems of those who must live close to their places of work. It is to this end that the Toronto City Planning Board has classified some areas as being slums and others as being 'blighted.' The board feels that extensive re-development, following the general pattern of the Regent Park project, would provide room for new homes and thus more economic use of available land" (11 May 1948).

Parkdale, along with most of central Toronto, continued to be classified as a neighbourhood in need of major renewal in master plans and urban renewal strategies of the late 1940s and early 1950s. While the 1946 Toronto City Planning Board's first annual report showed a new subway line along Queen Street, the second annual report replaced the subway line with an expressway. The 1949 third report and Official Plan map judged virtually all of North Parkdale to be "uneconomic" and cited Detroit's urban renewal as a model to be emulated (22-23). Plans to tear down housing continued even as surveys of housing conditions continued to show the stock in Parkdale was "fair to good" (CTPB 1956b, map 4). As Albert Rose, a Toronto-based public housing expert active from the 1940s to the 1970s, points out, adequate housing can be defined as "sufficient space to maintain a happy family life ... of sound construction, properly maintained," and the vast majority of Parkdale's housing stock met this physical standard, with adequate heat and ventilation, hot and cold running water, and space for stoves and refrigerators. However, Rose approvingly cites UK researcher J.M. Mackintosh, who said, "a 'home' in the proper sense of the word is a family living in a separate dwelling as an organic unit of society and permeated with human feeling" (A. Rose 1958, 3-4). By this social standard, Parkdale's housing stock was inadequate.

However, a shift can be identified in city planning reports from the mid-1950s. Some parts of central Toronto were successfully resisting urban renewal. For instance, from 1952 onwards, the West Annex and East Annex Neighbourhood Associations sponsored a campaign that proclaimed, "It's smart to live in the Annex." Along with advertising the neighbourhood to stores and homebuyers, the associations, led by woman homeowners and tenants, sponsored clean-up and beautification campaigns, and pushed local planners towards a 1958 neighbourhood plan with zoning that would preserve the neighbourhood's "distinct single family flavour" (Lemon 1986, 23-25; CTPB 1959b). Rosedale successfully fought for a change in zoning that would allow no new rooming houses (CTPB 1954).

Towards the end of the 1950s, the City of Toronto and the metropolitan government began what became a forty-year planning debate, with Metro Toronto stressing transportation improvements (especially expressways) in its master plan of 1959, while the City of Toronto's parallel master plan emphasized attracting the middle class to central neighbourhoods. In fact, by 1957, the city had quietly changed most zoning in central residential neighbourhoods from R3 and R4 to R2 and R1. The exceptions were St. James Town and South Parkdale, where apartment construction companies, particularly Meridian and Belmont, had assembled large holdings by the mid-1950s (Whitzman 1991; Land Registry Records). The president of Belmont Realty dated his interest in Jameson Avenue to 1951, when he noticed the wide street and large lots while driving to a wedding west of Toronto. He bragged that his company almost single-handedly increased the assessment value on the street from $1.5 million in 1954 to almost $7 million by 1959 (*Parkdale Citizen,* February 1971).

To give the example of one high-rise apartment redevelopment, two detached houses on Dowling were constructed by William Murray in 1898. One of the houses was sold for $4,400 cash to a widow, Barbara Cromer, who in turn sold it to another widow, Bessie Evans, for $7,000 cash in 1910. The Evans family lived there until 1955. The other house was rented to William Dockrill, who worked for the CPR, for ten years, at which point he bought the house for $5,000. In 1931, Phoebe, his widow, obtained a mortgage from Capital Trust Company for $4,800 and began to rent out the house. The trust company foreclosed in 1941, and two years later sold the property to William Vale, an inspector, for $500 cash and the value of the mortgage (a total of $5,300). This is one of a number of foreclosures found in land registry records from the time, suggesting that institutional lenders had good reasons to be reluctant to lend to private mortgage holders. In 1954, Agnes and John Zouzelka bought these two properties, along with a third adjacent property on Dowling, for $15,000. For fifty years, the increases in property prices and mortgages had been modest and gradual, but apartment development radically increased the value of property. By 1955, the Zouzelkas had a $680,000 mortgage from Prudential Assurance to construct two eight-storey apartment buildings, and five years later, they obtained an additional mortgage from Toronto-Dominion Bank for $500,000.

In 1959, Toronto's Planning Department projected a need for thirty-seven thousand new apartment suites, mostly serving single-person households, over the period 1956 to 1980, with Parkdale projected to receive the second-largest share of this new construction. Finally, the needs of lower-income single-person households were being recognized, albeit in the value-laden rhetoric of concentric zone theory: "As Metro Toronto grows, the natural tendency will be for larger numbers of the poor and unfortunate, and the floating element of the Metropolitan concentration to congregate in the City. They cannot and should not be planned out of existence or even out of town. Rather their needs and natural habitat in the city must be recognized" (CTPB 1959b, 25).

Why did the master plan include so much redevelopment for Parkdale? The increase in assessment values was one reason the city supported apartment buildings. In addition, federal government encouragement to institutional lenders supported massive housing change in this period. While owners of single-family houses found it difficult to find institutional lenders after World War Two, the federal government guaranteed and partly subsidized low-interest loans for almost all of Parkdale's new apartments through the Federal Limited Dividend program, designed to stimulate apartment construction for low- and moderate-income tenants (*City Planning,* Summer 1987). Even more critical was the fact that the area lay in the path of "Superhighway A," the most important of the expressway systems proposed by the new metropolitan government. Apartment dwellers would presumably use the expressway as a quick and easy way to reach downtown jobs.[4] Superhighway A would merely be the first in a ring of highways surrounding Toronto. Two northbound expressways, one to the west of the city and one running up the Don Valley in the central east, would extend from Superhighway A up to the new Trans-Canada Highway (the 401). The site of Sunnyside Amusement Park would become a parking lot for commuters wishing to transfer to a proposed Queen Street subway line. By the early 1950s, uncertainly about the lakefront's future led the THC to grant single-year instead of multi-year leases to concessionaires at Sunnyside. The boardwalk had become rundown, with the city refusing to repair or replace it, and the last Easter Parade to be held there took place in 1953 (Filey 1996, 91, 125). By 1954, the city had proceeded with expropriation plans that had remained more or less dormant since 1913, demolishing the remaining waterfront housing in Parkdale, dehousing eight hundred people in 170 houses, as well as tearing down Sunnyside Amusement Park.

Although I have located forty-five articles, dating from 1951 to 1958, that argue the pros and cons of Superhighway A options in terms of potential impact on Sunnyside, the Canadian National Exhibition, regional parkland, and industry, I have found only one article to give "the other side of the ... story ... a tale of 800 people who will lose their homes to civic progress." Those interviewed for the article were mostly unwaged women using their homes as a form of income. One resident, Mrs. Dorothy Wood of Jameson Avenue, had moved to her present address when her childhood home was expropriated for Lakeshore Boulevard in the late 1910s. Now she was being asked to move again, but the "house is my living as well as my home. I have an apartment here which I rent. This is awful." Another resident, Miss Viola Brown of Starr Avenue, echoed her neighbour's words: "This has been my home for 30 years. It is my income too. I keep boarders here." In contrast, a man who had obtained his house eighteen months earlier, possibly as the result of a will, said he did not "'care about moving so long as I get full value for the house' ... Mr. Kalika said he would not be one to stand in the way of progress" (*Star*, 4 May 1954). Parkdale's transformation from modern model suburb to obstacle in the way of progress was now complete.

## Conclusion: The Nature of Decline in Parkdale 1913-1966

In 1960, the future playwright and novelist M.T. Kelly was fourteen years old and had just moved with his widowed mother and brother to a new apartment in South Parkdale. By then, "Parkdale was a construction site. All the Victorian houses, including the one next door to where my best friend lived, were being torn down for apartment houses. The great trench of the Gardiner went through, further cutting us off from the Lake. While it was being built, we played there, pretending we were wolves; the ramp led up and fell off, as eerie and windswept as a desert" (cited in Gatenby 1999, 250).

After complaining about overcrowding and high densities in Parkdale for close to fifty years, the City of Toronto had devised a seemingly contradictory planning remedy: permitting the construction of forty-eight high-rise (eight-to-twenty-three-storey) apartment buildings in South Parkdale from 1953 to 1967. Next to Regent Park South, where a public housing superblock was constructed in 1956, South Parkdale had the highest population increase of any census district in the City of Toronto between 1956 and 1961 (Metropolitan Toronto Planning Board 1962).

The available evidence suggests that Parkdale was a mixed-income, mixed-tenure, mixed-use neighbourhood from its origin in the 1870s until the 1960s. The neighbourhood went through three changes in the early twentieth century that could be termed decline: discursive decline, socio-economic decline, and decline in the housing stock. First, it ceased to be spoken about as "a good place to live" by newspapers and government reports, and began to attract negative coverage because of the affordable housing options it provided. This change began in the 1910s with reaction to the construction of several dozen low-rise apartment buildings and the conversion of a limited number of single-family homes. The newspaper and government planning discourse on Parkdale was almost completely negative by the 1940s.

Second, the proportion of upper-middle-class household heads (businesspeople and professionals) declined from well above the city average in 1913 and 1921 to slightly below average by 1941, before stabilizing to the city average by 1951 (see Figure 2.1). The loss of a critical mass of upper-middle-class homeowners in the 1920s, 1930s, and 1940s meant that Parkdale was without influential advocacy during the period when the powers of planning and zoning increased in Toronto. However, during the period in which Parkdale was supposedly becoming a "serious slum," the socio-economic class of the neighbourhood was hardly that of communities traditionally thought of as slums. There were very few unskilled labourers as compared to the rest of Toronto, and police reports do not mention any particular problems in Parkdale, unlike their regular complaints about Cabbagetown and the Ward.

Third, conversion of single-family homes into flats, which had occasioned such a moral panic in the 1910s, became the norm for Parkdale before, during, and immediately after World War Two. Also, the close alliance between real estate interests and Parkdale's elite in the 1910s led to strong support for apartment houses, which were opposed in other neighbourhoods. There is, however, no evidence that the actual condition of Parkdale's multiple-unit housing was substandard in the period during which the area was repeatedly called obsolete and suitable for demolition. The 1934 Bruce Report and the 1940s housing reports found very few Parkdale homes in violation of health or fire codes. The 1951 census suggested that Parkdale homes were better than average in terms of plumbing and furnace heating. In fact, homes began to double and triple in value during the 1950s and early 1960s, and there is evidence of housing improvements at the time when the rhetoric of decline was at its apogee. Institutional mortgages were low throughout the period 1913 to 1966, but this trend appears to be true across the city. It seems fair to conclude that the forty-year discourse of decline that preceded an era of rapid social and housing change in Parkdale was based more on firmly held beliefs about the virtues and vices of various types of housing, and the absence of powerful local advocates for the neighbourhood, than on actual housing or social conditions.

So why was Parkdale called a slum? One factor was its movement in symbolic space from an outer-edge new suburb to the city's aging inner ring. During Parkdale's development, it was on the edge of the urban frontier. The as-yet-undeveloped open space to the south and west, with market gardens and lakeside views, made Parkdale seem more affluent and less industrial than it was, especially to the villa owners who promoted their community to the larger city. During Parkdale's supposed decline, it was seen as a part of the despised centre. The increasing street and rail traffic, with attendant noise, smoke, and bustle, the seeming disorder of small apartment houses, detached villas, row houses, commerce, and limited industry gave a cluttered impression to the outsiders who described the community, especially those who came from neat and orderly suburbs on the new urban frontier, where everything was in its "proper" place.

A more important factor seems to have been Parkdale's large stock of "flexible houses" (Harris 1994) on large lots, which could be easily converted into flats during times of economic recession and high housing demand (and, of course, just as easily de-converted in other times). The pursuit of a societal norm of perfect nuclear families, each encased in its own purchased and detached home, brought contempt on neighbourhoods, such as Parkdale, that accommodated differences from this norm. In the 1940s, after thirty years of housing reports, the city established a zoning system, supported by federal housing policies, that encouraged the redevelopment of "declining" mixed-use neighbourhoods with "obsolete" housing. The existence of a more complex picture, Parkdale residents who did not see their neighbourhood as a slum and people who counted on Parkdale for cheap housing and rental income, was ignored.

Neighbourhood decline was a two-edged sword for Parkdale. Calling the neighbourhood a slum may have depressed property values and made institutional home loans difficult, although the limited evidence available suggests that Parkdale sales prices and tendency towards vendor and other non-institutional mortgages matched the norm for Toronto in the early and middle twentieth century (Murdie 1991; Paterson 1991; Harris and Ragonetti 1998). But a bad reputation may have been a boon for lower-income renters and new property owners, especially newcomers to Toronto who might not otherwise have been able to buy or rent in the central city. Unmarried women and men working in the central city, older single women, Polish immigrants, and young couples all seem to have benefited from Parkdale's increasing reputation as a slum between 1913 and 1966.

What were the real differences between Parkdale as a suburb and Parkdale as a slum? Was it that the housing stock was once new, and then aged and went out of fashion? Rosedale and Forest Hill, developed slightly later, did not go out of fashion as they aged. Was it that land developers and home builders had more of a stake in promoting land in Parkdale, and once they disappeared, so did the good reputation of the neighbourhood? Again, the examples of Rosedale and Forest Hill seem to disprove that theory. Did the presence of non-British immigrants and woman-led households, in subdivided houses and apartment buildings, inevitably lead to decline? Both newspapers and planning reports of the time certainly thought so.

Once Parkdale had been a cynosure, a guiding star for Toronto's suburban development, with daily coverage in the newspapers. It drew visitors to the boardwalk for the annual Easter Parade, to the beaches at Sunnyside throughout the summer, to the Canadian National Exhibition in late summer. But by the 1960s, it was increasingly anonymous, viewed through the window of a car along the Gardiner Expressway, or cruised by people looking for parking at the CNE. It was dismissed by planning reports and ignored by newspapers. "It only takes 65 seconds to drive through Parkdale," said local historian Alan Skeotch (1979) after the Gardiner Expressway was built. Parkdale seemed barely worth a glance.

# 4

# From Bowery to Bohemia: The Urban Village, 1967-2002

Me: "I've just finished reading a book that talks about Parkdale. It's called *Landscapes of Despair*."
Real estate agent (quickly): "You can see why we prefer the term Roncesvalles Village."

"Tell me, would you be happy in Village Ghetto Land?"

– Stevie Wonder, "Village Ghetto Land"

## Bowery and Bohemia: Parkdale's New Double Life

On 8 August 1970, forty-five years after a highly symbolic Ku Klux Klan demonstration in Parkdale protested perceived negative change in the central city, and ninety-one years after an equally symbolic tree-planting ceremony announced the birth of the Flowery Suburb, the *Toronto Star* carried news of another publicity event. A housing developer was announcing his latest Parkdale offering with an open-house viewing. This, in itself, was not unusual. The 1950s and 1960s, like the 1910s and 1920s, had seen apartment buildings spring up by the dozen in Parkdale, all with their claims to greatness. For instance, West Lodge Apartments, two eighteen-storey towers in North Parkdale, had boasted an architectural award in 1963 (*Toronto Star,* 28 March 1974). In 1971, the "gleaming 23 storey" Lake Shore Place, "possibly the neighbourhood's last high rise," attracted tenants with saunas, an exercise room, and an outdoor pool (*Toronto Star,* 18 December 1971). However, there were two elements that were different about this developer, George Herczog. First, he was offering not some new apartment block, but modest two-storey row houses that had been described as tenements when they were built in 1883. Second, he was marketing these former working-class housing units by proclaiming what was, for Parkdale, a new way of seeing the neighbourhood.

Herczog claimed: "An unlimited number of older houses close to city conveniences can be modernized and provide reasonably priced living for scores of families." He had recently "reclaimed" more than two hundred houses and had no problem disposing of the refinished product. In his latest project, Melbourne Place, he was following his usual method of gutting the interior, with the "exception of things worth saving for effect."

Then he was adding modern kitchens, heating, wiring, and bathrooms. The houses would sell, he predicted, for $31,000 to $33,000. Not only would he profit, but the improvements would cause a positive "chain reaction to other properties" (*Toronto Star,* 8 August 1970).

To some extent, Herczog's claims were a return to Parkdale's early days, when reasonably priced houses with quick access to the city were marketed to families. In another sense, Melbourne Place was at the forefront of a new aesthetic. For the first time in Parkdale, age had become a virtue. Instead of destroying old-fashioned houses, modern conveniences could be added while preserving original features "for effect." Preservation and renovation might be as profitable as demolition. Herczog was hardly unique: Peter Williams (1986, 56) writes of how real estate agents in Australia and the United Kingdom began to use terms like "original features" and "period charm" in their marketing during the late 1960s and early 1970s.

There were already several chain reactions happening in Parkdale in the early 1970s. A Community Coalition had formed to "save the neighbourhood," a necessary step, suggested the *Globe and Mail,* for a "village that had lost its identity," a "disorganized community, with little community spirit," a place that might have become Rosedale, but did not (17 November 1970). Activist lawyers were creating the storefront Parkdale Community Legal Services, and a block away, South Parkdale Health Centre was being organized by equally activist health care workers. A Parkdale Tenants Association had formed. The revival of the Parkdale Business Men's Association was being supported by the recently revived South Parkdale Ratepayers' Association (now called the Residents Association, in tacit acceptance of the predominance of renters within the neighbourhood; *Parkdale Citizen,* September 1971). As it had been during its development, Parkdale was in the news on a daily basis. Parkdalians were reinventing a strong identity for the neighbourhood. But there were also hints of splits within this new community consensus: Mayor William Dennison had called Reverend Graham Cotter, chair of the Community Coalition, a "Marxist" at an October 1970 meeting at which a $6,000 municipal grant was refused. An attempt to set up a youth drop-in on Queen Street had foundered when local businesspeople made clear that they would prefer a vacant storefront to that particular use (*Globe and Mail,* 17 November 1970). As in every stage of the neighbourhood's history, identity would be forged through conflict.

While some groups within Parkdale were seeking to rebuild community spirit and tools for local control, outside institutions were visualizing the neighbourhood as part of a larger scheme of reform and control. In December 1969, the provincial government announced, as it did nearly every decade, that it was going to reform the Queen Street Mental Hospital (the former Provincial Lunatic Asylum). It hoped that the hospital would become a visiting clinic by 1973, rather than a place of permanent confinement for over six hundred people. A major renovation would take care of problems like fifty women in a ward sharing four toilet stalls with no doors on them, and patients sleeping in open wards with no privacy (*Globe and Mail*, 2 December 1969). This time, the changes took place. By 1976, Toronto-area psychiatric institutions had fewer than one-third of the beds than had existed in the early 1960s. Most of the twelve thousand patients discharged from institutions in southern Ontario found accommodations in rooming houses in central Toronto, over half of which were located in Parkdale (Dear and Wolch 1987, 97-108). There, many experienced inhumane conditions similar to those they had suffered in institutions: a dozen people sharing a bathroom without locks or towels, and three or four people sharing a room without a lock or even a private drawer (Capponi 1992). Increasingly hostile and well-organized neighbours were determined to eliminate even these substandard housing options, or any other housing alternative for the deinstitutionalized. Parkdale, supposedly in the process of "becoming a serious slum" since the 1930s, began to attract the rhetoric of an urban ghetto in which exclusion was measured not by race (as in US cities) but by dependence on social services (Dear and Wolch 1987). A "clash in values" was described by one reporter, with "houses, well kept by frugal immigrants who moved there 20 years ago" next to "decrepit apartment buildings," filled with "boisterous welfare recipients, drunks, and drug addicts" (*Globe and Mail*, 7 April 1972). Parkdale, once again, seemed to be getting out of control and in need of government intervention. And once again, Parkdale was hardly unique: Mele (2000b), Smith (1996), and Miller (2001) all describe how the highly charged language of "pathology" and "blight" drawn from an earlier generation of slum literature was reapplied to justify government intervention in US cities in the late 1960s and 1970s.

At this time, Parkdale began to develop a dual identity. A 1997 *Toronto Star* article spoke of the "bowery to bohemia" conversion that Parkdale had undergone in the last thirty years, but a more accurate description might be the conversion of the neighbourhood to a place where bowery *and* bohemia coexisted, a world of extreme poverty and powerlessness next to a world of individual and community creativity. In its formative years, Parkdale had had a strong identity as a model community of homeowners. It was the cutting edge of a suburban movement in which the values of middle-class wives and daughters would predominate. From the 1910s onwards, Parkdale began to be seen as a cautionary tale of decline. It was a community where difference in the form of woman-led households and non-British migrants was constructed as problematic. In the 1970s, Parkdale developed a third strong identity. It was the focus of a new generation of slum literature. At the same time, it was a battleground for neighbourhood control, a place that was fighting to regain a lost identity. One hundred years after Parkdale was incorporated as a village, it began to be spoken of as a village again. The nature of this special place was hotly contested, particularly with regard to who would be included and excluded in this newly empowered urban village.

## The Context for Change:
## Social Conditions in the 1950s and 1960s

In 1962, the *Parkdale Pictorial,* a community newspaper, bemoaned changes in South Parkdale. Before World War One, it claimed, Parkdale had been "a town unto itself," but "people moved on to North Toronto and Forest Hill Village." Now the neighbourhood had "a lot of dust" from new construction. But comparing the newspaper's advertisements with those in a community newspaper from forty years earlier (*Parkdale Topics,* June 1923), the overwhelming sense is of continuity rather than change. Hay's Men's Wear, the Kum-C Movie theatre, and Loblaw's Supermarket were among the many businesses that had not changed location since the 1920s, according to their advertisements in both newspapers. Dr. Stanley Haidasz, the Liberal candidate for the Parkdale-High Park provincial riding, bragged that his father had worked for the CPR for forty years and bought his home after seventeen years of hard savings, a common enough tale for Parkdale (*Parkdale Pictorial,* 11 April 1962). A 1961 report on ethnic origins in Toronto placed Parkdale in the lowest category for change, and furthermore added that the Germans, Poles, and Ukrainians who made up the predominant non-Anglo-Celtic immigrant groups were "minglers" rather than "displacers" (CTPB 1961).

The 1951 census is the first to use census tracts small enough to compare Parkdale with the rest of Metropolitan Toronto. In 1951, the social and economic conditions of the neighbourhood were average for the census metropolitan area, although Parkdale was more densely populated than the rest of Toronto. Despite the recent arrival of Eastern Europeans (Polish and Ukrainian immigrants each accounted for 6 percent of Parkdale's population), Parkdale's twenty-eight thousand residents were still overwhelmingly of British origin: 73 percent in both the neighbourhood and metropolitan Toronto. The proportion of those with a grade eight education or less was 42 percent in Parkdale and 41 percent in metropolitan Toronto. Occupational classifications, by and large, mirrored those of the greater city, and median household income was only slightly lower than the metropolitan Toronto average (Figures 4.1 and 4.2). Forty percent of the area's occupied dwellings were apartments or flats, double the rate for the rest of metropolitan Toronto. A little over half of the households in Parkdale owned their own homes, as compared with 71 per cent of metropolitan Toronto (see Figure 3.1). Parkdale's residents were slightly more stable than those in the rest of the city: 55 percent had lived in their homes for five or more years, as opposed to 49 percent for the rest of Toronto.

By the 1961 census, greater Toronto had begun to change, and Parkdale was once again at the forefront of change. The population of the City of Toronto was now, for the first time, a minority within the census metropolitan

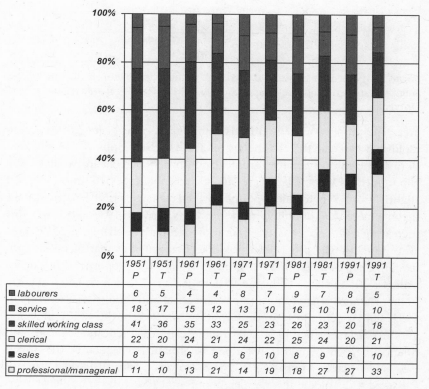

|  | 1951 P | 1951 T | 1961 P | 1961 T | 1971 P | 1971 T | 1981 P | 1981 T | 1991 P | 1991 T |  |
|---|---|---|---|---|---|---|---|---|---|---|---|
| ■ labourers | 6 | 5 | 4 | 4 | 8 | 7 | 9 | 7 | 8 | 5 |  |
| ■ service | 18 | 17 | 15 | 12 | 13 | 10 | 16 | 10 | 16 | 10 |  |
| ■ skilled working class | 41 | 36 | 35 | 33 | 25 | 23 | 26 | 23 | 20 | 18 |  |
| ☐ clerical | 22 | 20 | 24 | 21 | 24 | 22 | 25 | 24 | 20 | 21 |  |
| ■ sales | 8 | 9 | 6 | 8 | 6 | 10 | 8 | 9 | 6 | 10 |  |
| ☐ professional/managerial | 11 | 10 | 13 | 21 | 14 | 19 | 18 | 27 | 27 | 33 |  |

*Figure 4.1.* Occupational classification, Parkdale and Toronto, 1951-1991
*Note:* Figures for 2001 are not included because occupational classifications changed radically in the 2001 census. Toronto data are for the census metropolitan area.
*Source:* Census of Canada. Graph courtesy of Ric Hamilton, McMaster University.

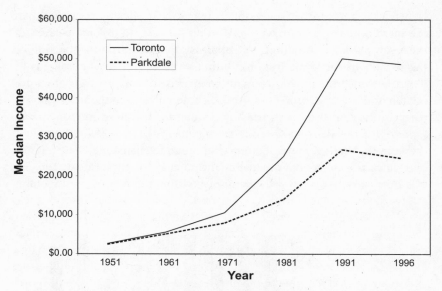

*Figure 4.1.* Median household income, Parkdale and Toronto, 1951-1996.
*Source:* Census of Canada. Graph courtesy of Ric Hamilton, McMaster
University

area. The proportion of non-British immigrants had begun to rise, more
rapidly in Parkdale than in the rest of Toronto. Now only 61 percent were
of British origin in greater Toronto, and only 55 percent in Parkdale. The
gap in median income between Parkdale and the rest of Toronto increased
slightly from 7 percentage points to 9 percentage points, with median
income more than doubling in the ten years between 1951 and 1961. This
increasing affluence was the result of occupation change among most
Torontonians. The proportion of workers classified as managerial or professional had doubled in 1961 from 1951, and the proportion considered
skilled working class had begun to decline. Parkdale, which had a slightly
higher-than-average proportion of managerial and professional workers in
1951, fell far behind the Toronto average by 1961. In the 1950s and early
1960s, the emergence of a new middle class of intellectual, social, and
financial leaders, which transformed neighbourhoods such as the Annex
(see below), largely bypassed Parkdale. However, South Parkdale was still
classified as a middle-income neighbourhood (the third quintile of average family income), with North Parkdale slightly poorer, in the fourth
quintile (Bourne 1967, figure 25, 87). Parkdale was less British, with fewer
middle-class people, than the rest of the Toronto metropolitan area.

The most significant changes between 1951 and 1961 were in housing
stock. Three-fifths of the dwelling units in Parkdale (90 percent south of

Queen Street) were apartments or flats by 1961, as opposed to a little over one-quarter in the rest of Toronto. And only one-third of Parkdale households owned their dwellings, as opposed to two-thirds in the rest of Toronto. As in the late 1930s and during World War Two, Parkdale could now be characterized as a community of tenants, and, as in that earlier era, there was an increasing number of absentee landlords. Unlike 1951, when Parkdale was above average for housing stability, in 1961, fewer than a third of Parkdalians had lived in their homes for five years or more, half the average for the census metropolitan area. Finally, there were significant differences in access to home financing between Parkdale and the rest of Toronto. Whereas 43 percent of Parkdale owner/occupiers reported a mortgage in the 1951 census, as compared to a metropolitan Toronto average of 57 percent, only 15 percent reported a mortgage in 1961, as opposed to the Toronto average of 51 percent (note: the six-block sample in Figure 3.7 does not reflect a similar decline, perhaps because of the large number of apartment buildings on Dowling and commercial buildings on Queen Street). While some of the difference could be attributable to short-term mortgages being retired by the post-World War Two influx of Parkdale homebuyers, the substantial gap does suggest some reluctance by both individual and institutional investors to put their money in Parkdale houses.

The changes between 1951 and 1961 do not support the argument, seen in planning documents and newspapers from the 1970s onwards, that Parkdale underwent sudden and precipitous decline in both public perceptions and social conditions in the mid-1950s, after eight decades of stability. As discussed in the previous chapter, the discourse of decline had been in place for four decades, and stability had never been the norm. Unlike earlier definitions of decline, based on housing type, the definition of decline from the 1960s onwards was measured in increasing poverty and decreasing community spirit. The causative factors of this decline, according to community organizations in the 1970s and 1980s, were the construction of the Gardiner Expressway and the high-rise apartment canyons of South Parkdale. The motor of decline was therefore assumed to be municipal urban planning decisions, such as zoning that allowed wholesale destruction of the historical housing stock.

Yet the first residents of the high-rise apartments in South Parkdale were not significantly different from the residents of low-rise apartments and houses in Parkdale in terms of income or occupation, and other neighbourhoods with high-rise apartments constructed in the 1950s and 1960s, such as Yonge-Eglinton, Yonge-St. Clair, and the Annex, did not go on to be called ghettoes. In 1961, when the average greater Toronto salary was $3,673, a little under one in five Parkdalians earned less than $2,000 annually (i.e., were designated "poor" by the census), the same proportion as the rest of Toronto. Parkdale may have had fewer middle-class residents than average, but it was by no means a community of poor people. A stronger argument can be made that the large landlords in Parkdale, who gradually began to provide cheap but nasty accommodation choices, eventually determined the social composition of the neighbourhood. The poor municipal decision making that led to "slum conditions" in Parkdale relates more to city inaction in the face of increasingly poor accommodation provided by the private sector than to allowing the construction of high-rise apartments and the continuation of multi-unit conversions. Providing more affordable housing elsewhere in Toronto, and enforcing housing standards within Parkdale, could have prevented the area from experiencing the first real decline in housing conditions in its history.

A 1967 report on Toronto, *Private Redevelopment of the Central City,* reinforces the contention that social conditions did not substantially change in Parkdale until the late 1960s and early 1970s. Using 1961 census figures, the report shows areas of poverty and affluence in Toronto. The census tracts immediately adjacent to the central business district, constituting the classic "zone of transition," are where most of the lowest quintile of family income is found (under $4,000 per year). North Parkdale, along with most "middle neighbourhoods" in terms of distance from the central city, is in the second-lowest quintile of income, between $4,000 and $5,000. South Parkdale, along with neighbourhoods to the north of High Park, east towards the Beaches, and in the Annex, is in the middle band of $5,000 to $6,000, while North Toronto is where most high-income tracts are found (Bourne 1967, figure 15, 87). South Parkdale, however, is noted in this report as the first neighbourhood outside the downtown area where widespread apartment construction occurred after World War Two, and the neighbourhood where the most substantial redevelopment had taken place. Forty-eight postwar apartment buildings were counted in South Parkdale, many more than in the other clusters: the Yonge-St. Clair area had thirty-eight properties, Yonge-Eglinton twenty-eight, the Annex twenty-five, the Beaches fifteen, Rosedale twelve, and upper Jarvis Street twelve (Bourne 1967, figure 28, 125). As in the apartment boom of 1912-1915, apartment construction in the 1950s and 1960s had been concentrated in middle-income areas, not in poor districts (Ley 1996, 239). But nowhere else, with the possible exception of Jarvis Street in downtown Toronto, would these apartments be as poorly maintained as in South Parkdale.

Significant economic differences between Parkdale and the rest of Toronto began to show up in the 1971 census. Median income in Parkdale was now 25 percent lower than the median income in greater Toronto. One in three Parkdalians earned less than half the average wage, twice the poverty rate of the rest of Toronto. Fewer than half of Parkdalians were now of British origin, indicating a growing importance as an immigrant reception area. The average rent in Parkdale was 12 percent cheaper than in the rest of Toronto (Census of Canada 1971). After six decades of record keeping, public health statistics began to diverge in the Parkdale public health district (i.e., all of west-central Toronto) only in the late 1960s. By 1970, the tuberculosis rate, often an indicator of poor housing conditions, was two and a half times the City of Toronto average (City of Toronto Public Health Department Annual Report 1970).

M.T. Kelly's autobiographical play *The Green Dolphin* (1982) describes Parkdale in the mid-1960s as "a paprika-reeking slum" of lower-income immigrants. Although the teenagers in the play are of Irish and Ukrainian heritage, they affect a "wannabe" look based on African American stereotypes, an "apprentice pimp" outfit of stovepipe pants, silk shirts, wool suits, and carved umbrellas. They listen to rhythm and blues music on Buffalo radio stations at their hangout, the Green Dolphin Restaurant, instead of attending Parkdale Collegiate. They sniff glue, drink cheap booze, flunk high school, and fancy themselves tough. A 1971 newspaper article on political changes within Parkdale described the southern portion of the riding as consisting of three-storey brick homes betraying their "past Anglo-Saxon prosperity. They're rooming houses now. Lunch bucket country." Moving north, the reporter found "smaller homes, rows of verandahs reminiscent of summer screen door bang, over-railing voices in English and Scottish accents. Now vivid colours, potted plants, foreign tongues" (*Telegram,* 6 June 1971). From some perspectives, Parkdale seemed to have fulfilled the Bruce Report prediction and become a slum dominated by new migrants. From other perspectives, Parkdale still seemed monocultural and exclusive: Mary Reid, when she immigrated in 1970 from Jamaica, thought that Parkdale was "a posh area, the rich lived here, you could not buy a house here" (interviewed in Parkdale Collegiate Institute 1996, 30).

## The Turning Point of 1967-1972:
## The Parkdale Community Coalition

Pierre Filion describes the international shift from modern to postmodern planning that began to occur in Toronto by the beginning of the 1960s. Ambitious modernist infrastructure programs had been pursued in the immediate postwar period, to coordinate industrial economic growth and provide a built environment suited to mass production and consumption. The Gardiner Expressway, along with the north-south Don Valley Parkway and Highway 401 running to the north of the city, helped disperse the city's population into "low density residential sectors offering households plentiful room to accumulate mass produced goods" (Filion 1999, 424). Then, in the shift towards postmodernism in the 1960s and 1970s, and as Warren Magnusson also describes, a new urban political reform movement based in central cities arose throughout North America. Concerns about destruction of urban heritage and increasing noise and traffic congestion in the central city, along with the desire to redefine and improve "neighbourhood character," led to a reconception of the role of urban planning (Magnusson 1983a, 33).

Toronto planners were slowly beginning to respond to this paradigm change among central city dwellers and their revived residential organizations. A 1960 City of Toronto Planning Board response to Metro's Urban Renewal Strategy stressed that "slum clearance will be increasingly seen as an element in urban renewal rather than an end in itself." In addition to "clearance of blighted properties and non-conforming uses," local planners wanted to improve roads, increase parks and recreation services, and beautify commercial streets (CTPB 1960).

A critical testing point for this shift from "urban renewal" to "urban revitalization" had been the Downtown Area Review and Plan for the Annex, the first of a series of neighbourhood planning exercises promised in the 1959 City of Toronto Official Plan. Even though the 1959 document was considered by the planning department to be a compromise with the newly unified Annex Residents' Association, with most buildings judged "sound and suitable" for family housing and the majority of the district zoned R2, the association was not pleased with the plan. It began a twelve-year campaign of opposition to new apartment buildings that resulted in several positive Ontario Municipal Board judgements, as well as successful opposition to the proposed Spadina and Crosstown Expressways. The leaders in the fight for a more liveable neighbourhood were professors living near the University of Toronto campus, social service workers, and people working in arts and media, exemplified by the Annex's two most famous residents: urbanist guru Jane Jacobs, and novelist, poet, and essayist Margaret Atwood (CTPB 1959a; Lemon 1986, 26-27).

The seventy-year era of unbroken political consensus in Toronto, which Harold Kaplan dates from the reform of civic government in the 1890s, was beginning to unravel. The City of Toronto had combined an activist local government, which municipalized hydro power and mass transit by 1920, with a relatively laissez-faire attitude towards developers. Occasional blazes of "Toronto the Good" moral fervour, such as the anti-apartment-building bylaw of 1913, were soon undone by the realpolitik of "old fashioned, pressure-group, oiling the squeakiest wheel politics," which meant that more affluent neighbourhoods successfully opposed most non-single-family-home development, while less affluent neighbourhoods got what developers wanted. An urban reform coalition consisting of organized labour, the Association of Women Electors, University of Toronto, the Board of Trade, the Bureau of Municipal Research, and the *Globe and Mail* achieved a relatively professional and uncorrupt municipal government, at least in comparison to other local governments of the time, throughout the first half of the twentieth century, but public discontent, led by a growing number of "anti-car, pro-neighbourhood, neo-reform" populists, was about to change the face of local politics (Kaplan 1982, 618-19, 656).

The new reform movement had begun with opposition to change in the middle-class and politically engaged Annex. By 1966, it was spreading to the more working-class neighbourhood of Trefann Court. There, late-nineteenth-century houses were going to be torn down for public housing, as had already occurred in much of east-central Toronto. North and South Regent Park, the first generation of public housing developed adjacent to Trefann Court, had been joined by three other large public housing projects: Moss Park and Don Mount east of downtown and Alexandra Park west of downtown. In contrast, Parkdale did not see much public housing development in the late 1950s and early 1960s, with the exception of a four-hundred-unit seniors' building that replaced the Magdalen Asylum. However, publicly subsidized private redevelopment was rapidly changing the neighbourhood, as it had the east downtown neighbourhood of St. James Town. In Trefann Court, residents organized by a young activist lawyer, John Sewell, achieved the first major victory for a neighbourhood that was not predominantly middle class. Instead of suffering the destruction of the housing stock and dispersal of the community, residents won money for a tenant-run non-profit co-operative that would rehabilitate much of the existing housing (Kaplan 1982, 647-56; Fraser 1972).

In 1967, the city's Official Plan proposals declared, "We must preserve and enhance the best of our older low density districts," illustrated with a photograph of the Annex. A study co-funded by the City of Toronto Planning Board and the federal Central Mortgage and Housing Corporation had concluded that housing rehabilitation should be supported through government funding mechanisms, a solution supported by the Social Planning Council (which included representatives from Parkdale social service agencies) in its response to the Official Plan proposals (CTPB 1966; 1967a, 8; 1967b, 87). The federal government shut off its subsidies for urban renewal and widespread destruction of the central city housing stock, and began to fund community organizers in neighbourhoods threatened by redevelopment (Magnusson 1983b, 114). Albert Rose describes such citizens' organizations as a new force, combining the neighbourhood focus of the older ratepayers' associations with the urban reform urges of previous charitable organizations like the Bureau of Municipal Research (1972, 169).

The paradigm shift was not yet evident in South Parkdale, where a Downtown Area Review and Plan was released in 1967. As in the case of the Annex, the Planning Department believed it was offering a compromise to the community. The area west of Jameson would be "stabilized," or protected from further apartment redevelopment, in exchange for additional high-rises in southeast Parkdale. The document argued that Parkdale could easily accommodate double the five thousand apartment units that had been constructed in the previous ten years, since transportation, water, and sewer infrastructure was good. The majority of houses remaining in southeast Parkdale, where development in the neighbourhood had first occurred, were over seventy years old and were of "declining suitability" due to the proximity of existing apartment buildings. In fact, although the properties were generally well maintained, "major repairs have not been extensive because of the uncertainty of the area's future redevelopment." Furthermore, the large volume of traffic on Queen, King, and Jameson, leading to the Gardiner Expressway, could be relieved by upgrading Dufferin Street as a regional connector road.

At least one apartment developer, Philip Roth of Meridian, who had bought nearly a dozen properties west of Jameson at Springhurst and Dowling, on the assumption that he would be able to create an apartment complex, was not amused. He argued for an extension of the high-density area westwards (CTPB 1967b, 33). Moreover, although the newly revived South Parkdale Residents Association considered the draft plan's zoning a workable compromise (while opposing the expansion of Dufferin Street as an arterial road), 220 other residents immediately gathered at a public meeting to protest the "land grab spectre" (*Globe and Mail*, 29 November 1967). It took five more years and dozens of public meetings, but South Parkdale finally began a new, resident-led process for a neighbourhood plan in 1973 (CTPB 1976b).

Kaplan, wrongly I think, suggests that the 1967 South Parkdale neighbourhood plan was the cause of massive private redevelopment. He says that both the Beaches and South Parkdale were slated for substantial apartment construction, yet "for some reason, apartment developers ignored the Beaches area but invaded Parkdale in full force. Parkdale residents fought back in each case, but they were too socially heterogeneous, poorly educated, and poorly organized to mount a countervailing campaign"

(Kaplan 1982, 677). I would argue that the opposite is true. The reaction to the 1967 draft neighbourhood plan (never adopted by City Council) marks the end of twelve years of high-rise urban renewal in Parkdale. Planning documents and assessment records show that the majority of high-rise apartments were constructed or approved before 1967. It is true that the Annex and Rosedale, described by Kaplan as "two relatively affluent areas lying close to the central core ... in contrast to Parkdale ... had well-organized, articulate ratepayers associations" (677), but it is also true that increasingly heterogeneous Parkdale was spurred by massive redevelopment to organize its own urban political movement.

Neighbourhood activism in Parkdale during the late 1960s grew out of two separate issues. The first was an attempt to preserve the neighbourhood's older housing stock and to renew the sense of the community as a special place. The second was a concern for the growing number of poor people living in the neighbourhood. At first, these two issues were linked: uncontrolled apartment construction was destroying affordable housing. Stabilizing the neighbourhood would benefit both those living in inexpensive rooming houses and flats, and the small but growing number of those interested in renovating older houses.

Howard Walker, a well-known architect and president of the revitalized South Parkdale Residents Association, was a key figure in late 1960s community activism. The SPRA's concerns included declining business along Queen Street, heavy car and truck traffic in the neighbourhood, and the uncertain future of Parkdale's older houses. Under Walker's leadership, the SPRA successfully pursued several short-term goals, such as banning truck traffic on Jameson and getting trees planted along that avenue, while pursuing a longer-term neighbourhood preservation plan that would be coupled with promotion of the neighbourhood's fine houses and "elite" history. By 1970, an alderman, Archie Chisholm, had been elected based on his involvement with the SPRA and the local chapter of the New Democratic Party. Like Walker, he espoused a "new community spirit" based on "issues" rather than "politics" (*Globe and Mail,* 17 November 1970; *Real Estate News,* November 1973).

A more radical approach was championed by two religious community leaders. Reverend G.R. Evans was the minister at the Parkdale United Church. When constructed in 1889, the church had been described as, "after the [downtown] Metropolitan Church, the finest structure for worship in the city" (Champion 1899, 246). By 1967, the "monstrous Victorian Cathedral," designed for 1,500 parishioners, served a congregation of less than 250, and Reverend Evans was attempting to give the land to the city or metropolitan government for a low-income singles housing development, to be called Phoenix Place. Although the city was happy to approve the twenty-three-storey Lakeshore Place one block to the south two years later, both levels of government agreed that an apartment building made up of single-room-occupancy units did not meet the building code, which specified a minimum standard for new units of 750 square feet. Evans retorted that "the building codes in the City are just as Victorian and outmoded as this cathedral" and that it was better to spend money on housing now than on penal institutions later (*Toronto Star*, 18 May 1967).

Reverend Graham Cotter was the priest at St. Mark's Anglican Church, and the leader of a movement to unite community agencies, religious institutions, and residents. The movement began with the re-establishment of the Parkdale Library, at the corner of Queen and Cowan Avenues, in 1964. The dynamic head librarian, Rita Cox, a recent immigrant from the Caribbean, ensured that books in sixty languages were available to the increasingly diverse Parkdale residents, and the library also offered ESL courses within the year (*Globe and Mail*, 22 October 1964; *Toronto Star*, 27 April 1965). The library became a gathering place for those interested in organizing the neighbourhood and was Parkdale's first publicly owned community centre since its days as an independent municipality. In 1965, Cotter and several other religious leaders were approached by Peter Loebel, a community organizer hired through the Parks and Recreation Department, to take part in a social planning study that would address recreation and other community services. Cotter said later (1978) that he had constantly "been challenged by the head of the SPRA" (identified as Gordon Thatcher, not Howard Walker) because of his position that middle-class residents must help their lower-income neighbours before they helped themselves.

Although he disagreed with the SPRA on strategy, Cotter and the SPRA shared a common vision of Parkdale's history. For Walker, Parkdale was a neighbourhood of fine houses and former wealth, which could still attain some of that past glory (*Real Estate News*, November 1973). According to Cotter, Parkdale had been intended as a commuter suburb of villas, a mix of prosperous merchants and holders of large estates who sought escape from a central city that was "going down." Meanwhile, "poor people did not live in early Parkdale, but were imported to work here." As "not so prosperous" people moved in, middle-class people moved out, "a function of the market system, but what of love of 'strangers'?" For Cotter, Parkdale's "recurrent pattern from the past" was of middle-class people moving outward to avoid rather than help the poor people in their midst. Cotter thus combined concentric zone theory with a passion for social justice, sounding very much as though he had read David Harvey's *Social Justice and the*

*City* (1973) before writing his memoir in 1978. But unlike Harvey's, and belying his reputation as a Marxist, Cotter's solutions were liberal rather than radical: in order for Parkdale to "come up again," it must recognize its strength in diversity and provide adequate housing and services for the poor. For Cotter, as for many other left-wing residents of Parkdale, the growing number of rooming houses, and the new self-contained single-room-occupancy apartments known as bachelorettes, were degrading and polarizing housing options, a dragon to be slain rather than viable elements in the housing mix. If bachelorettes and further rooming houses were made illegal and new apartment development stopped, then houses would once again "come on market at reasonable rates," family housing would become "stable," and the community could begin to rebuild (Cotter 1978). Cotter's perspective was shared by many North American neighbourhood activists in the early 1970s, who thought that privately owned high-rises would obliterate low-cost housing and replace it with more expensive housing. At this point, they did not realize that high-rise housing in places like Parkdale would become one of the few sources of new low-cost housing stock for poor families as well as singles, and that houses in gentrifying neighbourhoods would soon be unaffordable to the lower middle class (Caulfield 1994, 9-10).

Despite differences in strategy and outlook, the SPRA was able to work with the Social Planning Council, the West End branch of the YMCA, the Toronto Public Library and the two Protestant congregations to come up with a funding proposal in 1970 that included a part-time community worker to build links between agencies and a community newspaper. Their stated priorities were to organize "failing businesses," address "inadequate recreation" for youth, and stabilize the "shifting population." But despite the consensus approach, the Parkdale Community Coalition was attacked by some politicians for "excluding" the local police division, the Boulevard Club (an exclusive recreation club on the waterfront that was among the few buildings to survive the Gardiner Expressway's construction), and the area's three Catholic churches (*Toronto Star*, 9 October 1970). Of the three omissions, the most serious was the Catholic leadership. Catholic churches were by far the most active congregations in Parkdale by this time, and each of the congregations served as the central rallying point for a separate immigrant group. St. Stanislaus on Roncesvalles, the newest church, had served the Polish community since 1946. Holy Family, at the corner of King and Close since 1902, served a growing Filipino immigrant populace. St. Helen's, the former Brockton Catholic Church dating from the 1870s, had shifted to Portuguese-language services.

In 1971, the coalition received funding from both the city and the federal government, and it launched the *Parkdale Citizen* in September. The monthly newspaper combined articles on local history, to help instill a sense of community, with updates on new social services. By 1972, these services included a tenants' association, legal services, a community health centre, a single parents' group, a community information post housed in the Parkdale Library, the Atlantic Centre (a drop-in service for the large number of young single men who had recently migrated from the Atlantic provinces to Parkdale), and a joint project by George Brown College and the Queen Street Mental Health Centre to provide job counselling and training for "long term mental patients," who were also beginning to live in Parkdale in growing numbers.[1]

The *Citizen* took a strong editorial stance against any new high-rise construction, supporting a North Parkdale group that, with the help of Parkdale Community Legal Services, successfully fought to obtain a park instead of an apartment building on Lansdowne Avenue (*Parkdale Citizen*, October 1971; *Toronto Star*, 22 November 1971). The paper also began to advocate for a city-run recreation centre in the building originally constructed as the Parkdale Roller Skating Rink, later the Pavlowa Dance Hall and the John Inglis Recreation Club, and most recently the Jan Masaryk Centre, serving Czech immigrants.

The Community Coalition was not proceeding without challenges. In Toronto at the time, the two top candidates in each ward at municipal elections served as junior and senior aldermen. The latter also sat on Metro Council. There was a tradition of the two politicians being opposed (Kaplan 1982, 623), and Parkdale, by now part of Ward 2, was no exception. While Archie Chisholm, the junior alderman, came out of the SPRA and the resurgent reform movement, Senior Alderman Ben Grys was part of an older pro-development faction. He helped organize a parallel Ward Two Property Owner's Association that by early 1972 was calling for a police investigation of the coalition's dispersal of funds (*Toronto Sun*, 9 February 1972). At a raucous public meeting held at the end of February, the coalition was defeated in an attempt to obtain community input into the selection of a new principal for Parkdale Collegiate Institute. One resident, a former refugee from Eastern Europe, declared that the coalition was "a small group of newcomers ... [pursuing] a total program to gain control of all social services in the area. In Europe, they do this with armies; here they do it with the taxpayer's money" (*Community Schools*, March 1972; see also *Toronto Star*, 21 February 1972). Almost immediately after this debacle, a temporary youth centre run by the YMCA within Parkdale Collegiate was closed down after allegations that staff were not adequately controlling "glue sniffers" (*Toronto Star*, 9 June 1972).

Despite political and financial setbacks, the Community Coalition continued to attempt consensual reform politics within Parkdale. In 1973, organizations involved in developing the new community centre included police, Catholic Children's Aid, Catholic Lay Advocates, two new groups – Parkdale Home Renovators and an information centre for West Indians run out of St. Mark's Church – as well as the previous combination of Protestant religious organizations, residents' and business associations, and social services. But in February 1976, when the Masaryk-Cowan Community Recreation Centre opened, Grys' successor as senior alderman, Tony O'Donahue, was successful in overturning the election of the centre's first board, which residents called "Commies," in favour of a slate of conservative ratepayers (*Toronto Star,* 6 February 1976). By then, the Community Coalition was in disarray, its once consensual politics undermined by the battle that dominated Parkdale's tenth decade, the drive to ban bachelorette (single-room-occupancy) apartments.

## Housing Policy and Social Change

The consensual reform politics of Parkdale in the 1964-1973 period reflected larger political changes within the City of Toronto, which in turn stemmed from postwar urban economic and social transformations. From the end of the war, industrial employment began to decline while service, professional, and managerial jobs soared. According to the 1951 census, over 150,000 workers were employed by almost four thousand manufacturing firms within the central city. By 1971, the number of industrial workers and firms was halved, and by 1981, there was a further 28 percent decline in the industrial workforce. The Gutta Percha Rubber Company, whose opening and closing whistles at 8 a.m. and 5 p.m. helped keep time throughout the neighbourhood,[2] closed in 1960, followed by the local sheet metal, radiator, and furniture factories. The closures of the Massey-Ferguson and Inglis plants east of Parkdale by the early 1990s finally severed the neighbourhood's link with its industrial past. Meanwhile, the value of shares sold on the Toronto Stock Exchange increased from $2.1 billion in 1963 to $83.5 billion in 1990. By 1985, professional, managerial, and service occupations accounted for three-quarters of Toronto's employment (Caulfield 1994, 76-82).

These economic changes affected urban form, producing soaring land prices in the central business district and a new series of office towers. The growth in affluent white-collar workers led to a boom in central city restaurants and boutiques, and increasing interest in downtown living. The growing numbers of young people in the 1960s, products of the postwar baby boom, were delaying marriage, yet seeking (and able to afford) living space independent from their parents and close to downtown. They formed the demographic group most open to gentrification in Toronto. They were also the group most likely to support reform politics (Caulfield 1994).

The emergence of a strong citizen-led reform movement was institutionalized in local politics by the 1969 municipal elections, in which a number of activists were elected, including John Sewell, who had risen to prominence during the Trefann Court debate (Magnusson 1983b, 118). The 1972 municipal elections, which resulted in a reform majority on council and the election of moderate reformer David Crombie as mayor, brought together two potentially contradictory visions of urban reform, according to Jon Caulfield. One vision, exemplified by Crombie, was a new version of classic slow-growth politics, which feared that apartment redevelopment was occurring too quickly, developers were out of control, and the built form of the city needed to be preserved against the depredations of those out for a quick buck. A second vision, held by Sewell (who was elected mayor in 1978) was associated with left-populism. These so-called radicals on City Council combined planning concerns with a commitment to preserve low-income housing and industrial jobs in the central city. The second group was more likely to support paid community organizers, such as those requested by the Parkdale Community Coalition. There were, at this point, more grounds for political agreement than disagreement among the reform majority, just as at the neighbourhood level in Parkdale. For the moment, four quite disparate groups – the slow-growth advocates of the city's traditional elite in North Toronto, a new generation of urban activists influenced by Jane Jacobs, bohemians living in the countercultural hangouts of Yorkville, Church-Wellesley (by the early 1970s, Toronto's "gay ghetto"), and Queen Street West, and "townhousers" or "white-painters" (early 1970s terms for gentrifiers) – could together create a new plan for Toronto (Caulfield 1994, 61-75).

This consensus vision for Toronto surfaced in a 1973 document prepared for Toronto's newly formed Housing Department called *Living Room: An Approach to Home Banking and Land Banking for the City of Toronto.* According to *Living Room,* local government's previous concern with "the regulation of the quality of new housing produced and the policing of the existing stock to prevent the spillover of 'blight' to surrounding neighbourhoods with sound housing stock" needed to be replaced with a program that would build four thousand affordable housing units per year in the central city. An activist housing policy was needed to counteract "white-painting" (an early term for gentrification), which was transferring a thousand houses annually from low- and moderate-income households to middle- and upper-income ones. The program would not be driven by holding the invisible hand of the private development market, nor by large-scale public housing projects that stigmatized inhabitants. Rather, a range of smaller-scale housing initiatives were proposed to ensure that fully half of all new units created in the central city were affordable, with a high proportion of social housing (owned by government and non-profit organizations) and a significant amount of supportive housing (social housing with on-site staff and services, for people with psychiatric, physical, or intellectual disabilities). The programs included the encouragement of community-based non-profit housing companies, municipal "land banking" of all forms of housing ("older apartments, duplexes, townhouses and single-family buildings") in neighbourhoods where house prices were increasing rapidly, and use of most publicly owned land for new affordable housing construction. The report claimed that the federal government was "no longer prepared to rely simply on old houses 'filtering down' to low and moderate income families, in the same way as used cars do. It has stated that social housing is a right" (City of Toronto Housing Review Committee 1973, ii, 3, 8, 18, 33). The City of Toronto, in collaboration with other levels of government, should therefore act to make affordable housing an attainable right for all its citizens.

In the early 1970s, after federal government limited-dividend mortgages were extended to non-profit organizations and municipalities (Bacher 1993, 208), Parkdale saw a boom in social housing development. The John Bruce Co-operative renovated two low-rise apartment buildings on Elm Grove, while the Dufferin Grove Co-op bought two small apartment buildings and several houses in the vicinity of Melbourne Avenue. The new municipal public housing agency, Cityhome, purchased almost fifty houses in Parkdale from individual owners and large developers, renovating several for use by low-income families while maintaining others as rooming houses and flats pending eventual redevelopment into non-profit apartments. Beverley Lodge, a halfway house for young men who had been in trouble with the law, opened on Beaty Avenue in 1970, and Arrabon House, a boarding house run by nuns serving runaway girls, opened in 1973 on Wilson Park Road (*Evening Telegram*, 5 December 1970; *Toronto Star*, 27 October 1973). Churches and non-profit organizations also purchased houses in Parkdale. The provincial public housing program, still preferring massive public housing projects over small-scale infill, constructed a four-hundred-unit "tower in a parkette" on Dunn Avenue in 1974, the same year that Phoenix Place, the conversion of Parkdale United Church to 131 bachelorette units, was finally approved by City Council.

By 1975, Parkdale had twelve group homes: three serving children, two serving adolescents, five for psychiatric outpatients, one for seniors, and one for recovering alcoholics (CTPB 1976b, 60-61). There were also eleven privately operated nursing homes within Parkdale. Although these social housing initiatives accounted for less than 10 percent of Parkdale's total housing stock, there is no doubt that Parkdale was getting a dispropor-tionate share of some forms of social and supportive housing: one-third of the privately operated nursing homes in greater Toronto and five of the city's eleven group homes for psychiatric outpatients were in South Park-dale (CTPB 1974, 5). The problem was not that there was too much social housing in Parkdale, but that not enough supportive housing, social hous-ing, or indeed affordable housing was being built elsewhere. As early as 1954, a special bylaw had banned new rooming houses in Rosedale (CTPB 1954, 14). In the early 1970s, there were distance restrictions for room-ing houses and group homes in the Annex and Don Vale (*Toronto Star*, 5 August 1975; Lemon 1986, 29), and many other central city neighbour-hoods had been rezoned R1A, a designation that did not allow conver-sion into group homes or rooming houses.

Even where multiple occupancy was allowed, increasingly stringent standards made conversion of older houses into multiple units a bad investment, even as conversion to a single unit became more profitable to developers. The Ontario Building Code specified minimum sizes of 355 square feet for a rooming house unit and 750 (later 650) square feet for a legal apartment. One parking space was required for every three room-ing house tenants, and one parking space per legal apartment tenant. Every suburban municipality outside the City of Toronto had either an outright ban or extremely limited zoning (a few commercial streets only) for group homes, rooming houses, and even accessory units in single-family houses (*City Planning*, Winter 1979).

By 1980, Parkdale had lost 25 percent of its rental units in owner-occupied houses: 328 units north of Queen and 122 units south of Queen (City of Toronto Planning Department 1980). The 1986 evaluation of the *Living Room* policy gave a figure of 19,452 assisted housing units created by the City of Toronto, an impressive amount over thirteen years, if far short of the 4,000-unit annual goal set in 1973. At the same time, it estimated that over five thousand affordable housing units had been lost to luxury ren-ovation in the six years since 1980 alone, with the likelihood that at least as many had been lost in the late 1970s (City of Toronto Housing Work-ing Group 1986). But demand for low-cost units had increased even as supply decreased. Growing numbers of seniors, single mothers, people with disabilities living independently, and recent immigrants needed to be housed, as did the twelve thousand people who had been deinstitu-tionalized from psychiatric hospitals during the late 1960s and early 1970s.

In 1981, Ontario's health minister stated that "discharged psychiatric patients are independent citizens ... As private citizens, they can and do, choose to live where ever they choose." The promise of supportive housing had been forgotten, and 68 percent of recently discharged patients ended up in rooming houses or bachelorettes without social supports. Increasingly, Parkdale was one of the few places in the province where cheap small units and landlords willing to rent to discharged patients could be found (*Globe and Mail*, 13 March 1981, citing research for the Mayor's Task Force on Discharged Psychiatric Patients).

Land values rose rapidly throughout the central city. Caulfield (1994, 86) estimates that an "unremarkable" three- or four-bedroom house in central Toronto would have sold for $15,000 in the early 1950s, $25,000 in the early 1960s, $50,000 after the mid-1970s real estate boom, $100,000 after a second boom in the early 1980s, and $250,000 after still another boom in the late 1980s. Pressures were particularly acute within Parkdale. Large developers were continuing to pay high prices for properties, especially along streets where they had already been successful in building high-rise apartment buildings.

For instance, two sixty-year-old apartment buildings on Spencer Avenue, each with three units, had been converted to rooming houses in the early 1970s while the developer awaited permission to construct a new apartment house. Several families were living in the rooming houses, since children were not allowed in newer "adult-only" apartment buildings. Single men also lived there, renting on a weekly basis because they could not afford the first and last month's rent demanded by most apartment owners. Tensions were mounting between the occupants of these temporary rooming houses and neighbours who objected to the "filth and noise" emanating from the poorly maintained buildings. A fire had recently been started in one of the two "old decrepit garages filled with junk" behind the properties, and the body of a thirty-eight-year-old "hard drinking man" went undiscovered for several days after he died in one of the buildings. In April 1972, the developer had not paid the gas or electricity bills for the buildings, so there was no heat or power. The Parkdale Tenants Association was attempting to find new housing for the occupants, though without success. One neighbour, a Ukraine-born widow of a man who had worked in the nearby metal plating factory, was considering the developer's offer of $104,000 for her house (*Globe and Mail*, 7 April 1972). Soon after, Cityhome bought the rooming houses along with several other properties. It planned to renovate the properties while maintaining a mix of flats and rooming houses. Residents bitterly opposed the planned renovation and applauded the demolition of the properties in 1975, when the city decided it could no longer afford the renovations (*Globe and Mail*, 27 September 1973, 8 May 1975). The site was empty for twenty more years before it was redeveloped as non-profit housing.

Individual homebuyers, finally getting loans from banks and other institutional lenders (see Figure 3.7), were also fuelling house price inflation in Parkdale. One renovator, who worked as an estimator, according to the 1971 assessment rolls, bought a house on Gwynne Avenue for $8,043, fully covered by a vendor mortgage, in 1970. By 1975, he had borrowed a total of $28,000 based on the value of the property, including a $7,500 loan from the Ontario Home Renewal Program. A house on Galley that had sold for a $5,000 vendor mortgage in 1968 received a $25,600 second mortgage from an investment company five years later. A store on Queen Street, with two apartments above, sold for a $21,000 vendor mortgage in 1969, then was resold for a $70,000 mortgage, covered by the Toronto-Dominion Bank, in 1978 (Land Registry Records). These price increases of between 300 and 500 percent in less than a decade were reminiscent of the boom-town flavour of Parkdale in the 1880s.

As the city began to fall behind in its ambitious social housing targets, the population living within rooming houses started to change. A 1974 study on rooming houses counted 1,500 within the City of Toronto, with over two-thirds concentrated in four areas: east downtown, the Niagara neighbourhood east of Parkdale, Parkdale itself, and the Annex. Nine hundred and fifty houses were inspected, accounting for 9,900 rooms in 7,400 rentable units. This meant an average of eight units per house, with almost a third of the units consisting of more than one room. Two-thirds of the tenants were employed, and one-third had lived in their units for more than twelve months. Although two-fifths of the buildings had inadequate fire exits, the report suggested that additional fire exits could be constructed at a "not unreasonable cost." The report also recommended that all buildings with absentee landlords be licensed and subject to annual inspection (Peat Marwick 1974). These changes were incorporated in two new bylaws. Reports written twenty-five years later contend that these bylaws caused an immediate decrease in the number of legal units. Coupled with the release of a large number of mentally or physically disabled singles from institutional care, a qualitative change within Parkdale's rooming houses was soon evident (Starr Group 1998).

Pat Capponi, who moved to Parkdale in the mid-1970s, vividly describes conditions at her licensed rooming house in her memoir, *Upstairs at the Crazy House* (1992). After her release from the Queen Street Mental Hospital, her welfare worker assigned her to Channon Court, a block of three adjacent houses on King Street West. Seventy people lived there, crammed three or four to each bedroom. The front door had no lock, nor did the individual rooms. Petty theft was common, and when one woman was sexually assaulted, the police told her to lock the door and clearly disbelieved her claim. The rooming house was licensed to receive former inmates of psychiatric institutions, but apart from an occasional visit from a welfare worker, no social services were available at the house. Capponi tells of one friend, Gary, who spent seventeen years (half of his life), at an institution in Whitby, thirty miles east of Toronto, before being discharged with no more than a bus ticket and the address of Channon Court. After attempting suicide soon after arriving, he spent the night at Queen Street Mental Health Hospital, then was sent back to the rooming house. A repeat arsonist was continually sent to new rooming houses, whose operators were not told of his previous history. He nearly succeeded in burning down Channon Court, along with its occupants, one night. Welfare cheques were sent directly to the landlord, who doled out the ten or twelve dollars left after the rent payment. There were no laundry facilities and no money for tampons or deodorant, let alone coffee or cigarettes or bus tickets. The bathroom had no lock, no plug for the sink or tub, no hand soap, towels, or shower curtain. Conditions, in short, were squalid and dehumanizing, conducive to an atmosphere of violence that replicated what many inhabitants, including Capponi, had gone through in their childhood.

Something needed to be done. Capponi, who had been a social worker, attended a public meeting on group homes at Masaryk-Cowan Community Centre one night in 1978. She heard a flurry of speakers blast the province for all the "weirdos and crazies" that had been "dumped" in Parkdale. When she spoke up on behalf of her fellow "weirdoes and crazies," she was told that she must be pretending to be crazy, a Communist social worker sent to such meetings to stir the pot (Capponi 1992). The problem of absent social supports, inadequate income, and horrific living standards had become transformed for many Parkdale residents into an issue of how best to eliminate a particular form of low-income housing they had not invited into the neighbourhood.

## Class Warfare: The Bachelorette Clean-Up Squad, 1977-1986

The consensus politics of the SPRA, the Parkdale Tenants Association (PTA), and various social agencies continued into the mid-1970s. In 1972, both the SPRA and the PTA wrote letters strongly urging the provincial government to prioritize local residents for the Dunn Avenue public housing, since 1,300 local applicants for the four hundred units had been identified by family and friends, congregations, and physicians (Parkdale Tenants Association 1972; South Parkdale Residents Association 1972). Parkdale

Community Legal Services supported the SPRA in its efforts to ban conversions to bachelorette apartments as late as 1976, because of the need for family housing in the face of adult-only apartment buildings (Parkdale Community Legal Services 1976). However, the consensus broke down as broadly based social improvement battles were replaced by issue-specific advocacy, both in Parkdale and across central Toronto. As David Ley (1996, 246) analyzes the situation, local political movements turned from a focus on neighbourhood improvement underpinned by a commitment to social mix, to neighbourhood protection, as middle-class newcomers faced a much stiffer entry fee to gentrifying communities and concomitant investment risk. Stephan Kipfer and Roger Keil (2002) have discussed the "urbanisation of neoliberalism" that emerged in Toronto's local politics by the early 1980s. While the urban social movements of feminism, anti-poverty, and queer politics were still apparent, local government response seemed to shift from "reform-minded" to "entrepreneurial" planning.

Residents' associations, supported by homeowners and some tenants, began to fight for restrictive bylaws banning further conversions of houses into apartments and rooming houses. In 1973, residents of North Parkdale, with a new association of their own, obtained a bylaw limiting new construction to thirty feet or three storeys (CTPB 1973a). Also in 1974, the City of Toronto Planning Board issued *A Report on the Desirability of the Intense Proliferation of Group Homes, Rest Homes, Halfway Houses and Children's Homes in the South Parkdale Area* (CTPB 1974). The report recommended an end to "as of right," or automatically approved, applications for institutional use in the parts of South Parkdale still zoned R4, and suggested a bylaw similar to the ones in the Annex and Don Vale, disallowing new group homes within four hundred feet of an existing group home. The report argued that de-concentrating group homes would improve "therapeutic effectiveness" for their residents. This specious rationale ignored the fact that few other areas in Toronto were zoned to allow this form of housing. The 1976 neighbourhood plan, *Trends and Planning Goals for South Parkdale* took restrictive zoning a step further. The "primary objective" of the plan was "to strengthen the residential character of the neighbourhood" by limiting "the expansion of institutions and institutional-related uses," including group homes and bachelorette apartments (CTPB 1976a).

While some advocacy groups continued the newest version of the hundred-year-old discourse on "tenements," other neighbourhood groups focused on deteriorating housing conditions. The Parkdale Tenants Association, in conjunction with Parkdale Community Legal Services, began what became a twenty-year struggle with the owners of Parkdale's largest apartment complex. West Lodge Apartments, two eighteen-storey buildings in North Parkdale, had been bought by Phil Wynn in 1968 for $8 million. In 1973, Wynn attempted to sell the two buildings for over $10 million to a German consortium, but soon took them back when the consortium defaulted on the vendor mortgage. By 1975, the buildings had 1,100 outstanding building code violations, including malfunctioning front-door locks, no intercom system, unreliable elevators, and filthy garbage rooms (*Toronto Star*, 16 November 1973; *Canadian*, December 1975). The PTA, assisted by local councillor Archie Chisholm and Parkdale Community Legal Services, organized a rent strike in late 1973, but only 18 of 720 households participated (*Toronto Star*, 21 January and 28 March 1974). Wynn, who was called "a contemptible landlord" by a judge and "The Most Hated Man in Town" by *Canadian* magazine, claimed that he took a personal interest in his tenants and that they trusted him to sort out the problems. The PTA claimed that he personally beat up local organizers and that tenants lived in fear of eviction (*Canadian*, December 1975). What is certain is that Wynn rented his units to new immigrant families who were shunned by other local apartment managers. When the PTA telephoned thirty-one buildings in west-end Toronto in early 1975, only one was willing to rent to a family (Parkdale Tenants Association 1975). By 1977, the city had stepped in to repair the "bottomless pit" building, adding the costs to the property tax bill. Despite Wynn being behind in both mortgage payments and property tax, the city refused to expropriate the buildings as the PTA requested (*Toronto Star*, 21 January 1974, 4 February 1977; *Toronto Sun*, 10 October 1974).

The growth of bachelorette buildings in South Parkdale during the early 1970s was the outcome of a range of citywide and local factors. First, despite the proliferation of high-rises with one-bedroom and bachelor units in Parkdale, there was a large and growing unmet demand for cheap single-person accommodation throughout the central city. In 1957, 10 percent of Toronto's population had lived in single-person households; by 1976, the proportion had risen to 30 percent, and many of these households were living in poverty (*Toronto Star*, 8 May 1979). Parkdale, having gained a reputation as a cheap place to live, attracted many of these singles. Second, the bylaws governing rooming houses were increasingly restrictive throughout the city, and aside from a limited municipal program, there were few attempts to preserve large older houses from the depredations of renovators. So choices were narrowed. Third, rooming house owners could add a kitchen or bathroom and claim that a room was a self-contained apartment, thus increasing their rent while avoiding the costly and contentious licensing process for rooming house operators.

Fourth, a 1974 provincial land speculation tax on residential invest-ment properties held for less than ten years, intended to prevent property flipping, led some larger developers to maximize interim profit from their poorly maintained old houses in Parkdale by conversion to bachelorettes pending apartment redevelopment. Fifth, and possibly most important, institutional mortgages were readily obtainable for illegally converted properties (illegal because the units were smaller than the minimum size for an apartment in the Ontario Building Code). In 1978, for instance, 6 Elm Grove was one of seven properties that accounted for a total of $2 million in mortgages held by Sterling Trust, a reputable lender whose direc-tors included a well-known Canadian publisher specializing in left-wing urban-themed books (*Toronto Star,* 1 November 1978). Finally, conversion to an illegal use was facilitated by a corrupt civic bureaucracy. The chief plumbing inspector and several other building inspectors were charged with taking bribes in 1978, after fifty-seven files concerning over forty buildings vanished from City Hall (*Toronto Star,* 1 and 8 November 1978; *Toronto Star,* 19 December 1979). By 1977, city officials estimated that there were three hundred illegally converted buildings in South Parkdale. While some build-ings had only one or two bachelorette apartments, one Cowan Avenue house reportedly contained thirty single units, while a house on Spencer Avenue contained forty-three (*Toronto Sun,* 27 February 1977).

Although some bachelorette buildings were owned by large developers, many other buildings had been converted from rooming houses or larger apartments by small developers specializing in bachelorettes. One devel-oper eventually charged with illegal conversions, Benislav Ivanovic, had immigrated to Canada from Croatia when he was twenty-three, in 1968. His career as a bachelorette owner began in 1972, when he was given a stake in a building as payment for his services as a drywall contractor. In 1978, he lived in a suite in one of the fourteen Parkdale properties he had converted. He described his tenants as better off now that he had installed kitchens, since they couldn't afford to eat out and had previously cooked on hotplates and washed up in communal bathroom sinks. However, his claim that he was "buying a slum and converting it into luxury accom-modations" was nonsense. There was nothing luxurious about leaking toilets not properly bolted to the wall, kitchens without cupboards, and plywood unit dividers, all of which were found by building inspectors (*Toronto Star,* 5 April 1979). The business was profitable. Ivanovic boasted that a building he bought for $180,000 would be worth over $1 million after his renovations (*Globe and Mail,* 1 June 1977). Tenants might be spending $160 a month where previously they had paid $100 for a room or a half a large two-bedroom apartment. Of course, these new conversions exerted upward pressure on neighbourhood rents (letter from W.M. Piper to *Globe and Mail*, 10 June 1977).

Bachelorettes were a step up for many of the tenants living in the squalid conditions of some group homes and rooming houses in Parkdale. Capponi (1992), for instance, treats the move from Channon Court into a bachelorette apartment at the end of *Upstairs at the Crazy House* as the start of her new life. Bachelorettes met a growing need for small, self-contained units, a need that had been recognized in 1974, when City Council approved Phoenix Place, with an average apartment size of 240 square feet, and in 1975, when a Planning Board report, *Housing Low-Income Single People,* recommended that 20 percent of all new accommodation built by the city consist of self-contained units with a minimum size of 225 square feet, including bath and cooking facilities (CTPB 1975). The city could have created new standards for small apartments and legalized the apartments that met these standards, although this change would have required enabling legislation from the provincial government. The city could then have cracked down on maintenance violations in all rental units, including high-rise apartments and licensed rooming houses in South Parkdale. Toronto had already been given provincial permission to make repairs and add the cost to the landlord's property tax bill, and rent controls in place at the time would have allowed small rent increases to cover improved maintenance. Instead, City Council decided to placate a new residents' group called the Parkdale Working Group on Bachelorettes (PWGB).

The PWGB, made up of local home and business owners as well as owners of legal rooming houses (such as Channon Court), opposed the legalization of bachelorettes on the basis that they "threaten the stability of family neighbourhoods, strain community facilities through overcrowding, destroy streetscape, and bring a host of social problems because of the often rowdy transients they attract as tenants" (PWGB, cited in *Globe and Mail*, 25 June 1979). In 1977, the city proposed setting standards such as a minimum unit size of 145 square feet as a preliminary to legalizing some units. This was an extremely low minimum unit size; even the Toronto Guest Home Association, the bachelorette owners' lobby group, said they would be happy with a 190 square foot minimum (City of Toronto Committee on Buildings and Development 1978). The PWGB responded with recommendations that were clearly untenable, not to mention contradictory: a minimum 25 percent of any lot should be landscaped open space, there should be no alterations to the exterior, and there should be a minimum of one on-site parking space for every two units (CTPB 1977a; PWGB 1977). The dispute formed the backdrop to a municipal election in which Barbara Adams, the chair of the PWGB, successfully unseated

Ed Negridge, who supported policies that encouraged "bedsits" throughout Toronto, as the junior alderman for Ward 2 (*Toronto Star,* 28 April 1977). The local campaign was bitter and full of dirty tricks. According to the *Toronto Sun* (18 November 1977), photocopied documents distributed to the media detailing Negridge's arrest for impaired driving several years earlier bore the same Queen's Park legislative postage meter code as letters of support for Barbara Adams signed by Jan Dukszta, the NDP member of provincial parliament for Parkdale. John Sewell, the reformer who had helped organize Trefann Court, became mayor in the same election.

Although the council majority was now considered progressive if not radical, this composition did not translate into policies friendly to the growth of affordable housing for those most in need of it. Sewell had been the lone dissenting voice at council when Phoenix Place was approved in 1974, saying that a lower building with more family units was appropriate. Adams had made the elimination of illegal bachelorettes a major plank in her platform. Immediately after the election, in January 1978, a bylaw banned all new and converted boarding or lodging houses in Parkdale, with the exception of those legalized before that date (City of Toronto Council 1978).

Like the apartment building legislation of 1913, the bylaw had little effect on the number of unwanted units, nor did it seem to stop further conversions in Parkdale. Barbara Adams wrote a stream of letters to City Council, passing on complaints from constituents. For instance, 156 Dowling, once a traditional boarding house with one self-contained dwelling unit, ten rooms, three kitchens, and three and a half bathrooms, had received a permit for "small alterations" in 1977. A sixteen-by-thirty-three-foot addition was built, and now there were a total of eighteen self-contained units with bathroom and space for a kitchen in each unit, although the gas and water lines were capped. Their average size was 240 square feet, and the building had only four parking spaces instead of the required thirteen (Adams 1979). What seemed missing from all of these accounts of "bombed out buildings," as Adams called them, was a discussion of acceptable standards, whether based on neighbourhood character or public health, for all buildings in Parkdale. After all, many single-family houses were getting building permits for much larger additions. And the required ratio of parking spaces appeared groundless: an early 1980s study found that one parking space for every three units was more than ample for single-room-occupancy units (Bureau of Municipal Research 1982). Nor was there any substantive discussion of the rationale behind various minimum unit sizes.

In January 1979, Sewell created a Mayor's Task Force on Bachelorettes.

Its recommendations, released in April of that year, included the estab-lishment of a "clean up team" to "speed up the process of getting rid of about 300 properties in South Parkdale that currently violate by-laws" (*Globe and Mail,* 27 April 1979). Clayton Ruby, a civil liberties lawyer asso-ciated with progressive causes, was hired to lead the process, at a rate of $90 per hour. He was later replaced by Ian Scott, the future Liberal attorney-general of Ontario, who charged $900 a day. By September 1979, hundreds of charges had been laid, against not only twenty bachelorette owners, but also twenty-eight tenants (*Globe and Mail,* 14 September 1979). After that initial splash of publicity, the process bogged down. Fourteen months later, fewer than half the landlords charged had been convicted, only five buildings had been closed down, and the process had cost $211,000, not including the wages of nine City Hall staff seconded to the project (*Toronto Star,* 14 September 1980; *Globe and Mail,* 2 December 1980). Ivanovic, one of the landlords convicted of multiple charges, faced a $2,750 fine, hardly a deterrent to future action (*Toronto Star,* 31 May 1980). Sterling Trust, fac-ing twenty charges of violating bylaws, was fined $525, considerably less than one week's rent on any building the company owned and managed (*Toronto Star,* 24 May 1980).

The Bureau of Municipal Research, the business-supported think tank that had been one of the few voices against slum demolition in the 1930s, spoke up once again for the rights of low-income tenants with a report entitled *A Case for Bachelorettes* in 1982. The report pointed out that the city had the legislative ability to expropriate and manage buildings that persistently violated fire and health and safety regulations once it estab-lished minimum standards for single-room-occupancy units, instead of closing down buildings or letting landlords abandon them, which was the practice of the Clean-Up Squad (see, for instance, *Toronto Star,* 28 May 1980). Parkdale Community Legal Services had also swung around to em-brace bachelorette tenants, helping to organize a separate Parkdale Bach-elorette Tenants Association affiliated with the PTA (*Globe and Mail,* 28 May 1980). Newspapers, led by the *Toronto Star,* began to provide sympa-thetic coverage of the approximately twelve hundred "elderly widows and war veterans, welfare mothers with small children, and unemployed per-sons" who would lose their homes if bachelorette buildings were closed down. Juliane Dubay, a twenty-nine-year-old mother of three, had been told to leave her Cowan Avenue apartment, but "I got used to it here ... To find a new place you need your first and last month's rent." A thirty-two-year-old single tenant on Dowling Avenue, Jim Donelly, feared that "all that will be left are flophouses with 15 people using one bathroom. At least you have your own bathroom here" (cited in *Toronto Star,* 19 April

1980). At a bachelorette building on Wilson Park Avenue owned by Sterling Trust (the redevelopers having defaulted on a mortgage), tenants were told that the building was substandard, in part because it needed to provide twelve parking spots for the forty tenants. Yet only two of the tenants owned cars. Beare Weatherup, a seconded City of Toronto employee whose sole task was to find alternative accommodations for tenants displaced by the crackdown, admitted that it was "not realistic to get rents" as low as the $55 a week charged for the condemned units (*Toronto Star,* 28 May 1980). By 1986, when the Clean-Up Squad was effectively disbanded, the cost for the five-year project was $315,000 in legal bills and at least $600,000 in employee hours. A total of sixty buildings had been closed down, and approximately three hundred people evicted (*Toronto Star,* 19 May 1983; *Globe and Mail,* 9 September 1986). The Gardiner Expressway had accomplished more in the way of "slum" dehousing in less time for less money, and at least it left behind a road.

Not only was the Bachelorette Clean-Up Squad an ineffective and costly regulatory exercise that harmed the most vulnerable members of the neighbourhood without improving housing conditions for the majority, it was remarkably divisive, creating scars among neighbourhood groups that remain to this day. Alderman Adams and the PWGB felt that despite the crackdown, they had been betrayed by a "change in focus" as Sewell's office slowly came around to the idea that regulations needed to be relaxed to ensure the viability of single-room-occupancy units in the city (*Globe and Mail,* 25 June 1979). As Mark Connelly, from the Parkdale Village Residents Association (the new name of the SPRA), said when the Clean-Up Squad was formally shut down in 1986, "This is like saying to a drug-dealer that his goods should be legitimized because the people want his product" (*Globe and Mail,* 24 April 1986). In turn, housing agencies charged that the same small group of homeowners and local politicians stirred up "local hysteria" every time a social housing project came along (*Globe and Mail,* 12 January 1983). By the time the city attempted to legalize bachelorette units on a building-by-building basis in the late 1990s, Parkdale Community Legal Services and the Parkdale Tenants Association refused to sit down at the table with the residents' and business associations, claiming that any attempt to regulate these buildings would amount to "social cleansing" (*Eye Magazine,* 29 October 1998). One bachelorette owner, caught in an uneasy alliance with his tenants and anti-poverty organizations, asked plaintively: "What about the bastard slumlords in the legal highrises?" (*Toronto Star,* 16 November 1998). A tenant said, with an air of resignation, that he had been pushed from house to house by renovators and regulators, "and the next thing you know, we'll all be in the fucking lake" (*Eye Magazine,* 29 October 1998).

## The Resurgent Urban Village:
## The Renovation of Parkdale's History

How did a small group of homeowners dominate politics in a neighbourhood that was so overwhelmingly made up of tenants? Why did bachelorettes face the lion's share of opprobrium and municipal government action while conditions in legal rooming houses and apartment buildings were steadily declining? What justification was offered for a million-dollar dehousing program in Parkdale during a period when the supply of affordable small units in Toronto was demonstrably evaporating in the face of growing demand, leading to growing homelessness (Metropolitan Toronto Planning and Community Services Departments 1983; Metropolitan Toronto Task Force on Housing for Low-Income Singles 1983; Starr Group 1988)?

Graham Cotter (1978) had written of the "recurrent patterns" in Parkdale's history, and the Parkdale Working Group on Bachelorettes can be seen as the latest and most successful step in a century-old dance of images and planning policy within the neighbourhood. In the 1880s, row houses along alleyways were described as tenements by residents who unsuccessfully fought the construction of this form of housing. In the 1910s, the term *tenement* was applied to new apartment buildings and conversions of villas into flats in another unsuccessful attempt to stop a particular form of housing. The signage bylaw in the early 1930s was an attempt to control a third form of housing, rooming houses, in Parkdale. By that time, the city had decided that all houses within Parkdale were declining and on the road to obsolescence. In the 1970s, the municipal government, institutional lenders, and developers found new value in Parkdale's older houses. Banning bachelorettes, the latest type of housing to be vilified, was a way to accelerate the process of reclaiming these older houses for the single-family market.

In each case, an expressed concern about housing conditions was soon transformed into single-minded hatred for a particular housing form. These despised housing forms were associated with particular social groups who were felt to threaten Parkdale's identity. In the 1880s, it was feared that row houses would attract "mechanics," who in turn would frighten away middle-class families from the developing suburb. In the 1910s, it was feared that apartment buildings and rooming houses would be lived in by single women and men and childless couples, who were perceived as a threat to family formation and an invitation to moral disorder. In the 1970s, it was feared that bachelorettes would attract "transients" with mental illness or addictions, who would prevent Parkdale Village from regaining its communal identity.

When Parkdale was first described as becoming a serious slum in the 1930s, its supposedly stable middle-class residential past was recalled as a contrast to present conditions. As Parkdale gentrified in the early 1970s, its mythic past began to assume ever greater importance. In April 1973, the Parkdale Baptist Church sponsored a Toronto Historic Night, and by 1974, the *Citizen* was reporting on meetings of the Parkdale Local History Club (*Parkdale Citizen,* April 1973, May 1974). In 1976, a non-profit Parkdale Village Foundation was created to channel federal funds for a 1979 celebration of the centennial of Parkdale's incorporation as a village. In the same year, a $1 million Neighbourhood Improvement Program grant went towards installing a fountain and benches at "the historic centre of Parkdale" in front of the public library and across the street from the new community centre. *Parkdale: A Centennial History* was produced in 1978. These local histories, planning reports, and newspaper coverage of the neighbourhood's current issues gave authenticity to one version of Parkdale's history through sheer repetition. Like George Herczog renovating the old houses on Melbourne Place, this redeveloped history gutted much of the record while keeping certain details in place for effect.

Oddly enough, given the secular nature of Canadian society by that time, the story of Parkdale that emerged was rife with religious imagery. An affluent and stable past was referred to as a state of grace, lost through hubris and greed. The new generation was trying to find future meaning through turning away from the sins of the fathers and rediscovering the virtues of the forefathers. "Parkdale: Where Graciousness Fell Victim to the Greed of Progress" read a *Toronto Sun* headline in 1977 (27 February). "The passing years have seen Parkdale's slow fall from grace," said the *Toronto Star* in 1979 (17 June). This article begins: "The past is present again for the three young women in T-shirts and jeans ... Morning 'til night, they work over faded photographs, ancient land surveys, old records ... Not a word is spoken about Parkdale's current blights: Illegal bachelorettes, oppressive traffic, more and more transients ... It's Parkdale's centennial celebration this year, and hope for the future is being sought through a backward glance at the neighbourhood's romantic and optimistic beginnings." Although the local historians did not talk of Parkdale's "current blights," their enquiry was an attempt to place a pattern on the past in order to explain the present and suggest a future.

Carole Corbeil, the novelist and arts critic who wrote an elegiac newspaper article on Parkdale's past and present in 1980, described the former state of grace: "Parkdale, with its lake view, its old houses, with its shoreline of boardwalks, of bathing pavilions and dance halls ... [was] possibly the only true vision of beauty that Toronto ever had." Corbeil quoted a "Parkdale resident of 36 years, a 78 year old retired bricklayer" who remembered walking "home from work at five o'clock [to] see all these old ladies on the porch gettin' served tea and biscuits by their maids. It was a village, not a slum" (*Globe and Mail*, 13 September 1980). A 1976 Neighbourhood Improvement Program report claimed that South Parkdale originally "housed a class of wealthy, well-educated professionals" living in "large homes on large properties" (CTPB 1976a, 3). The industrial workers in row houses, the lodgers in the villas, and the seamstress in the shack had all been forgotten, as had the fights over tenements, foreigners, and "room for rent" signs.

The actual moment of the fall from grace was disputed. A November 1973 *Real Estate News* article by Howard Walker, the president of the SPRA, described the "early twentieth century rivalry with Rosedale" ending in the 1930s, as the second generation of Parkdale residents moved on. The *Parkdale Citizen*, in a two-part history of the neighbourhood published in July 1974, said that by 1950, "Parkdale was losing ground almost daily in its feud with Rosedale as first choice of the wealthy in Toronto." In 1978, another two-part series in the *Real Estate News* similarly contended that by 1950, people who inherited the "huge, gracious homes, well-kept gardens, and well-maintained streets" found them difficult to maintain (4-10 August). The loss of an articulate middle class is thus implicitly blamed for the planning follies that followed, as in Reverend Cotter's history (1978). The 1976 neighbourhood plan for Parkdale also gave the 1950s as its turning point, using as an example Jameson Avenue, with "no apartments" in 1955, two by 1957, sixteen by 1959, and only two original houses left by 1962. Yet this example was completely false: the six-storey Kingsway Apartments and at least two other apartment buildings fronting Jameson dated from the 1910s, and most of the villas had become rooming houses by the 1930s (CTPB 1976b). The *Toronto Sun* claimed that in 1974, with the sudden growth of illegal bachelorettes, "three quarters of a century of relative stability came to an end" (27 February 1977). Newspaper articles and planning reports thus posited a sudden change from middle-class stability as occurring some time between the 1930s and 1974. However, the research on social conditions in this book leads to a different conclusion: Parkdale was never entirely middle-class or stable, and a decisive change in the health and welfare of neighbourhood residents in the late 1960s and early 1970s had more to do with housing conditions, insufficiently policed by local government, than with any particular housing form, such as bachelorettes.

All these articles agreed that the present was unpleasant. Corbeil used another religious comparison, Parkdale as the scapegoat for Toronto's sins: "All other parts of town can bask in the illusion of urban victory, but illusions always exist at the expense of something, and that something often turns out to be Parkdale." Parkdale had become a "dumping ground," first for a much-needed urban expressway, then for low-cost housing and group homes (*Globe and Mail*, 13 September 1980). Another article in this genre said that Parkdale, with its "leafy" streets and "jewel" like homes, had become a "dumping ground" (that phrase again) for the poor (*Toronto Star*, 16 June 1982). Parkdale had had its life drained out of it along with its wealth. Jameson Avenue's high-rise corridor was, to Corbeil, a "mini Jane Finch," referring to the suburban public housing project northwest of the central city: "unrelentingly sunny, barren and sterile."

Thus Parkdale was a scapegoat, a dumping ground, barren and sterile. But as one rooming-house resident, Pat Capponi (1992), put it, if Parkdale was a dumping ground, then poor people like her must be garbage. The new poor of Parkdale were dehumanized by these terms, and middle-class residents drew on other slum literature tropes that denied citizens their identity as people. According to the long-time resident who had described the afternoon tea parties, the older houses were "cut up into bachelorettes" filled with "two legged rats," who "sleep all day and roam the streets at night." "You don't get families" in bachelorettes, another resident complained, "you get riff raff" (*Toronto Star*, 5 April 1979). Even for those who granted the poor some human characteristics, they really were a breed apart. Corbeil interviewed a former "tough guy" (possibly M.T. Kelly) who described the old Parkdale Hotel, now called OV's, with its "clientele in and out of jail ... [who] never do a day's work in their lives" (*Globe and Mail*, 13 September 1980). Another resident said in 1979 that Parkdale had become "an unbearable hell not fit for decent people," although a year later, after the start of the crackdown on bachelorette apartments, she amended her views (*Toronto Star*, 14 September 1980).

In contrast to previous campaigns against affordable housing, the locus of immorality had shifted gender, from bad women to bad men. The early-twentieth-century campaigns against lodging and apartment houses, with their emphasis on sex and the single woman, were being replaced by fears of the "hard drinking men" who presumably inhabited bachelorettes. Despite reports of female prostitution, the archetypal image of Parkdale's poor was a single man, probably mentally ill, probably involved in some form of substance abuse. As in the first phase of Parkdale's history, women were associated with a kinder and gentler time, older women being served tea by their maids on their front porches in the 1940s and 1950s, "young women in t-shirts and jeans" in the 1970s poring over the past in order to find and restore Parkdale's lost order. Even in the slough of despond, a reawakening or rebirth could be predicted by some journalists. In 1977, a *Toronto Sun* journalist in search of "chic streets" described Melbourne Avenue, adjacent to Melbourne Place. Now that the Dominion Radiator Factory was gone, it was "so quiet you can hear your footsteps at 5 o'clock in the afternoon." Aside from "fat cats" and "kids setting out street hockey nets," there was a quiet peacefulness, with trees rustling in the gentle lake breeze. It could be a "scene from a planning student cribbing Jane Jacobs." Parkdale, like the Annex, Riverdale, and Don Vale (the gentrifying area that took the name Cabbagetown from the slum to its south when that was redeveloped as public housing), offered a fine prize to a new genera-tion of urban "pioneers" (*Toronto Sun,* 2 December 1977). In 1980, Corbeil similarly wondered whether Parkdale could, like some neighbourhoods, rise "phoenix-like ... out of their ashes." Parkdale was certainly showing "signs of picking up on its own." The "attractive homes," including those subdivided into bachelorettes, were finding middle-class buyers. A local real estate agent proclaimed: "For value, nothing in the city can beat Park-dale right now. You're paying as much as $35,000 less for houses of com-parable size and condition to other areas ... It's a very good area right now." An art gallery owner living on Cowan Avenue, only the second owner of his house since 1915, told Corbeil: "I've lived in American cities, in pretty bad areas, and compared to those this is a suburb" (*Globe and Mail,* 13 September 1980). In 1981, the *Toronto Star* proclaimed, "Old Park-dale reborn in new splendour," and, profiling a gay couple's conversion of a rooming house, predicted that it would once again become "the Rosedale of the west end" (1 July 1981). A long-time resident was quoted in 1982: "Parkdale is like a sleeping Cinderella waiting for a fairy god-mother to wave a magic wand and bring back the good old days" (*Globe and Mail,* 10 March 1982).

Almost alone among writers of the period, Corbeil expressed doubts about some of the plans for revival, such as a private consortium bury-ing the Gardiner Expressway, and the complete elimination of bachelorette apartments. She wondered whether these ideas were merely "mammoth bureaucratic measures to correct previous mammoth bureaucratic mea-sures." And where would the poor people go if bachelorettes were elimi-nated? Why had a $1 million Neighbourhood Improvement Program grant gone to create a fountain and benches in front of Parkdale Library, which were almost immediately removed because of the low-income people sitting on the benches and using the fountain to wash themselves and their clothes? Would it not have made more sense to use the money to make existing housing better? Could Parkdale find a "middle ground" between "arrogant suburb and neglected dumping ground"? (*Globe and Mail*, 13 September 1980).

Across North America, resuscitated slum rhetoric was used to justify exclusionary housing policies in gentrifying neighbourhoods by real estate agents, newspapers, local government planners, and residents themselves (Smith 1996). In the early 1980s, local newspaper coverage featured Parkdale almost daily, as it had a hundred years earlier. A scan of the *Toronto Star*'s "Pages from the Past" searchable database shows 415 "hits" for Parkdale in its news section in 1981, compared with 128 for Rosedale and 114 for the Annex. An explanation for this attention is suggested by an article on "Parkdale as a neighbourhood to watch" in the November 1984 issue of *Toronto Life*. "For longer than we care to recall, gung ho realtors, local activists, and this magazine have been proclaiming that Parkdale is on the brink," it began, "to which it is fair to reply, 'of what?'" It described the "pitiful rubbies [who] congest a park designed to commemorate the village's centenary" and how the "group home juggernaut" was rolling on. "Parkdale is a Cautionary Tale, an example of how well-meaning planning can go awry," and this was certainly one strand of contemporary coverage. Then the article turned to the other strand: "And yet when two years ago we suggested Parkdale as a possible next Hot Area for middle-class renovators, we weren't whistling totally in the dark." Parkdale seemed to represent both the best and the worst of what the central city had to offer. On the one hand, it contained a fine stock of affordable houses to be renovated, potentially constituting a rediscovered peaceful suburb for brave urban pioneers. On the other hand, it was the home of a growing urban underclass of (literally) shiftless "two legged rats."

Parkdale seemed to offer an either-or choice for the future. Surely these two land uses could not coexist for long, especially if there was competition for the same limited stock of old houses. The fact that both had coexisted uneasily for most of Parkdale's history had been forgotten. The newly renovated version of Parkdale's history helped guide and justify city planning efforts that gave special treatment to Parkdale's middle-class minority.

## Parkdale at the Turn of the Twenty-first Century

By the late 1980s, Parkdale had been rendered safe for gentrification, even as median incomes continued to decline and health and housing conditions worsened for the majority of residents. By 1981, 25 percent of families with children in Parkdale lived below the poverty line, as compared to 11 percent throughout greater Toronto. Claims that Parkdale was losing its family housing to bachelorettes were belied by the fact that 9 percent of Parkdale's population was under five years of age, as compared to 7 percent in the rest of Toronto. Disparities within the neighbourhood continued to increase over the next twenty years. The household median income in northwest Parkdale, now called Roncesvalles Village by real estate agents, was $18,608 in 1981, while the median in south-central Parkdale was only $10,129. By 1991, 40 percent of northwest Parkdale wage earners were classified as professional/managerial, as compared to 21 percent in south-central Parkdale and 33 percent across Toronto (Census of Canada 1981, 1991). Ten years later, the unemployment rate in northwest Parkdale was 5.6 percent, in line with the census metropolitan area's 5.9 percent, but half the 11 percent unemployment rate in south-central Parkdale. Similarly, the proportion of low-income individuals was 18.1 percent in northwest Parkdale, 16.7 percent in the CMA, and 44.6 percent in south-central Parkdale.

The decades since the 1980s have seen improvements in the neighbourhood that have benefited all residents. Attempts have been made to reconnect Parkdale with its Lake Ontario shoreline. The lakeshore finally obtained a new boardwalk, and the Sunnyside Bathing Pavilion was restored as a free municipal swimming pool. A pedestrian bridge over the Gardiner Expressway at Roncesvalles has enabled access to the boardwalk and pool. New downtown expressway plans had been shelved by 1975 (*Toronto Star*, 19 June 1975), and a plan to deck over the Gardiner Expressway and improve access to the lakeshore was first raised in 1980, reappearing at intervals ever since (*Toronto Star*, 10 April and 5 June 1980; also see *Toronto Life*, June 2002). Several parks and playgrounds were created in the neighbourhood from the late 1970s onwards, and Parkdale Public School was rebuilt with a community centre and pool open to the public in the early 1990s. The Flowery Suburb thus obtained its first public parks and recreation facilities after one hundred years of settlement.

As in the first years of the Village of Parkdale, the policing of public morality has assumed great importance, with several well-publicized crackdowns on the Queen Street drug and sex trade. On the first night of the "prostitute patrol" in 1984, Alderman Chris Korwin-Kuczynski was a bit embarrassed when the group, armed with T-shirts, whistles, and cameras, were unable to find any women plying their trade (*Toronto Sun*, 2 August 1984). The Ku Klux Klan reappeared during the early 1980s, attempting to distribute leaflets at schools on "morality issues," but was soon evicted from its Springhurst Avenue base of operations by a multicultural community coalition (Sher 1983, 143). In 1991, the New York City-based

Guardian Angels, a vigilante group, attempted to open an office in Parkdale, but they disbanded after a few months (*Toronto Star*, 5 February 1991). Parkdale Focus Community, a provincially funded community development organization set up in the early 1990s, shifted from an early emphasis on crime prevention through environmental design (with campaigns to remove phone booths on the grounds that they were encouraging the drug trade) to "softer" anti-drug campaigns in the schools by the end of the decade.

Regular newspaper coverage referred to the ongoing tension between wealthy enclave and dumping ground, with a 1987 article suggesting that Parkdale was well on its way to becoming "another Cabbagetown, ejecting down-and-outers." According to this article, a house on Cowan that had sold for $130,000 the previous year had been renovated, flipped twice, and was now selling for $259,000 (*Globe and Mail*, 12 January 1987). Some bohemians were drawn to the area by the picturesque contrast between rich and poor. One artist, Sandor Ajzenstat, told an interviewer in 1996, "I think that if the community accepts someone who is walking down the street with their pyjamas on, then that means the community will accept me" (Parkdale Collegiate Institute 1996, 68). By 1997, an article on Parkdale's "Bowery to Bohemia" conversion could point to 1313 Queen, the former Six Division police station converted to artist's apartments and a ground-floor gallery, the Pia Bouman School of Dance in one of Parkdale's former churches, various local arts festivals, and a growing number of fashionable cafes and restaurants (*Toronto Star*, 16 January 1997). Three years later, the same newspaper claimed that the "gentrification of Parkdale" had effectively squeezed out artists from homeownership, while live-work lofts in the older industrial buildings were being transformed into condominiums and expensive offices. Artists, having successively made Yorkville, Queen and Spadina, and Parkdale fashionable, would have to find a new bohemia (*Toronto Star*, 4 July 2000).

Opposition to local affordable housing and social services continued. The Parkdale Village Residents Association and the Parkdale Business Improvement Association, active members of the anti-bachelorette movement, opposed the relocation of the Archway drug and alcohol rehabilitation program from one Queen Street site to another in 1980 (*Toronto Star*, 6 June). The following year, Alderman Korwin-Kuczynski tacked an amendment onto the end of a report from the Mayor's Task Force on Discharged Psychiatric Patients, reiterating a ban on future legal rooming houses in Parkdale, despite the report's finding that 10 percent of the remaining rooming house stock in Toronto was being lost every year (*Toronto Star*, 27 March 1984; 10 percent figure from *Globe and Mail*, 12 November 1981). When St. Mark's Church attempted to buy six houses (including one legal rooming house and one bachelorette building) for conversion to rooming houses in 1983, it was blasted by both the senior alderman and the member of provincial parliament for Parkdale, the latter opining that "the more [rooming houses] you build, the more you need" (*Toronto Star*, 9 September).

The Wynns, Phil and his sons, continued to provide conditions as bad as those of any bachelorette or rooming house in their apartment building complex. In January 1994, a woman burned to death at 103 West Lodge when her space heater caught fire; the city's inspections unit had already reported that heat and electricity had been turned off in the buildings, and indoor temperatures had fallen to ten degrees Celsius (*Globe and Mail*, 13 January 1994). After rent controls were lifted by the province in 1998, Wynn sent notices increasing rents by an average of 38 percent. Parveen Moussa, a single mother with two children, claimed she caught ten mice one sleepless night in her one-bedroom West Lodge apartment (*Toronto Star*, 22 October 1999). Other apartment managers vied with Phil Wynn for the title of worst Parkdale landlord. The Toronto Apartment Building Company, owner of four buildings on Jameson Avenue, called itself a hotel provider in 1983 and began to charge tenants an average of $180 a week instead of $338 a month (*Toronto Star*, 2 and 27 May 1983). After being convicted in 1986 of defrauding $240,000 from over two hundred tenants, it evicted many of the tenants for "overcrowding" one-bedroom and bachelor apartments with families (without these units being inspected by the city), then leased these units to the federal government for use as short-term refugee family accommodation at $24 per day, or $720 a month (*Toronto Star*, 20 July 1986).

There were occasional oases of hope within this landscape of despair for low-income Parkdale residents A number of social agencies, notably Houselink and First Step Homes, were funded in the late 1980s and early 1990s to provide housing with on-site supportive services for ex-psychiatric patients (see, for example, *Toronto Star*, 5 August 1986, on the sale of Channon Court, Pat Capponi's former home, to Houselink), although funding dried up from 1995 to 2003 after the election of a neoconservative provincial government. From 1985 onwards, an organization called Sistering offered a drop-in centre to homeless and socially isolated women at Masaryk-Cowan Community Centre, joining Parkdale Activity and Recreation Centre, another drop-in centre that served both homeless men and women, and Creating Together, a drop-in centre for low-income mothers with young children. The latter two agencies moved to Queen Street storefronts in the late 1990s. St. Francis Table and Shalom House, two organizations affiliated with Catholic ministries, continue to provide low-cost meals in the neighbourhood. There are several food banks and community economic development initiatives.

Successive exposés of "nineteenth-century European slum conditions" in licensed group homes and rooming houses followed repeated deaths and suspicious fires, without causing any meaningful changes to maintenance, ownership, or legislation related to these forms of housing.[3] A City Hall study on single-room housing for low-income singles was sparked by the 1989 Rupert Hotel fire in east-central Toronto, in which ten roomers lost their lives. A task force on homelessness was created after Mel Lastman, the successful candidate in Toronto's 1997 mayoralty race, stated, "There are no homeless people in North York," on the same night a woman was found dead behind the North York gas station where she had been sleeping (City of Toronto Alternative Housing Subcommittee 1992; Golden, et al. 1999).

Parkdale homeowner and business associations continued to insist that the neighbourhood had more than its fair share of small, low-cost, housing units, and the city's Planning Department continued to listen. The 1998 neighbourhood plan said that zoning must permit no more than three units per lot in Parkdale, since otherwise the neighbourhood's "vital diversity" would be lost. The challenge was to restore Parkdale's "stability," to recreate an "environment where children can be raised and where home life can be enjoyed in relative peace and quiet, where neighbour can get to know neighbour over time, where pride in the place you live leads to good property maintenance, where change over time is incremental rather than abrupt" (City of Toronto Urban Development Services 1998).

With this planning report, we return to 1879 and the first manufactured images of Parkdale: the scent of flowers, the sound of trees rustling in the lake breeze, the reassuring sight of children playing together in their stable neighbourhood, the sense of pride in being a good, healthy, and family-friendly place to live. Thirty-five years of neighbourhood conflict, of political choices and failure of political will, of retrieved and renovated history, had gone into that hard-won image. Parkdale, the renascent urban village, would be restored to its golden era with the help of planning policy. If Carole Corbeil were still alive, would she call Parkdale an arrogant suburb or a neglected dumping ground? Perhaps it had become both.

# 5
# Why Does Parkdale Matter?

There is a quality even meaner than outright ugliness or disorder, and this meaner quality is the dishonest mask of pretended
order, achieved by ignoring or suppressing the real order that is
struggling to exist and be served.

– Jane Jacobs, *The Death and Life*
*of Great American Cities*

Every new time finds its legitimation in what it excludes.

– Michel de Certeau

## The Tyranny of the "Descript Community"

In September 2002, during the Toronto International Film Festival, the
*New York Times* went "on the party whirl in Tinseltown North." As the
reporter pointed out, the real business of the festival was taking place in
the "chic stores ... over-designed restaurants ... and louche hangouts for
serious drinkers" found in this "bustling city." In a Queen Street West bar,
alongside "new galleries and clubs" that "seem to pop up overnight," the
reporter met up with a "filmmaker, musician and budding game-show
host" named Nobu Adilman. Adilman had recently moved to the "old Polish" neighbourhood at the end of Queen Street West, "where – as fast as
you can say Greenpoint, Brooklyn – young artists are buying up two-storey
houses on Roncesvalles Avenue for $200,000," or $300,000 in Canadian
dollars. "You have to wash the smell of kielbasas off yourself every morning," Adilman said, "but it's worth it. You even get a basement and a backyard" (*New York Times*, 15 September 2002).

In the international cocktail circuit of cultural capital, Parkdale had come
of age, rating an indirect mention in the *New York Times* as a hip place to
live and work. Once again, reporters were singing the praises of the Flowery Suburb. The neighbourhood was commended for combining the virtues
of an older suburb – space (a basement and a backyard) and affordability
– with proximate access to galleries and clubs, places of business as well as
pleasure in the new economy. The reminders of a slum past, the louche
bars and kielbasa (Polish sausage), were signifiers of pleasurable, because
contained, heterogeneity and authenticity, much sought after by those who
despise the homogenous new outer suburbs. The urban village of Parkdale
was now part of the global village of mass cultural consumption.

In 1929, Harvey Zorbaugh, a member of the Chicago school of sociology, introduced one of the first studies of neighbourhood transition by saying that "a descript community is 'a place of unity and charm.'" Parkdale, however, is what Zorbaugh would call a "nondescript community," one that "has physical proximity rather than unity" (Zorbaugh 1976, xvii). Throughout its 125-year history, Parkdale has been diverse in terms of class, gender, sexuality, ethnicity, and physical and mental health. This study of how, when, and why labels were attached to this place demonstrates how successive descriptors papered over diversity and conflict. The image of Parkdale as a Flowery Suburb, a place for families, innocent amusements, and retreat from the city, ignored the fact that the majority of residents walked to work in nearby industrial jobs. When Parkdale was condemned as becoming a serious slum, it was also providing good-quality affordable housing for a range of moderate-income households. The most recent image of Parkdale as a revitalizing village seems, at first glance, to celebrate diversity. But it is based on a grossly simplified image of the past that informs discriminatory planning practices and accepts diversity only within narrow limits. The desire to create a descript community of unity and charm, a single and simplified neighbourhood character out of the complexity of urban life, continues to have exclusionary consequences (see Young 2000).

## A Return to the Research Questions: Image over Time

As explained in the Introduction, there is a renewed interest in longitudinal studies of neighbourhood transition. This renewed interest is sparked by two factors: the gentrification of many neighbourhoods in Anglo-American central cities, which confounds earlier theories of inevitable decline, and a postmodern concern with changing discourses or images of place (Mele 2000a, 2000b; Miller 2001). Christopher Mele (2000a, 628) says that in the 1990s, "urbanists have begun to address the processes in which rhetoric, images, symbols, and representations that cohere as conventions simultaneously reflect and shape social practices within specific spaces and time frames." I would argue that there is a long minority tradition of examining complexity within communities and investigating the relationship between perceptions and social conditions over time (such as Firey 1948; Jacobs 1992; Dyos 1961; S. Clark 1966; Sennett 1974). However, it is true that the postmodern turn within the social sciences has greatly expanded the number of neighbourhood and comparative studies that take a critical look at images of place (such as Mayne 1993; Zukin 1989; Howe 1994; Smith 1996; Mele 2000a, 2000b; Miller 2001; McFarland 2001; Beauregard 2003).

I began with a central research question: what were the relationships between images of place, social conditions, and planning policy? My initial hypothesis was idealist, and somewhat mechanistic as well. I expected to find that images of place had little relation to social conditions, but that these inaccurate images would influence planning policy, which in turn would have an impact on social conditions. This initial hypothesis was based on the ideas of writers like Jane Jacobs (1992), Christine Boyer (1994), Alan Mayne (1993), and Robert Beauregard (2003), who, for me, raised compelling arguments about the importance of discourse, often contradicted by actual social conditions, in influencing planning policy. Indeed, Parkdale's successive labels of middle-class residential suburb, declining slum, and rediscovered urban village have been based more on stereotypes about gender, ethnicity, and disability, and on half-hidden social agendas related to housing type and "a good place to live" than on social conditions. Images of place may have influenced local government policy. But local government policy, in the form of restrictive zoning, bylaws, and other planning tools, had little impact on housing stock for the first hundred years of Parkdale's history.

To a considerable extent, the evidence from my case study supports the materialist view of writers such as Smith (1996), Harvey (1973, 1985), and Mele (2000b), wherein the forces of capital shape images that help determine social policy. The recurrent conflicts over Parkdale's image were often led by two different groups of property owners and developers: those who sought to immediately maximize profit from their investment in the neighbourhood and those who preferred exclusivity in the hopes that this would maximize long-term profitability. Parkdale was called a middle-class residential suburb from the 1880s until the 1910s by those who sought to market it: real estate agents, developers, journalists, and local politicians. The nickname the Flowery Suburb seems to have been invented by Parkdale's reeve in May 1879, just as the name Parkdale had been invented by the Toronto House Building Association when it registered its initial subdivision in 1875. Parkdale's image as a morally and physically separate place, a haven for the wives and daughters of middle-class commuters, was an example of successful marketing by some of its residents, particularly journalists and land developers. Simultaneously, other developers, sometimes assisted by labour leaders, promoted a minority image of Parkdale as a place of working-class homeownership, a haven for the prudent mechanic and his family. The existence of this "other" Parkdale, where mechanics walked to work with their lunch buckets, passing middle-class commuters waiting for the streetcar, was largely forgotten over time.

Parkdale was called a slum in the early twentieth century by housing reformers, politicians, and others seeking to use it as an object lesson in central city decline. In many cases (the most blatant being Robert Home Smith), these political forces were concurrently pursuing profit maximization through new housing development in the suburban fringe. In the early 1910s, Parkdale began to attract negative attention in newspapers and government reports because of its apartment buildings (both purpose-built and villa conversions), then, in the early 1930s, because of conversions to rooming houses. In 1934, an influential local government report labelled Parkdale as "becoming a serious slum." There were few powerful resident voices raised in opposition to this label, although after World War Two, the Polish community quietly embraced North Parkdale as a haven for working-class homeownership. The institutional lenders associated with this ethnic community did not agree with the consensus that the neighbourhood was inevitably declining. But local and senior government policies assumed that urban renewal was the only answer to the neighbourhood's decline, and they supported wholesale redevelopment into high-rise apartment buildings through zoning, institutional loan guarantees, and the destruction of older houses along the lakeshore for an expressway. This redevelopment was also supported by major lending institutions and by a new generation of apartment developers.

In the late 1960s, there was a resurgence of neighbourhood activism, with a theme of Parkdale returning to its past suburban glory. Politicians and some journalists listened to the voices of those developers who were renovating Parkdale's older houses into expensive single-family homes for their own use or resale. They ignored other voices, those of the tenants who were living in increasingly poor housing conditions and their social service advocates, government reports that warned of the loss of affordable housing throughout the central city, as well as some developers who were seeking to increase the stock of small units in the neighbourhood for their own immediate profit. By the 1970s, institutional lenders were happy to support all manner of redevelopment within Parkdale, both middle-class renovations and subdivision into bachelorettes. The latest stage of conflict over image was avidly reported in newspapers throughout the 1970s and 1980s. The conflict resulted in a victory for "the resurgent urban village," a shift in government policy that prioritized the needs of the minority – higher-income single-family homeowners – and ignored the needs of the majority – lower-income families and singles living in rented accommodation.

So what matters more in the determination of how neighbourhoods get their labels: evolving social norms or structural economic forces? This particular case study could be used to support either a materialist or an idealist viewpoint. The initial battle over Parkdale's image was led, on both sides, by real estate interests: not only agents, but landowners, developers, and mortgage holders. On the other hand, ordinary citizens seem to have participated to an extraordinary degree in village improvement, educational, and religious activities that reinforced the suburb's social and moral separation from the central city.

In the apartment house debate of the early 1910s, Parkdale's local political leaders, with their many linkages to apartment house construction and ownership, fought less hard than leaders of other communities to restrict this housing type. Political figures like Home Smith supported the destruction of South Parkdale's houses for a highway in order to provide easier access to his landholdings in the new suburbs west of the city. On the other hand, the moral furore over apartment housing had very little to do with economic cycles of investment and disinvestment, and much more to do with anxieties over the changing economic and social roles of women.

In the 1950s, a second wave of apartment construction in Parkdale was supported both by federal policy and by banks, while an equally important transformation was being supported by immigrant capital. By the 1970s, banks were willing to invest in both gentrified housing and bachelorettes, and the leaders of the revived Parkdale Village Residents Association were the new gentrifiers. However, during a brief period, community consensus around "reviving the lost village" extended to advocates for low-income tenants, and the ideology of gentrification seemed to have as much to do with a new set of dreams around particular housing types as with increasing profit and reducing risk in land investment. I conclude that both economic and social factors, both transnational structural trends and local agents, led to Parkdale's changing image over time.

As for the question of turning points, my examination of Parkdale closely resembles Zane Miller's 2001 history of the Cincinnati suburb of Clifton. Like Parkdale, Clifton was developed in the late nineteenth century as a socio-economically mixed "outer city neighbourhood," although its image was of a wealthy community with "parklike grounds, splendid residences, magnificent prospects" (5, 10). From the 1910s onward, the rise of comprehensive planning in Cincinnati, as in Toronto and other Anglo-American cities, was informed by the notion that, in the words of a mid-twentieth-century planning report, "older developments will gradually give place to more intensive development and the best type of housing will move further out" (cited 45). By the late 1940s, widespread apartment redevelopment was being promoted by metropolitan planners in the "middle aged" neighbourhood (54). In 1961, a new community coalition called the Clifton Town Meeting began to advocate for the preservation of this "in-town suburb" (68). Over the past forty years, there have been continuing tensions over demographic "balance" in the community, with planning initiatives aimed at limiting the number of low-income households within the neighbourhood (131).

I do not think it coincidence that Miller and I identify similar decades as turning points. Lemon (1986) gives 1912 as the date when Toronto's Annex neighbourhood ceased to "develop" and began to "decline." As in Parkdale, the Annex's larger houses began to be converted to rooming and boarding houses, despite the interventions of newly formed ratepayers' associations. Cleveland Heights, Ohio, in the case study of Marion Morton (2002, 678-82), was at the height of its affluence as a model community in the 1910s, yet clusters of inexpensive housing developments, including apartments along streetcar lines, were attracting foreign-born members of the working class and leading to ethnic and class conflict. Lemon (1986, 23-24) says that Annex residents pursued the "politics of protection" from the early 1950s, with both tenants and a new generation of "whitepainters" promoting a "renaissance" in their neighbourhood. Similarly, community associations in Cleveland Heights were successful in fighting off proposed freeways in the 1960s (M. Morton 2002, 689).

I would argue that the second decade of the twentieth century, and the 1950s and 1960s, were times when the contradictions of urban social *and* economic change were at their most unmanageable. The rhetoric of Hastings' 1911 slum report and the subsequent discourse on apartment buildings in Toronto can only be understood within a context in which a rapid increase in the number of women in the paid workforce, and growing concerns about immigration, led to a condemnation of housing forms that might accommodate these different households. I agree with both Christine Boyer (1983) and Robert Beauregard (2003) that the growth of planning instruments in the early twentieth century was an attempt to place greater disciplinary order on an increasingly complex set of citizens and households. Parkdale had been sold as a morally different community during its development in the 1880s, but in the 1910s its diverse housing forms defied an increasingly stringent concept of what a good place to live might look like. Although mortgage lenders were moving outwards in Toronto in search of green fields in which to invest capital (Paterson 1991), the new images of decline owed more to ideas than to the presence or absence of development money.

Similarly, the 1950s and 1960s were a time when households and individuals were changing rapidly. The urban social movements of the time, which seemed at first to be broad-based and inclusionary, gradually turned into exclusionary battles that hid an agenda of homogenization under the rhetoric of social balance (Smith 1996, 2002). The fight to make Parkdale a good place to live again required that, in the words of Christine Boyer (1983, 68), "contradictory strategies and information [be] contained within a veneer of rationality and compatibility." Part of the story in Parkdale may have been increasing costs to buy into a gentrifying community, leading to increased protection of investments by homeowners and real estate interests. But I would argue, based on my research, that the historical myth of Parkdale as a stable, middle-class, residential, somehow "good" community both justified and shaped strategies to "return" its houses to single-family occupancy. Once again, both structural socio-economic forces and local agents shaped the debate over Parkdale's character.

## Social Conditions and the Impact of Policy over Time

Images may have had an impact on planning policy, but policy in turn was remarkably ineffective in changing social conditions, at least in the short term. I do not know of any other longitudinal neighbourhood studies that have been backed up by roughly comparable empirical data over a 125-year period. The use of assessment samples, street directories, land registry records, and (after 1951) census information has allowed me to determine, at least within the confines of this case study, whether image-led policy changed social conditions.

Let me begin by summarizing the data on social conditions in relation to images. When Parkdale was first described as a residential suburb for middle-class commuters in the 1880s, the majority of household heads worked within walking distance, and there were more skilled labourers than businesspeople or professionals. The Parkdale homeownership rate was extremely high (75 percent in the 1881 sample, 60 percent in the 1891 sample), over double the Toronto rate. Property prices rose rapidly throughout the 1870s and 1880s, only to plummet during the 1890s depression. Property profits rebounded slightly during the 1906-1913 housing boom, when the northwestern portion of the suburb was developed and apartment buildings began to be constructed along the main commercial streets.

Parkdale had its highest proportion of businesspeople and professionals from the 1890s to the 1910s, after it was annexed by the City of Toronto and its initial image as the Flowery Suburb had begun to fade. When Parkdale was first being developed, the majority of land and home mortgages were held by institutional lenders. By 1913, the proportion of mortgages held by institutions had declined, as had the proportion of professional and managerial households. This coincided with the first concerns about decline in the community.

Throughout the 1921 to 1961 period, Parkdale was a mixed community, relatively affluent in relation to the rest of the central city, in terms of the socio-economic class of household heads. The neighbourhood continued to have a lower proportion of unskilled labourers than the City of Toronto, and in 1951, average income was not substantially lower than the average for greater Toronto, and relatively high for central Toronto. Property prices increased during the 1920s, then remained stagnant until the early 1950s, which matches what we know about general Toronto price trends. Very few Parkdale houses did not meet the health and safety standards of the day. Thus Parkdale was not a classic slum of poor people and substandard housing conditions during this period, despite being described as "becoming a serious slum." It was, however, a place where the conversion of houses to multiple units soared and homeownership plummeted in the 1930s. Even after the housing crisis of World War Two had ended, it remained a community of tenants in the City of Homes.

Beginning in the early 1950s, Parkdale property prices began to rise steadily. From the 1960s, institutional mortgage lending increased, and house prices continued to climb above the greater Toronto average. At the same time, median household income was beginning to decline in Parkdale, and the occupational classification of workers was beginning to diverge from the average for greater Toronto. A small proportion of Parkdale homeowners and landlords were making good profits on their investments. But most residents were becoming poorer during the time that the neighbourhood began to be called an urban village.

I do not want to overstate my case. To some extent, the common images were a faithful reflection of social conditions. Parkdale was a haven of homeownership at the time that it was called a suburb, although its houses were occupied by industrial walk-to-workers as much as middle-class commuters. Parkdale did experience some investment decline at the time it began to be described as declining. And descriptions of Parkdale as an increasingly divergent community over the past thirty-five years, simultaneously a gentrifying area and a social service ghetto, are supported by empirical data.

Images sometimes predated, and to some extent determined, social conditions. Parkdale's image as a Flowery Suburb predated the construction of most of its villas. Its image as a declining community justified disinvestment in its houses and planning policies that encouraged the wholesale destruction of affordable housing. A simplified image of Parkdale's past fuelled homeowner activism and planning responses that made the lives of poor residents much more difficult, while supporting the gentrification of older houses in the community.

But while changing images of "a good place to live" did inform social conditions and housing policy, local government planning policy was essentially ineffective, at least until the end of the twentieth century. Successive attempts to regulate row houses in the 1880s, apartment buildings in the 1910s, boarding houses in the 1930s, and bachelorettes in the 1980s all proved ineffective in stopping these housing forms. It can be argued that a broadly based community coalition helped end high-rise apartment construction in the late 1960s and early 1970s, and later, a less broadly based community coalition was able to stymie many affordable social housing projects from being built in Parkdale. But in the second case, it can also be argued that the success of these campaigns resulted from broader political and social changes in the City of Toronto and, indeed, in large cities in Canada and other countries as well (see Ley 1996 and Caulfield 1994). The local forces of gentrification may have mattered less than the inexorable market forces in the late twentieth century that were transforming older houses into commodities for the upper middle classes.

A disturbing continuity is apparent behind this century of planning policy campaigns. Each time, the rhetoric talked about creating good housing while the regulations sought to limit housing choices for low-income people. There were only two short periods when local government policy seemed to react constructively to the social conditions of those most in need. The actions of the independent Parkdale Council and some residents during the 1880s supported the establishment of good public education facilities for all ages and a commitment to public amenities such as trees and a lakeside boardwalk. In the early 1970s, the City of Toronto's house and land banking program, along with the local community's social service innovations, produced a brief moment of support for the growing population of people in need of affordable housing in Parkdale. But these short periods were exceptions to the rule of fear of poor and somehow "different" people who might be accommodated by particular housing forms. As Pierre Filion (1999) has discussed in relation to modern versus postmodern planning, the discourse changes, but the planning practices remain remarkably continuous over time, perhaps pointing to the underlying stability of the profit motive and property relations over the past two centuries.

## Rediscovering the Nondescript Community:
## A Preliminary Research Agenda

As I began to gather information, the story of Parkdale began to appear as a story of "stubborn housing diversity," in the words of Harris (1996, 1994). If one of the great challenges that face cities today is the accommodation of difference (Hayden 1984; Young 1990, 2000; Wilson 1991;

Sibley 1995; Fincher and Jacobs 1998), then it might help to look back at the past, not only to understand why we have the exclusionary planning policies that we do, but also to uncover alternatives, sites of resistance, places that did not fit the dominant models.

Despite local government hostility and institutional memory loss, Parkdale has always provided a range of affordable housing to the people who needed it most. Aside from the hidden history of housing diversity, an equally hidden history of gender, ethnicity, disability, and power differences began to emerge in this research. Recent scholarship has examined how beliefs about gender shaped nineteenth- and twentieth-century suburban development, and moral panics over lodging houses and apartments in the early twentieth century.[1] Although single women have been given their due as gentrifiers in recent literature (D. Rose 1984 and 1989 helped accomplish this), considerably less information exists on earlier generations of women as actors in the housing process: as landowners, housing developers, and mortgage holders in the late nineteenth century (but see Green 2000), or as landladies and housing reform advocates in the mid-twentieth century (but see Harris 1993; Dennis 1987). Nell Gwynne and Pamela Noble's subdivision efforts in the late nineteenth century, Mrs. Virtue building her tenements despite opposition in the 1880s, the widow Sophie Dunn and her mortgages, are not unique. The stories of Mrs. Rawcliffe the Queen Street grocer and landlady in the 1880s, Martha Crooks operating her Jameson Avenue rooming house in the 1920s, Dorothy Wood and Viola Starr losing their livelihoods as well as their homes with the construction of the Gardiner Expressway in the 1950s, are glimpses of a hidden world of businesswomen as well.

While many US urban histories focus on racial and ethnic conflict over urban resources in the early twentieth century (Philpott 1978; Jackson 1967), a great deal more remains to be discovered about Canadian nativist movements in the late nineteenth and early twentieth centuries, and about conflicts over difference in urban space. For instance, there are no published works on the brief life of the Toronto Ku Klux Klan in the 1920s (although Robin 1992 and Sher 1983 focus more generally on nativist and fascist movements in Canada). Little is known about the lives of people institutionalized in the Magdalen Asylum for Fallen Women, Central Prison, the Provincial Lunatic Asylum, or the Mercer Reformatory for Women and Girls (although Splane 1971 is a classic work on the establishment of these institutions).

In general, we know very little about the basic struggles to obtain adequate and affordable housing over time (although Harris 1996 is an excellent work on affordability struggles in Toronto in the early twentieth century). Empirical studies of mortgage financing and property prices in Canadian cities before World War Two are scarce (but see Doucet and Weaver 1991; Harris and Ragonetti 1998). The stories of Alan Skeotch's father running barefoot in the snow to the nearest cheap hotel in the 1930s, Joseph Brunelle and his various housing affordability strategies (home repair, taking in boarders, walking to work) from the 1910s to the 1960s, Pat Capponi trying to survive in her rooming house in the 1970s, and Parveen Moussa spending a sleepless night catching mice in her apartment in the 1990s come from little-known memoirs or brief mentions in newspaper articles. All of these stories are important, however, not only because they illuminate housing conditions in a way that neither reports nor statistics can, but because they speak to us of the importance of home and the lengths to which people go to find one.

Iris Marion Young (1990, 229), a political philosopher, cites Michel Foucault on the Enlightenment dream of a "transparent society, visible and legible in each of its parts, the dream of there no longer existing any zones of darkness [or] disorder." This dream, which Young also calls the "ideal of community ... expresses a desire for social wholeness, symmetry, a solid identity." It is an "understandable dream ... with serious political consequences" (232). In this book, I have talked about the 125-year life of a neighbourhood in which the changing ideal of community was in constant conflict with the politics of difference. From the first naming of Parkdale as a suburb separate from industrial Brockton, there were attempts to control housing types as a mechanism of social filtering. The fact that these attempts were largely unsuccessful, at least in the short term, does not make them any less discriminatory in intent. The fact that these attempts involved coalitions of government, business, academics, reformers, and local communities, in various combinations and identifying with different political parties, does not make them any less repressive in nature.

Instead of a focus on good housing conditions and the welfare of citizens, instead of efforts towards an inclusive community that would accommodate different households in different forms of housing, local government – abetted by some property-related businesses, some residents, and some academic researchers – repeatedly attempted to impose a false unity through regulation of housing type, successively row houses, apartment houses, rooming houses, and bachelorettes. One group, such as local government, progressive reformers, or residents' associations, would legitimate a positive vision of the neighbourhood's identity by excluding another group, such as industrial workers, boarders, single women, or single men. The slow-growth Tories in the early years of Parkdale Council in the 1880s identified row houses as a threat to the Flowery Suburb. In the

1910s, the City of Toronto's Public Health Department, the University of Toronto's Social Work and Architecture Departments, and the Toronto Council of Women, all progressive institutions, declared apartment buildings to be the harbingers of immorality in Parkdale. By the 1930s and 1940s, the same reform coalition had decided that only wholesale destruction and rebuilding would save the neighbourhood and its inhabitants. The Parkdale Working Group on Bachelorettes in the 1970s, supported by councillors on the left wing of City Council and progressive local planners, saw the main threat to Parkdale's revitalization, its return to suburban dreamtime, as single-room-occupancy units, not deteriorating housing conditions in legal apartments.

With the exception of a brief period in the 1980s, Parkdale's population continued to rise over 125 years, with an increasing number and variety of people calling it home. Houses were used and reused in many different ways. To use terms coined by Iris Marion Young (1990, 238), against all odds, the neighbourhood was often able to provide the cardinal virtues of city life: social difference without exclusion, variety and diversity in land use, eroticism (the pleasure and danger of the strange and surprising), and publicity (the encounters with difference that are the hallmark of public space). Parkdale was neither particularly beautiful nor particularly famous. Despite moments of fame, during its brief moment as a model suburb in the 1880s and the heyday of Sunnyside in the 1920s, it was generally a utilitarian rather than a showpiece suburb. It provided housing, opportunity, belonging, and a measure of social life to its residents. It appears to have "worked" as a neighbourhood, perhaps because it never quite embodied its successive labels of middle-class suburb, declining slum, and renascent urban village.

Parkdale is not a special place, except in the sense that all places that people call home are special. It is a nondescript community in the best sense of the term. It is a complex place, where diversity has thrived despite repeated attempts to impose false unity through a simple label. The question remains how to nurture that diversity, within neighbourhoods and within cities. The challenge remains finding a set of urban images and policies that do not legitimize themselves by excluding the "other."

# Notes

## Introduction

1 In this book, I will be dealing mostly with the experience of cities in relatively wealthy English-speaking nations: Canada (particularly English Canada), the United States, the United Kingdom, and Australia. Despite the significant differences in the urban histories of these four countries, cross-cultural stereotypes help shape not only representation and public perception, but also policy.

2 For neighbourhoods that resisted decline in Chicago, New York City, and Boston, see Jacobs 1992. In addition, McFarland 2001 discusses Greenwich Village in New York City; Firey 1947 looks at Beacon Hill in Boston; and Teaford 1990 gives other examples of US neighbourhoods that resisted decline.

3 Parkdale consists of six regular census tracts and one special tract, the Toronto Rehabilitation Hospital, whose 247 residents are not included in income or housing calculations. Median income and other statistics for the neighbourhood are derived from census tract figures.

4 James Lemon's short history (1986) of the neighbourhood in Toronto which most resembles Parkdale, the Annex, identifies similar periods, although the current era of what Lemon calls the "politics of protection" is dated back to 1959.

## Chapter 1: A Good Place to Live?

1 I am referring here to Marxist formulations of the city in the late 1970s and early 1980s, such as Walker 1981.

## Chapter 2: The Flowery Suburb

1 The Americans landed at Humber Bay. The name of Grenadier Pond in High Park commemorates the British troops who fell through the ice during an unsuccessful attempt to stop the invasion.

2 As Gunter Gad (1994, 113; 2004) has pointed out, the movement of industries to what was then the western fringe of Toronto took place well before the turn of the twentieth century, in seeming contradiction to many urban historians' emphasis on central city concentration. Robert Lewis (2002) has also argued that industry began to decentralize in North American cities much earlier than previously assumed.

3 But see Green 2000 and Rodger 2001 for a discussion of women's roles in the development of London and Edinburgh, respectively.

4 Letter from long-time resident A. Gowanlock (1905), in Parkdale's local history collection. Lest this be dismissed as suburban legend, the *Globe* reported on 25 July 1878 that "A camp of Gypsies have occupied three tents at the village of Parkdale for some days past. The men seem to do business in the buying and selling of horses."

5 Parkdale's medical officer of health, Charles Playter, a Liberal, applied for the position,

but lost to William Caniff, who was a Conservative and thus a more palatable patronage appointment for the Tory majority on Toronto's council (MacDougall 1990, 13).

6   R.C. Libby's oral history was taped by the Toronto between the Wars Project (1971-1972), and can be heard at the Baldwin Room, Toronto Reference Library, along with the memoirs of Ethel Abel, Dorothy Goddard, and many others cited in this and the following chapter.

7   The development of Sunnyside in 1922 did include a swimming pool, which remains in use today.

8   The case, deserving of a book in itself (which I hope to write), is described by Strange (1992, 1995).

### Chapter 3: "Becoming a Serious Slum"

1   See letter from city solicitor, 12 July 1912, indicating that the Magann estate is being bought for park purposes (City of Toronto Board of Control 1912); the properties do not appear in the 1913 assessment records.

2   The Kum-C, Parkdale Theatre, and Odeon, all on Queen Street west of Sorauren, advertised in the local paper, *Parkdale Topics*, in 1923. The Brighton, at Roncesvalles and Pearson, also dates from this period. The Revue, further north on Roncesvalles, has been in continuous operation as a movie theatre since 1911.

3   As of 1951, census tract information is available for the 1879-1889 boundaries of Parkdale.

4   The 1967 South Parkdale planning proposals explicitly state that further high-density development in Parkdale would be served by the Gardiner Expressway along with the proposed Queen Street subway line.

### Chapter 4: From Bowery to Bohemia

1   For more information on the job trailer, see *Telegram*, 23 March 1971; for more on the Atlantic Centre, see *Globe and Mail*, 15 April 1971.

2   The Gutta Percha whistle is mentioned in many oral histories, such as Albert Crosswell's contribution to the Oral History Project (1974-1978).

3   See, for example, a five-part *Toronto Star* exposé on rooming house conditions by a reporter who went "undercover" as a former psychiatric patient (24-28 August 1981); inquests of tenant deaths covered in *Toronto Star* (30 November 1985) and *Globe and Mail* (5 August 1986); and reports on fatal fires in *Globe and Mail* (25 June 1981, 27 March 1986) and *Toronto Star* (17 September 1998).

### Chapter 5: Why Does Parkdale Matter?

1   See Marsh 1990, Hayden 1984, and Wright 1980 on general suburban history, and Sendbuehler and Gilliland 1998 on a specific piece of Toronto legislation; see Strange 1995 and Valverde 1991 on turn-of-the-century moral reform and women.

# References

**Unpublished Sources**
All reports are to be found in the City of Toronto Archives (CTA), the Urban Affairs Library (UAL), Toronto Reference Library (TRL), or the Local History Collections of Parkdale (PDL) and High Park (HPL) branches of Toronto Public Library, unless otherwise noted.

A note on Toronto planning bodies: There were no long-term planning bodies in the City of Toronto until the early 1940s. In 1942, an independent committee on zoning created Toronto's first city-wide zoning bylaw, which was accepted, after considerable modification, in 1943. From 1943 to 1946, the City Planning Board, an appointed committee reporting to Council, created Toronto's first master plan, which was never formally adopted by Council. In 1949, the re-organized Toronto City Planning Board presented a modified master plan (Official Plan), which was adopted by City Council. Other master plans followed in 1959, 1974, and 1992. From 1953 to 1997, a regional level of government, Metropolitan Toronto, encompassing the City of Toronto and the inner ring of suburban municipalities, also developed master plans which increasingly diverged from the City of Toronto's "central city neighbourhood preservation" perspective. The Toronto City Planning Board, an independent body, became the City of Toronto Planning Department in 1980, and the City of Toronto Planning and Development Department soon after. In 1997, the Province of Ontario amalgamated all six municipalities within Metro Toronto into a new City of Toronto, and planning was subsumed within Urban Development Services. An Official Plan for the new City of Toronto was adopted in 2003.

Abbott, A.R. 1880-1905. Notebooks (10 volumes, transcribed but unpublished). Baldwin Room, TRL.
Abel, E. 1971. Parkdale: The making of a community. *Parkdale Citizen,* 5 September. PDL.
Adams, Alderman B. 1979. Memo to City Council re: 156 Dowling Avenue. PDL.
Arthur, E., et al. 1942. Report of the Advisory Committee Studying Housing in the City of Toronto. Toronto Board of Control. CTA.
Bruce, Lord, et al. 1934. Report of the Lieutenant-Governor's Committee on Housing Conditions in Toronto [The Bruce Report]. CTA.
Brunelle, J. 1972. *The Brunelles of Wright Avenue.* Self-published. HPL.
Bureau of Municipal Research. 1918. What is the Ward going to do with Toronto? CTA.
–. 1982. A case for bachelorettes. UAL.
Carver, H. 1946. How much housing does greater Toronto need? Toronto Metropolitan Housing Research Project. CTA.
Census of Canada. 1951, 1961, 1971, 1981, 1991, 2001.
Chaddah, C. March 2002. Roncesvalles Village real estate report (flyer). Personal collection of author.

City of Toronto. 1912. Report of the Charities Commission. Toronto: Carswell Publishing. CTA.

City of Toronto Alternative Housing Subcommittee. 1992. Rooming House Review. UAL.

City of Toronto Assessment Commissioner. 1927. Report of the Assessment Commissioner. CTA.

City of Toronto Assessment Rolls. 1891, 1901, 1913, 1921, 1931, 1941, 1951. CTA.

–. 1961, 1971, 1981, 1991, 2001. Toronto Records Office, basement of Toronto City Hall, 100 Queen Street West, Toronto.

City of Toronto Board of Control. 1911-1913. Correspondence boxes. CTA.

City of Toronto Board of Health. 1912-1914. Monthly reports to Council. CTA.

City of Toronto Committee on Buildings and Development. 1978. Deputations re: bylaw to control conversions of boarding or lodging houses to bachelorettes, 18 April. PDL, Parkdale Tenants Association file.

City of Toronto Council. 1893, 1910-1912, 1931-1932. Minutes. CTA.

–. 1913a. By-law 6061 concerning apartment and tenement houses. CTA.

–. 1913b. By-law 6109, an amendment to by-law 6061. CTA.

–. 1978. By-law 67-78 restricting boarding and lodging houses in South Parkdale. 30 January. CTA.

City of Toronto Housing Commission. 1918. Report of the Housing Commission. CTA.

City of Toronto Housing Department. 1980. Vanishing options: The impending rental crisis in Toronto. UAL.

–. 1981. Building challenges: Confronting Toronto's rental crisis. UAL.

City of Toronto Housing Review Committee. 1973. Living room: An approach to home banking and land banking for the City of Toronto. UAL.

City of Toronto Housing Working Group. 1986. Living room 2: A city housing policy review. UAL.

City of Toronto Independent Committee on Zoning. 1942. Draft zoning by-law. CTA.

City of Toronto Planning Board. 1952. Fourth annual report. CTA.

–. 1954. Fifth annual report. CTA.

–. 1956a. Report on review of the Official Plan. CTA.

–. 1956b. Urban renewal. CTA.

–. 1959a. The Annex planning district appraisal and plan. UAL.

–. 1959b. The changing city: A forecast of planning issues for the City of Toronto 1956-1980. CTA.

–. 1960. Urban renewal, redevelopment and housing. UAL.

–. 1961. Ethnic origins, based on 1961 census data. UAL.

–. 1966. Prospects for the rehabilitation of housing in central Toronto. UAL.

–. 1967a. Proposed plan for South Parkdale. UAL.

–. 1967b. Proposed plan for Toronto. UAL.

–. 1967c. Submissions received on proposed plan for Toronto. UAL.

–. 1973a. Report on height limitations in North Parkdale. UAL.

–. 1973b. Study designed to ascertain parking requirements for lodging and rooming houses. UAL.

–. 1974. Report on the desirability of intense proliferation of group homes, rest homes, halfway homes and children's homes in the South Parkdale area. UAL.

–. 1975. Housing low-income single people. UAL.

–. 1976a. Neighbourhood improvement plan for Queen-Lansdowne. UAL.

–. 1976b. Trends and planning goals: South Parkdale. UAL.

–. 1977a. Conversion of Boarding or Lodging Houses to Bachelorettes, 18 May. PDL, Bachelorette folder.

–. 1977b. Report of the working committee on group homes. UAL.

City of Toronto Planning Department. 1980. Housing deconversion. Research bulletin 16.

City of Toronto Planning and Development Department. 1982. Neighbourhood plan proposals for South Parkdale. UAL.

–. 1983. South Parkdale plan. UAL.

–. 1990. Update on South Parkdale proposals. UAL.

City of Toronto Police Department. Annual reports of the Chief Constable 1901-1951. CTA.

City of Toronto Public Health Department. 1921-1975. Annual public health reports. CTA.

City of Toronto Social Survey Commission. 1915. Report of the Social Survey Commission. CTA.

City of Toronto Subcommittee on Housing Needs of the Homeless Population. 1986. Housing needs of the homeless population. UAL.

City of Toronto Survey Committee on Housing Conditions. 1943. Report of the City Council's Survey Committee on Housing Conditions in Toronto 1942-1943. CTA.

City of Toronto Urban Development Services. 1998. Parkdale planning initiatives final report. UAL.

Cotter, Graham. 1978. Reminiscences (unpublished manuscript). PDL.

CTPB. *See* City of Toronto Planning Board.

Golden, A., W. Currie, E. Greaves, and J. Latimer. 1999. Taking responsibility for homelessness: An action plan for Toronto. Mayor's Task Force on Homelessness. UAL.

Greater Toronto and the men who made it. 1911. Toronto: Inter-provincial Publishing Company. TRL.

Harris, R. 1992. Assessment roll samples. 1901, 1913, 1921, 1931, 1941, 1951.

Hastings, C. 1911. Report of the medical officer of health dealing with the recent investigation of slum conditions in Toronto, embodying recommendations for the amelioration of same. City of Toronto Department of Health. CTA.

Howard, J.G. 1883. My autobiography. Self-published. TRL.

Land Registry Records. 1793-2002. Can be viewed for a charge at Land Registry Office #66, Ontario Ministry of Consumer and Business Services, 20 Dundas West, 3rd floor.

Lillie, B.A. 1971a. Parkdale man recalls the past. *Parkdale Citizen*, September, 3. PDL.

–. 1971b. BA Lillie continues Parkdale memories. *Parkdale Citizen*, October, 3. PDL.

Mayor's Task Force on Bachelorettes. 1979. Report of the Mayor's Task Force on Bachelorettes. UAL.

Metropolitan Toronto Planning Board. 1959. Official Plan for the Metro Toronto planning area. CTA.

–. 1962. Analysis of 1961 census data for Toronto. UAL.

Metropolitan Toronto Planning and Community Services Departments. 1983. No place to go: A study of homelessness in Metro Toronto. UAL.

Metropolitan Toronto Task Force on Housing for Low-Income Singles. 1983. Final report. UAL.

*Might's Directory*. 1878-1951 editions. TRL.

Oral History Project. 1974-1978. Audiotaped memoirs of Alfred Bolt, Aubrey Bone, Albert Crosswell, Ruth Ellis, Stan Mamek, Jessie Johnson, John Jose. Baldwin Room, TRL.

Parkdale Collegiate Institute. 1996. Profiles in Parkdale. PDL.

Parkdale Community Legal Services. 1976. Submission on proposed amendment to zoning by-law re: bachelorettes. 30 August. PDL, Bachelorette file.

Parkdale Council (Village of Parkdale 1879-1885; Town of Parkdale 1886-1888). Minutes. CTA.

–. 1881. Assessment roll. CTA.

Parkdale Liberty Economic Development Committee. 2000. Parkdale Liberty: History, arts, culture (flyer). Author's personal collection.

Parkdale Tenants Association. 1972. Letter to Ontario Housing Commission re: Dunn Avenue. PDL, Social Housing folder.

–. 1975. Newsletter, 10 February. PDL, Tenants folder.

Parkdale Working Group on Bachelorettes. 1977. The basis of a solution to bachelorette conversion. 31 May. PDL, Bachelorette file.

Peat Marwick. 1974. City of Toronto rooming house study. UAL.

Potts, B. 1971. Down memory lane. *Parkdale Citizen*, June, 3. PDL.

Skeotch, A. 1979. It only takes 65 seconds to drive through Parkdale (unpublished manuscript). PDL.

South Parkdale Residents Association. 1972. Letter to Ontario Housing Commission re: Dunn Avenue. PDL, Social Housing folder.
Starr Group. 1988. West end rooming house study: Final report. UAL.
–. 1998. Housing supply and affordability: Rooming houses and second suites (background report to Golden, et al. 1999). UAL.
Toronto between the Wars. 1971-1972. Audiotaped memoirs of Ethel Abel, Dorothy Goddard, R.C. Libby, Bella Townsend. Baldwin Room, TRL.
Toronto City Planning Board. 1946. First annual report. CTA.
–. 1947. Second annual report. CTA.
–. 1949. Third annual report and Official Plan. CTA.
Toronto Harbour Commission. 1913. Toronto waterfront development 1912-1920. CTA.
Toronto Housing Commission. 1918. Report of the Housing Commission. CTA.
Toronto Planning Board. 1943. Master Plan for the City of Toronto. CTA.
–. 1944. Third annual report. CTA.
York Township. 1874-1878. Minutes. CTA.

**Newspaper and Magazine Articles**

Toronto has three daily newspapers that existed throughout the study period. The *Globe and Mail* is the result of a 1936 merger between the *Globe*, aligned with the Liberal Party and founded in 1844, and the *Mail and Empire*, itself the product of a merger of two papers aligned with the Conservative Party. It is generally considered the "pro-business" newspaper. The *Toronto Star*, with small-l liberal tendencies, has been publishing since 1892. The *Evening Telegram*, a populist broadsheet since 1878, became the *Sun* in 1971.

The Parkdale Branch, Toronto Public Library (PDL) has hundreds of Toronto local and neighbourhood news clippings from 1970 onwards, and a scrapbook of newspaper clippings, lovingly hand-transcribed, from 1878 to 1910. A scrapbook of Toronto local news clippings from 1910 to 1930 can be found in the Baldwin Room, Toronto Reference Library (TRL). Many of these clippings and transcripts have lost their original page numbers. The Urban Affairs Library (UAL) has hundreds of news clippings about the "Parkdale Planning Area" from 1965 onwards. The *Toronto Star* has a searchable database, called *Pages of the Past*, covering the period since 1892. This database can be accessed free of charge at TRL and UAL. Because of the number of newspaper articles cited, I merely list the newspaper and publication date. All newspapers can be found on micro-fiche at Mills Library, McMaster University, with the exceptions of those so noted.

*Canadian,* December 1975. Clipping at PDL.
*City Planning.* Clippings at PDL
*Community Schools,* 1972-1973. Clippings at PDL.
*Empire* (Toronto), 1887-1895.
*Evening Telegram* (Toronto), 1878-1969.
*Eye Magazine* (Toronto), 1998. Clippings at PDL.
*Globe and Mail* (Toronto), 1936-2002.
*Labour Gazette,* 1901-1951.
*Mail* (Toronto), 1878-1895.
*Mail and Empire* (Toronto), 1895-1936.
*Parkdale Citizen,* 1971-1977. PDL.
*Parkdale Gazette and Brockton Advocate,* 1881. PDL.
*Parkdale Pictorial,* 11 April 1962. TRL.
*Parkdale Topics,* June 1923. TRL.
*New York Times,* 2002.
*Real Estate News* (Toronto), 1973-1999. Clippings at PDL.
*Telegram* (Toronto), 1971. Clippings at PDL and UAL.
*Toronto Life,* 1982-2002.
*Toronto Star,* 1892-2002. Online database at TRL and UAL.
*Toronto Sun,* 1971-2002. Clippings at PDL and UAL.

*Worker*, 28 February 1925. Thomas Fisher Rare Books Collection, Robarts Library, University of Toronto.
*World*, 1878-1898.

## Published References

Adam, G.M. 1891. *Toronto old and new: A memorial volume historical, descriptive and pictorial*. Toronto: The Mail Printing Company.

Ahlbrandt, R., and P. Brophy. 1975. *Neighbourhood revitalization*. Lexington, MA: Lexington Books.

Allen, I. 1984. The ideology of dense neighbourhood redevelopment. In J. Palen and B. London, ed., *Gentrification, displacement and neighbourhood redevelopment*, 27-42. Albany: SUNY Press.

Anderson, M. 1964. *The federal bulldozer: A critical examination of urban renewal 1949-1962*. Cambridge, MA: MIT Press.

Armstrong, C., and V. Nelles. 1977. *Revenge of the Methodist Bicycle Company: Sunday streetcars and municipal reform in Toronto*. Toronto: P. Martin Associates.

Bacher, J. 1993. *Keeping to the marketplace: A history of Canadian housing policy*. Montreal: McGill-Queen's University Press.

Ball, M., and A. Wood, 1999. Housing investment: Long run international trends and volatility. *Housing Studies* 14(2): 185-209.

Baxandall, R., and E. Ewen. 2000. *Picture windows: How the suburbs happened*. New York: Basic Books.

Beauregard, R. 1986. The chaos and complexity of gentrification. In Smith and Williams 1986, 35-55.

–. 1990. Trajectories of neighbourhood change: The case of gentrification. *Environment and Planning A* 22: 855-74.

–. 2003. *Voices of decline: The post-war fate of U.S. cities*. Cambridge, MA: Blackwell.

Berry, B. 1985. Islands of renewal in seas of decay. In P. Peterson, ed., *The new urban reality*, 69-96. Washington: Brookings Institute.

Bondi, L. 1991. Gender divisions and gentrification: A critique. *Transactions, Institute of British Geographers*, 16, 190-98.

Booth, C. 1971. *Charles Booth's London: Excerpts from "Life and labour of the people of London."* London: Penguin Books. Originally published 1889-91.

Bourne, L.S. 1967. *Private redevelopment of the central city: Spatial processes of structural change in the City of Toronto*. Chicago: University of Chicago Department of Geography Research Paper 112.

–, ed. 1971. *Internal structure of the city*. New York: Oxford University Press.

Boyer, C. 1983. *Dreaming the rational city: The myth of American urban planning*. Cambridge, MA: MIT Press.

–. 1994. *The city of collective memory: Its historical imagery and architectural entertainments*. Cambridge, MA: MIT Press.

Briggs, A. 1993. *Victorian cities*. Berkeley: University of California Press. Originally published 1963.

Burgess, E. 1974. The growth of the city: An introduction to a research project. In R. Park, E. Burgess, and R. Mackenzie, eds., *The city*, 47-62. Chicago: University of Chicago Press. Originally published 1925.

Burnett, P. 1973. Social change, the status of women and models of city form and development. *Antipode* 5(2): 57-62.

Canniff, W. 1968. *Illustrated atlas of the County of York 1878*. Toronto: P. Martin.

Capponi, P. 1992. *Upstairs at the crazy house: The life of a psychiatric survivor*. Toronto: Viking.

Careless, J.M.S. 1984. *Toronto to 1918: An illustrated history*. Toronto: James Lorimer.

Carr, E.H. 1961. *What is history?* New York: Vintage Books.

Castells, M. 1977. *The urban question: A Marxist approach*. Cambridge, MA: MIT Press.

–. 1983. *The city and the grass-roots: A cross-cultural history of urban social movements*. Berkeley: University of California Press.

Caulfield, J. 1994. *City form and everyday life: Toronto's gentrification and critical social practice*. Toronto: University of Toronto Press.

Champion, T. 1899. *The Methodist churches of Toronto*. Toronto: G.M. Rose and Sons.

Chaucer, G. 1974. *Canterbury Tales*. London: University of London Press.

Chorney, H. 1990. *City of dreams: Social theory and the urban experience*. Toronto: Nelson Canada.

Clark, C.S. 1898. *Of Toronto the good: A social study [of] the queen city of Canada as it is*. Montreal: Toronto Publishing Company.

Clark, S.D. 1966. *The suburban society*. Toronto: University of Toronto Press.

Copp, T. 1974. *The anatomy of poverty: The condition of the working class in Montreal 1897-1929*. Toronto: McClelland and Stewart.

Crawford, B. 2000. *Rosedale*. Toronto: Dundurn.

Dear, M., ed. 2002. *From Chicago to L.A.: Making sense of urban theory*. Thousand Oaks: Sage.

Dear, M., and.J. Wolch. 1987. *Landscapes of despair: From deinstitutionalization to homelessness*. Princeton, NJ: Princeton University Press.

Dennis, R. 1987. *Landlords and rented housing in Toronto 1885-1914*. Toronto: University of Toronto Centre for Urban and Community Studies Research Paper.

–. 1989. *Toronto's first apartment housing boom: An historical geography 1900-1920*. Toronto: Centre for Urban and Community Studies, University of Toronto.

–. 1998. Apartment Housing in Canadian cities, 1900-1940. *Urban History Review* 26(2): 17-31.

–. 2000. Zoning before zoning: The regulation of apartment housing in early 20th century Winnipeg and Toronto. *Planning Perspectives* 15: 267-99.

Dominion Coach Line. 1910. *Handbook of Toronto*. Toronto: Dominion Coach Line.

Doucet, M., and J. Weaver. 1991. *Housing the North American city*. Montreal: McGill-Queen's University Press.

Douglass, H. 1970. *The suburban trend*. New York: Arno Press. Originally published 1925.

Downs, A. 2000. Comment on Metzger. *Housing Policy Debate* 11(1): 41-55.

Dreier, P., J. Mollenkopf, and T. Swanstrom. 2001. *Place matters: Metropolitics for the 21st century*. Lawrence: University of Kansas Press.

Duany, A., E. Plater-Zyberk, and J. Speck. 2000. *Suburban nation: The rise of sprawl and the decline of the American dream*. New York: North Point Press.

Dyos, H.J. 1961. *Victorian suburb: a study of the growth of Camberwell*. Leicester: Leicester University Press.

Dyos, H.J., and D.A. Reeder. 1973. Slums and suburbs. In H.J. Dyos and M. Wolff, ed., *The Victorian city: Images and realities*, 359-88. London: Routledge and Kegan Paul.

Edel, M., E. Sclar, and D. Luria. 1984. *Shaky palaces: Homeownership and social mobility in Boston's suburbanization*. New York: Columbia University Press.

Ehrenreich, B. 1983. *Hearts of men: American dreams and the flight from commitment*. Garden City, NJ: Anchor Press.

Einhorn, R. 1991. *Property rules: Political economy in Chicago 1833-1872*. Chicago: University of Chicago Press.

Engels, F. 1969. *The Condition of the working classes in England*. Chicago: Academy Chicago. Originally published 1845.

Filey, M. 1996. *I Remember Sunnyside: The rise and fall of a magical era*. Toronto: Dundurn Press.

Filion, P. 1999. Rupture or continuity? Modern and postmodern planning in Toronto. *International Journal of Urban and Regional Research* 23(3): 421-44.

Fincher, R., and J.M. Jacobs, eds. 1998. *Cities of difference*. New York: Guilford Press.

Firey, W. 1948. *Land use in central Boston*. Cambridge, MA: Harvard University Press.

Fishman, R. 1987. *Bourgeois utopias: The rise and fall of suburbia*. New York: Basic Books.

–. 2000. The American metropolis at century's end: Past and future influences. *Housing Policy Debate* 11(1): 199-214.

Florida, R. 2002. *The rise of the creative class*. New York: Basic Books.

Ford, L. 1994. *Cities and buildings: Skyscrapers, skid rows, and suburbs*. Baltimore: Johns Hopkins University Press.

Franklin, J. 1998a. John Howard's secret children. *High Park Quarterly* (Spring): 8-9.

–. 1998b. Railroad carnage rocks High Park in 1884. *High Park Quarterly* (Fall): 8-9.

Fraser, Graham. 1972. *Fighting back: Urban renewal in Trefann Court*. Toronto: Hakkert.

Fulford, R. 1995. *Accidental city: The transformation of Toronto*. Toronto: Macfarlane, Walter, and Ross.

Gad, G. 1994. Location patterns of manufacturing in Toronto in the early 1880s. *Urban History Review* 22(2): 113-38.

–. 2004. Suburbanisation of manufacturing in Toronto, 1881-1951. In Lewis 2004, 143-77.

Galster, G. 2000. Comment on Metzger. *Housing Policy Debate* 11(1): 61-66.

Gans, H. 1962. *The urban villagers: Group and class in the life of Italian-Americans*. New York: Free Press.

Ganton, I. 1982. Land subdivision in Toronto, 1851-1883. In A. Artibise and G. Stelter, eds., *Shaping the urban landscape: Aspects of the Canadian city-building process*, 200-231. Ottawa: Carleton University Press.

Gatenby, G. 1999. *Toronto: A literary guide*. Toronto: McArthur.

Gibson, S. 1984. *More than an island: A history of Toronto Island*. Toronto: Irwin Publishing.

Glazebrook, G.P. 1971. *The story of Toronto*. Toronto: University of Toronto Press.

Goheen, P. 1970. *Victorian Toronto: Pattern and process of growth*. Chicago: University of Chicago Department of Geography.

–. 2001. The struggle for urban public space: Disposing of the Toronto waterfront in the nineteenth century. In A. Murphy and D. Johnson, eds., *Cultural encounters with the environment: Enduring and evolving geographic themes*, 59-78. Lanham, MD: Rowan and Littlefield.

Gottdiener, M. 1985. *The social production of urban space*. Austin: University of Texas Press.

Green, D. 2000. Independent women, wealth, and wills in 19th century London. In A. Owens and J. Stobart, eds., *Urban fortunes: Property and inheritance in the town 1700-1900*. Aldershot: Ashgate Publishing.

Groth, P. 1994. *Living downtown: The history of residential hotels in the United States*. Berkeley: University of California Press.

Gunn, J. 1990. The lawyer as entrepreneur: Robert Home Smith in early 20th century Toronto. In W. Caroll, eds., *Beyond the law: Lawyers and business in Canada 1830-1930*. Toronto: Osgoode Society.

Hall, P. 1996. *Cities of tomorrow: An intellectual history of urban planning and design in the twentieth century*. Oxford: Blackwell.

–. 1998. *Cities in civilization: Culture, innovation and urban order*. New York: Pantheon Books.

Harris, R. 1993. The end justified the means: Boarding and rooming in a city of homes 1880-1951. *Journal of Social History* 26(2): 331-58.

–. 1994. The flexible house: The housing backlog and the persistence of lodging 1891-1951. *Social Science History* 18(1): 31-53.

–. 1996. *Unplanned suburbs: Toronto's American tragedy 1900-1950*. Baltimore: Johns Hopkins University Press.

Harris, R., and R. Lewis. 2001. The geography of North American cities and suburbs 1900-1950: A new synthesis. *Journal of Urban History* 27(3): 262-92.

–. 1998. Constructing a fault(y) zone: Misrepresentations of American cities and suburbs 1900-1950. *Annals of the Association of American Geographers* 88(4): 622-39.

Harris, R., and M. Luymes. 1990. The growth of Toronto: A cartographic essay. *Urban History Review* 18(3): 244-53.

Harris, R., and D. Ragonetti. 1998. Where credit is due: Residential mortgage finance in Canada, 1901-1954. *Journal of Real Estate Finance and Economics* 16(2): 223-38.

Harney, R., ed. 1985. *Gathering place: Peoples and neighbourhoods of Toronto 1834-1945*. Toronto: Multicultural History Society of Ontario.

Harvey, D. 1973. *Social justice and the city*. Baltimore: Johns Hopkins University Press.

–. 1985. *Consciousness and the urban experience: Studies in the history and theory of capitalist urbanization.* Baltimore: Johns Hopkins University Press.

–. 1989. *The condition of post-modernity: An enquiry into the origins of cultural change.* Oxford: Blackwell.

Hayden, D. 1984. *Redesigning the American dream: The future of housing, work, and family life.* New York: Norton.

–. 2000. Model houses for the millions: The making of the American suburban landscape 1820-2000. Lincoln Institute of Land Policy Working Paper.

–. 2003. *Building suburbia: Green fields and urban growth 1820-2000.* New York: Pantheon Books.

Hill, D. 1985. The blacks in Toronto. In Harney 1985, 41-60.

Hinchcliffe, T. 1981. Highbury New Park: A nineteenth century middle class suburb. *London Journal* 7: 29-44.

Hoover, E.M., and R. Vernon. 1959. *Anatomy of a metropolis.* Cambridge, MA: Harvard University Press.

Howe, R. 1994. Inner suburbs: From slums to gentrification. In Johnson 1994, 141-59.

Hoyt, H. 1970. *One hundred years of land values in Chicago.* New York: Arno Press. Originally published 1933.

–. 1939. *The structure and growth of residential neighbourhoods in America.* Washington, DC: Federal Housing Administration.

Hudson, E., ed. 2000. *The Provincial Lunatic Asylum in Toronto: Reflections on social and architectural history.* Toronto: Toronto Regional Architectural Conservancy.

Hutcheson, S. 1978. *Yorkville in pictures 1853-1883: The early history of Yorkville.* Toronto: Toronto Public Library Board.

Jackson, K. 1967. *The Ku Klux Klan in the city 1915-1930.* New York: Oxford University Press.

–. 1985. *Crabgrass frontier: The suburbanization of the United States.* New York: Oxford University Press.

Jacobs, J. 1992. *The death and life of great American cities.* New York: Random House. Originally published 1961.

James T. Little and Associates. 1975. *The contemporary neighbourhood succession process.* St. Louis: Institute for Urban and Regional Studies.

Johnson, L., ed. 1994. *Suburban dreaming: An interdisciplinary approach to Australian cities.* Geelong: Deakin University Press.

Jonas, A., and D. Wilson, eds. 1999. *The urban growth machine: Critical perspectives two decades later.* Albany: State University of New York Press.

Kaplan, H. 1982. *Reform, planning, and city politics: Montreal, Winnipeg, Toronto.* Toronto: University of Toronto Press.

Kealey, G. 1980. *Toronto workers respond to industrial capitalism, 1867-1892.* Toronto: University of Toronto Press.

Keating, A.D. 1988. *Building Chicago: suburban developers and the creation of a divided metropolis.* Columbus: Ohio State University Press.

Kelly, M.T. 1982. *The Green Dolphin.* Toronto: Playwrights Canada.

Kipfer, S., and R. Keil. 2002. Toronto Inc.? Planning the competitive city in New Toronto, *Antipode* 34(2): 227-64.

Lampard, E. 1973. The Urbanizing World. In H.J. Dyos and M. Wolff, eds., *The Victorian city: Images and realities*, 3-58. London: Routledge and Kegan Paul.

Laycock, M., and B. Myrvold. 1991. *Parkdale in pictures: Its development to 1889.* Toronto: Toronto Public Library Board.

Lees, L. 2000. A reappraisal of gentrification. *Progress in Human Geography* 24: 389-408.

Lemon, J. 1985. *Toronto since 1918: An illustrated history.* Toronto: James Lorimer.

–. 1986. The Annex: A brief historical geography (unpublished manuscript).

–. 1996. *Liberal dreams and nature's limits: Great cities of North America since 1600.* Toronto: Oxford University Press.

Leo, C., and L. Shaw. 2002. What causes inner city decay and what can be done about it? In C. Andrew, K.A. Graham, and S.D. Phillips, eds., *Urban affairs: Back on the policy agenda*, 119-50. Montreal: McGill Queen's University Press.

Lewis, R. 2002. The changing fortunes of American central city manufacturing. *Journal of Urban History* 28(5): 573-98.

–, ed. 2004. *Manufacturing suburbs: Building work and home on the metropolitan fringe.* Philadelphia: Temple University Press.

Ley, D. 1996. *The new middle class and the remaking of the central city.* Oxford: Oxford University Press.

Lubove, R. 1962. *The progressives and the slums: Tenement house reform in New York City, 1890-1917.* Pittsburgh: University of Pittsburgh Press.

Lundell, L. 1997. *The estates of old Toronto.* Eden Mills: Boston Mills Press.

MacDougall, H. 1990. *Activists and advocates: Toronto's health department 1893-1993.* Toronto: Dundurn Press.

Magnusson, W. 1983a. Introduction: The development of Canadian urban government. In W. Magnusson and A. Sancton, eds., *City politics in Canada*, 3-57. Toronto: University of Toronto Press.

–. 1983b. Toronto. In W. Magnusson and A. Sancton, eds., *City politics in Canada*, 94-139. Toronto: University of Toronto Press.

Marcuse, P. 1989. "Dual city": A muddy metaphor for a quartered city. *International Journal of Urban and Regional Research* 13: 697-708.

–. 1997. The enclave, the citadel and the ghetto: What has changed in the post-Fordist U.S. city. *Urban Affairs Review* 33(2): 228-64.

Marsh, M. 1990. *Suburban lives.* New Brunswick, NJ: Rutgers University Press.

Martyn, L. 1980. *Aristocratic Toronto: More stories of fascinating homes and elegant people of early Toronto.* Toronto: Gage.

Mayne, A. 1993. *The imagined slum: Newspaper representation in three cities 1870-1914.* London: Leicester University Press.

McFarland, G. 2001. *Inside Greenwich Village: A New York City neighbourhood 1898-1918.* Amherst: University of Massachusetts Press.

Mele, C. 2000a. The materiality of urban discourse: Rational planning in the restructuring of the early 20th century ghetto. *Urban Affairs Review* 35(5): 628-48.

–. 2000b. *Selling the Lower East Side: Culture, real estate and resistance in New York City.* Minneapolis: University of Minnesota Press.

Metzger, J. 2000. Planned abandonment: The neighbourhood life-cycle theory and national urban policy. *Housing Policy Debate* 11(1): 7-40.

Middleton, J.E. 1923. *The municipality of Toronto: A history.* Toronto: Dominion Publishing.

Miller, Z. 2001. *Visions of place: The city, neighbourhoods, suburbs, and Cincinnati's Clifton, 1850-2000.* Columbus: Ohio State University.

Mills, C. 1993. Myths and meanings of gentrification. In J. Duncan and D. Ley, eds., *Place/culture/representation*, 149-70. London: Routledge.

Mollenkopf, J., and M. Castells. 1991. *Dual city: Restructuring New York.* New York: Russell Sage.

Moore, P. 1979. Zoning and planning: The Toronto experience 1904-1970. In A. Artibise and G. Stelter, eds., *The usable urban past: Planning and politics in the modern Canadian city*, 316-42. Toronto: Macmillan.

Morris, S. 2000. J.G. Howard, architect. In E. Hudson, ed., *The Provincial Lunatic Asylum in Toronto: Reflections on social and architectural history*, 109-24. Toronto: Toronto Regional Architectural Conservancy.

Morton, D. 1973. *Mayor Howland: The citizen's candidate.* Toronto: Hakkert.

Morton, M. 2002. The suburban ideal and suburban realities: Cleveland Heights, Ohio, 1860-2001. *Journal of Urban History* 28(6): 671-98.

Morton, S. 1995. *Ideal surroundings: Domestic life in a working-class suburb in the 1920s.* Toronto: University of Toronto Press.

Mulvaney, G.P. 1884. *Toronto past and present: A handbook of the city.* Toronto: W.E. Craiger.

Murdie, R. 1986. Residential mortgage lending in Metropolitan Toronto: A case study of the resale market. *Canadian Geographer* 30(2): 98-110.

–. 1991. Local strategies in resale home financing in the Toronto Housing Market. *Urban Studies* 28(3): 465-83.

Newman, P., and J. Kenworthy. 1999. *Sustainability and cities: Overcoming automobile dependency*. Washington: Island Press.

Nicolaides, B. 2002. *My blue heaven: Life and politics in the working-class suburbs of Los Angeles, 1920-1965*. Chicago: University of Chicago Press.

Park, R. 1926. The urban community as a spatial pattern and a moral order. In E. Burgess, ed., *The urban community*, 3-18. Chicago: University of Chicago Press.

–. 1974. The city: Suggestions for the investigation of human behavior in the urban environment. In R.E. Park, E.W. Burgess, and R.D. McKenzie, *The city*, 1-46. Chicago: University of Chicago Press. Originally published 1925.

Parkdale Centennial Research Committee. 1978. *Parkdale: A centennial history*. Toronto: Parkdale Centennial Research Committee.

Paterson, R. 1991. Housing finance trends in twentieth century suburban Toronto. *Urban History Review* 20(2): 63-71.

Patterson, C., C. McDougall, and G. Levin. 1986. *Bloor-Dufferin in pictures*. Toronto: Toronto Public Library Board.

Peel, M. 1995a. *Good times, hard times: The past and future in Elizabeth*. Melbourne: Melbourne University Press.

–. 1995b. The urban debate: From "L.A." to the urban village. In P. Troy, ed., *Australian cities: Issues, strategies and policies for urban Australia in the 1990s*, 39-64. Cambridge: Cambridge University Press.

Peterson, J. 2003. *The birth of city planning in the United States, 1840-1917*. Baltimore: Johns Hopkins University Press.

Philpott, T. 1978. *The slum and the ghetto: Neighbourhood deterioration and middle class reform*. New York: Oxford University Press.

Piva, M. 1979. *The condition of the working class in Toronto 1900-1921*. Ottawa: University of Ottawa Press.

Purdy, S. 1997. Industrial efficiency, social order, and moral purity: Housing reform thought in English Canada. *Urban History Review* 23(2): 30-40.

Rapkin, C., and W.G. Grigsby. 1960. *Residential renewal in the urban core*. Philadelphia: University of Pennsylvania Press.

Reeves, W. 1992a. *Regional heritage features on the Metro Toronto waterfront*. Toronto: Metropolitan Toronto Planning Department.

–. 1992b. *Visions for the Metro Toronto waterfront I: Towards comprehensive planning*. Toronto: University of Toronto Centre for Urban and Community Studies Research Paper.

–. 1993. *Visions for the Metro Toronto waterfront II: Forging a regional identity 1913-68*. Toronto: University of Toronto Centre for Urban and Community Studies Research Paper.

Relph, E. 1976. *Place and placelessness*. London: Pion.

Richards, P.M. 1926. How the Ku Klux Klan came to Canada. *Saturday Night*, 26 June.

Riis, J. 1957. *How the other half lives*. New York: Hill and Wang. Originally published 1898.

Robin, M. 1992. *Shades of right: Nativist and fascist politics in Canada 1920-1940*. Toronto: University of Toronto Press.

Robinson, C.B. 1885. *History of Toronto and County of York*. Toronto: Rose Publishing Company.

Robson, G., and T. Butler. 2001. Coming to terms with London: Middle-class communities in a global city. *International Journal of Urban and Regional Research* 25(1): 70-86.

Rodger, R. 2000. Suburbs and slums: The persistence of residential apartheid. In P. Waller, ed., *The English urban landscape*, 233-68. Oxford: Oxford University Press.

–. 2001. *The transformation of Edinburgh: Land, property and trust in the nineteenth century*. Cambridge: Cambridge University Press.

Rose, A. 1958. *Regent Park: A study in slum clearance*. Toronto: University of Toronto Press.

–. 1972. *Governing Metropolitan Toronto: A social and political analysis 1953-1971*. Berkeley: University of California Press.

Rose, D. 1984. Rethinking gentrification: Beyond the uneven development of Marxist urban theory. *Environment and Planning D* 2(1): 47-74.

–. 1989. A feminist approach on employment restructuring and gentrification: The case of Montreal. In J. Wolch and M. Dear, eds., *The power of geography: How territory shapes urban life*, 118-35. Boston: Unwin Hyman.

Rose, G.M. 1886. *A cyclopedia of Canadian biography: Being chiefly men of the time.* Toronto: Rose Publishing Company.

Rybczynski, W. 1995. *City life: Urban expectations in a new world.* New York: Scribner.

Sante, L. 1991. *Low life: Lures and snares of old New York.* New York: Farrar Straus Giroux.

Scott, J.C. 1881. *The Parkdale register.* Toronto: Bengough, Moore, and Bengough.

Sendbuehler, M., and J. Gilliland. 1998. "To provide the highest type of manhood and womanhood": The OHA 1919 and a new suburban ideal. *Urban History Review* 26(2): 42-55.

Sennett, R. 1974. *Families against the city: Middle-class homes of industrial Chicago.* New York: Vintage Books.

Sewell, J. 1993. *The shape of the city: Toronto struggles with modern planning.* Toronto: University of Toronto Press.

Sher, J. 1983. *White hoods: Canada's Ku Klux Klan.* Vancouver: New Star Books.

Sibley, D. 1995. *Geographies of exclusion: Society and difference in the West.* London: Routledge.

Sies, M.C. 2001. North American suburbs 1880-1950: Cultural and social reconsiderations. *Journal of Urban History* 27(3): 313-46.

Smith, N. 1978. Toward a theory of gentrification: A back to the city movement by capital. *Journal of the American Planning Association* 45(4): 538-48.

–. 1996. *The new urban frontier: Gentrification and the revanchist city.* London: Routledge.

–. 2002. New globalism, new urbanism: Gentrification as global urban strategy. *Antipode* 34(3): 427-49.

Smith, N., and P. Williams, eds. 1986. *Gentrification of the city.* Boston: Allen and Unwin.

Sobel, D., and S. Meurer. 1994. *Working at Inglis: The life and death of a Canadian factory.* Toronto: James Lorimer.

Splane, R.B. 1971. *Social welfare in Ontario 1791-1893: A study of public welfare administration.* Toronto: University of Toronto Press.

Spragge, S. 1979. A confluence of interests: Housing reform in Toronto 1900-1920. In A. Artibise and G. Stelter, eds., *The usable urban past: Planning and politics in the modern Canadian city*, 247-67. Toronto: Macmillan.

Stedman-Jones, G. 1984. *Outcast London: A study in the relationships between classes in Victorian society.* Oxford: Clarendon Press.

Stilgoe, J. 1988. *Borderland: Origins of the American suburb 1820-1939.* New Haven: Yale University Press.

Stimpson, C., E. Dixler, C. Nelson, and K. Yatrakis. 1981. *Women and the American city.* Chicago: University of Chicago Press.

Strange, C. 1992. Wounded womanhood and dead men: Chivalry and the trials of Clara Ford and Carrie Davis. In M. Valverde and F. Iacovetta, eds., *Gender conflicts: New essays in women's history*, 149-88. Toronto: University of Toronto Press.

–. 1995. *Toronto's girl problem: The perils and pleasures of the city 1880-1930.* Toronto: University of Toronto Press.

Swan, H.B. 1944. *The housing market in New York City.* New York: Reinhold.

Teaford, J.C. 1986. *The twentieth century American city: Problem, promise, and reality.* Baltimore: Johns Hopkins University Press.

–. 1990. *The rough road to renaissance: Urban revitalization in America 1940-1985.* Baltimore: Johns Hopkins University Press.

Temkin, K. 2000. Comment on Metzger. *Housing Policy Debate* 11(1): 55-60.

Toronto Street Railway Company. 1894. *Toronto as seen from the streetcars.* Toronto: Toronto Street Railway Company.

Valverde, M. 1991. *The age of soap, light and water: Moral reform in English Canada 1885-1925.* Toronto: McClelland and Stewart.

Von Hoffman, A. 1994. *Local attachments: The making of an American urban neighbourhood 1850-1920.* Baltimore: Johns Hopkins University Press.

Walden, K. 1997. *Becoming modern in Toronto: The Industrial Exhibition and the shaping of the late Victorian culture.* Toronto: University of Toronto Press.

Walker, R. 1981. A theory of suburbanization: Capitalism and the construction of urban space in the United States. In M. Dear and A. Scott, eds., *Urbanization and urban planning in capitalist society*, 383-420. Montreal: Black Rose Press.

Ward, S. 1998. *Selling places: The marketing and promotion of towns and cities 1850-2000.* London: Routledge.

Warner, S.B. 1978. *Streetcar suburbs: The process of growth in Boston 1870-1900.* Cambridge, MA: Harvard University Press and MIT Press. Originally published 1962.

Weiss, M. 1987. *The rise of the community builders: The American real estate industry and urban land planning.* New York: Columbia University Press. Originally published 1967.

Wekerle, G., R. Peterson, and D. Morley, eds. 1980. *New space for women.* Boulder, CO: Westview Press.

White, J. 1980. *Rothschild buildings: Life in an east-end tenement, 1889-1920.* London: Routledge and Kegan Paul.

–. 1986. *The worst street in North London: Campbell Bunk, Islington, between the wars.* London: Routledge and Kegan Paul.

White, R. 1993. *Too good to be true: Toronto in the 1920s.* Toronto: Dundurn Press.

Whitzman, C. 1991. Community and design: Against the solution in St. James Town. In K. Gerecke, ed., *The Canadian city: The best of City Magazine*, 163-74. Montreal: Black Rose Press.

Wiese, A. 2003. *Places of their own: African-American suburbanization in the twentieth century.* Chicago: University of Chicago Press.

Williams, P. 1978. The role of institutions in the inner London housing market: The case of Islington. *Transactions, Institute of British Geographers* 1: 23-34.

–. 1986. Class constitution through spatial restructuring? A re-evaluation of gentrification in Australia, Britain, and the United States. In Smith and Williams 1986, 56-77.

Williams, R. 1973. *The country and the city.* New York: Oxford University Press.

–. 1976. *Keywords: A vocabulary of culture and society.* New York: Oxford University Press.

Wilson, E. 1991. *The sphinx in the city: Urban life, the control of disorder, and women.* London: Virago.

–. 1995. The rhetoric of urban space. *New Left Review* 209: 145-60.

Wright, G. 1980. *Moralism and the model home: Domestic architecture and cultural conflict in Chicago 1873-1913.* Chicago: University of Chicago Press.

Wyly, E., and D. Hammel. 1999. Islands of decay in seas of renewal: Housing policy and the resurgence of gentrification. *Housing Policy Debate* 10(4): 711-71.

Young, I.M. 1990. *Justice and the politics of difference.* Princeton: Princeton University Press.

–. 2000. *Inclusion and Democracy.* Oxford: Oxford University Press.

Zorbaugh, H. 1976. *The gold coast and the slum: A sociological study of Chicago's Near North Side.* Chicago: University of Chicago Press. Originally published 1929.

Zukin, S. 1989. *Loft living: Culture and capital in urban America.* New Brunswick, NJ: Rutgers University Press.

# Index

Printed and bound in Canada by Friesens

Copyedited by Sarah Wight

Set in Stone by Robert Kroeger, Kroeger Enterprises

Proofread and indexed by Dianne Tiefensee

## ENVIRONMENTAL BENEFITS STATEMENT

**UBC Press** saved the following resources by printing the pages of this book on chlorine free paper made with 100% post-consumer waste.

| TREES | WATER | ENERGY | SOLID WASTE | GREENHOUSE GASES |
|---|---|---|---|---|
| 7 | 2,704 | 5 | 347 | 651 |
| FULLY GROWN | GALLONS | MILLION BTUs | POUNDS | POUNDS |

Calculations based on research by Environmental Defense and the Paper Task Force. Manufactured at Friesens Corporation